Work-based Practice in the Ea

Bringing together the essential theory, research and policy with examples from practice, *Work-based Practice in the Early Years: A Guide for Students* provides a complete guide to successful work placements for early years students. It makes links to the Occupational Standards for the Early Years Educator and the Teacher Standards for early years, and integrates examples of effective, universal and inclusive practice throughout.

Following an overview of the research and policy context which has shaped the sector since the 1990s, this new text is designed to prepare and support you, the student, as you embark on your placement, which is an integral part of your early years degree. It covers the key information you need about safeguarding and the curriculum frameworks, EYFS and the National Curriculum KS1, alongside chapters on reflective practice and research to support your developing professional and practical skills.

Written with the student in mind, this book draws on first-hand student experiences and introduces the idea of working towards being a leader of practice and the wider role in working with parents and families. This comprehensive guide also considers the views of placement providers, examining the roles and responsibilities of both the student and provider, and offering insight into their expectations and what factors make a work placement successful.

Including reflective activities, student's views and evidence from student portfolios, this is an essential text for all early years' students undertaking their work placement.

Samantha McMahon is Principal Lecturer and Complex Pathway Leader for a range of early years courses at the University of Huddersfield, UK.

Mary Dyer is Senior Lecturer in early years at the University of Huddersfield, UK.

Work-based Practice in the Early Years

A Guide for Students

Edited by
Samantha McMahon and Mary Dyer

Routledge
Taylor & Francis Group

LONDON AND NEW YORK

First published 2018
by Routledge
2 Park Square, Milton Park, Abingdon, Oxon OX14 4RN

and by Routledge
711 Third Avenue, New York, NY 10017

Routledge is an imprint of the Taylor & Francis Group, an informa business

British Library Cataloguing-in-Publication Data
A catalogue record for this book is available from the British Library

Library of Congress Cataloging-in-Publication Data
A catalog record for this book has been requested

ISBN: 978-1-138-67364-9 (hbk)
ISBN: 978-1-138-67365-6 (pbk)
ISBN: 978-1-315-56180-6 (ebk)

Typeset in Sabon
by Apex CoVantage, LLC

Printed in the United Kingdom
by Henry Ling Limited

Contents

Figures

Tables

Contributors

Amanda Crow is an early years practitioner with 35 years of experience ranging from local authority day care, schools, pre-school play groups and integrated children' centres. In 2000 she became employed in one of the trailblazer Sure Start projects, and was involved in developing integrated childcare and education services for children and their families. Amanda has been working at the University of Huddersfield as a Senior Lecturer since 2014, supporting students on the BA (hons) Early Years and BA (Hons) Childhood Studies programmes. A particular aspect of her role is to prepare students for placement, this involves offering individual support to ensure they gain positive work based experiences and feel prepared for future employment.

Mary Dyer is a Senior Lecturer in Early Years and has been teaching and training early years practitioners for over 25 years. She has also worked in the early years sector as a Development Officer, then Project Co-ordinator, supporting early years settings in developing and improving provision. Her research focuses on how practitioners develop and describe their professional identity, particularly at this time of significant change for the sector.

Nicola Firth is a Senior Lecturer in Early Years at the University of Huddersfield. She has worked in higher education for 11 years, working with undergraduate students on Foundation Degree Programmes and BA Honours. Prior to working in higher education Nicola qualified as a Nursery Nurse in 1993 with the NNEB and worked in early years settings as a Nursery Nurse, then Nursery Manager from 1995 to 2006. Nicola is currently studying the Doctorate in Education with a research focus on boys' underachievement in their early years.

Tina Froggett has worked in early years for 15 years managing a pre-school in the PVI sector where she also acted as mentor to a wide range of students from local schools and colleges. In addition, Tina has worked in partnership with the University of Huddersfield mentoring undergraduates and Early Years Teachers. In 2015 she was awarded the Sir Al Aynsley-Green Scholarship by the University and returned to full-time study. As part of her doctoral programme, she is currently researching the impact of play and formal learning on children's well-being in the UK and Finland.

Jo McEvoy is an early Years specialist with a passion for improving quality and outcomes for young children. Jo joined the university in 2013 and leads the courses for Early Years Teacher status. Prior to this she worked as the Early Years team leader for a local authority quality improvement service and as a deputy headteacher in a primary school. She has held many early years teaching posts after starting her interest in early years through running a voluntary independent pre-school. Jo's research interests are effective early years pedagogy with a focus on quality interactions and positive relationships.

Samantha McMahon is a Subject Leader in the School of Education and Professional Development and has been instrumental in the growth and development of early years provision from the Foundation degree to EYPS and the BA (Hons) Early Years. She is responsible for the student experience across a number of courses and understands the importance of a successful transition into university. She has been teaching children and young people for more than 20 years in a variety of contexts including HE, FE, Primary and pre-school. Samantha's research interests are leadership in early years and young children's physical development.

Alison Ryan is a Senior Lecturer in School of Education and Professional Development. Since joining the University in 2002 she has been responsible for teaching on a number of programmes across the school focusing on Literacy, Maths and Inclusive Learning. Alison's teaching career started in 1988. Her first role as a tutor for young people with learning difficulties and disabilities in a London Further Education college led to a subsequent career in Adult Education where she taught on and developed family learning programmes in partnership with the local authority.

Lindsey Watson is a Senior Lecturer in early Years at the University of Huddersfield. She works with undergraduate students on the BA Early Years programme. Prior to working at the University, Lindsey worked as an Early Years Teaching Assistant, spending time within mainstream and special school settings. Lindsey in currently studying for a Doctor of Philosophy with research focusing on "What younger children really think and understand about internet safety: The value of stories and role play as research methods".

Andrew Youde is Acting Head of Department for the Department of Education and Community Studies. He has particular research interests in the skills and qualities of online tutors with his doctoral research exploring the relationship between a tutor's emotional intelligence and their success in blended learning environments. He lectures on various courses including MSc Technology Enhanced Learning, BA (Hons) Early Years, BA (Hons) Leading in the Children's Workforce, and BA (Hons) Educational Management and Administration.

Preface

Why this book?

This book has been written with a first year undergraduate student who is studying on an early years or early childhood studies course, firmly in mind. We know that students are often excited about starting university and particularly look forward to going out on placement. However, they can also feel overwhelmed and anxious about these new experiences. This handbook is designed to prepare and support you, the student, as you embark on your placement. Placement is an important element of this type of course as it provides you with invaluable first-hand experiences and the opportunity to make links between practice, research and theory, an essential degree-level skill. By developing this type of higher level theoretical perspective on practice, you are empowered to become reflective Early Years Educators and graduate leaders of the future. The qualifications of those working with young children matter to children's outcomes, and the team writing this book are passionate about workforce development to ensure future generations of children have the best start in life.

In compiling this book, the authors have drawn extensively on our many years of experience of working with students and our knowledge of early childhood education and care (ECEC). We have also drawn on first-hand student experiences, by holding a focus group to ascertain student's views, and including evidence from student portfolios. Uniquely, we have also spoken to placement providers to ensure that their perspectives are represented in this book and, as a result, you are made more aware of their expectations. In addition, we have made links to the relevant National Occupational Standards for the Early Years Educator (EYE) and the Teacher Standards for early years.

What this book contains

The book provides an overview of the ECEC sector in England, and the policy and research context which have shaped the sector since the 1990s. The book then turns its focus to you, the student, and the information you need to be successful on placement. It introduces reflective practice and some key models of reflection and provides guidance on communicating effectively and working in a team. An essential introduction to the early years curriculum and some underpinning theoretical perspectives are included. As a result, you should develop an initial understanding of how you can support a child's learning and development. To ensure you are prepared for different placement experiences, the book also includes a brief overview of the National Curriculum in England with an in-depth consideration of Key Stage 1. It will consider pedagogical approaches you might use, particularly, to develop your practice in teaching English and maths. The book explains what safeguarding means in practice for you and provides a brief overview of the current policy and legislative framework in this vital area. There is a chapter that outlines the purpose of observation in the assessment and planning cycle, and provides an overview of a range of observational methods. The book introduces the idea of working towards being a leader of practice, and encourages you to consider the skills and attributes you need to develop as a leader. It then turns to focus on how you, the student, might engage in research and how this helps you to develop as a critical, reflective practitioner. Finally, the book considers the perspective from placement, and explains the responsibilities of the placement and their expectations of the student.

Many of the chapters include case studies drawn from the experiences of real students on placement to support you in developing professional and practical skills. Examples of universal inclusive practice are embedded into the chapters and threaded throughout the book. Your learning is further supported through suggested activities interspersed throughout the chapters. These are designed to scaffold the reflective process and encourage you to make links between experience and theory. As it is impossible to include everything you need to know, we have also identified additional sources of reading and research, which can be readily accessed, to extend your knowledge and understanding.

This is an exciting time and we hope you have a challenging and fulfilling learning experience. Enjoy!

Samantha McMahon and Mary Dyer

Chapter 1

Development of the early years sector

Mary Dyer and Samantha McMahon

Aims of the chapter

By the end of this chapter you will be able to:

- describe the development of the early years sector over the last 60 years
- identify key policies and legislation and explain how they have combined to shape the role of the early years practitioner
- understand how research within the sector has contributed to our understanding today of the role of the early years practitioner.

Introduction

This chapter provides an overview of how the early years sector has developed, what it comprises today and what policy and legislation has shaped its current form. This will help you to understand the role of the graduate practitioner and how this has developed. Whilst it is easy to focus on the early years sector in terms of the services and experiences it provides for very young children outside the family home, it should not be overlooked that this provision can only be provided by a workforce that is appropriately trained, qualified and registered, and which has in-depth knowledge and understanding of children's learning and developmental needs. To understand what this knowledge base includes means considering what the early years sector itself is, with its complex and wide-ranging responsibilities, and how it has evolved into the provision we see today. We will do this by considering key policy initiatives, wide-ranging research projects and landmark legislation and the impact they have had on the role of the early years practitioner.

The modern early years sector

The early years sector in England today comprises provision registered with Ofsted to provide stimulating, play-based care and education for children outside the family home aged from birth to 5 years, and out of school care for children aged 5–7 years. Such provision may take the form of:

- childminder services, delivered in a home setting to small groups of children
- day care provision offered by private and voluntary organisations, for all or part of a day

- breakfast club, after school and holiday provision run by schools, private, voluntary and independent providers
- Sure Start Children Centre provision run by local authorities, charities and social/ health services lead bodies.

It also includes the free nursery education provided to children aged from 2–4 by schools either under local authority control or within the independent, free school and academy sector.

Thus the early years sector is a mix of government-controlled and -funded provision, privately owned and managed businesses, and voluntary, community-run provision and social service. Anything that is not local-authority controlled is referred to as private, voluntary or independent (the PVI sector), as it is owned either by individuals; independent groups such as charities, community groups and religious bodies; or education providers outside local-authority control, i.e. independent schools, academies and free schools. Whilst all providers must meet the same registration and inspection requirements overseen by Ofsted, the differences in the management structure and ownership of early years settings means that practitioners may have very different titles, job descriptions and terms and conditions of employment. However, in one respect they all come together – to meet the needs of young children and promote their learning and development as set out in the statutory Welfare Requirements (DfE, 2017) and Development Matters of the Early Years Foundation Stage (EYFS) (Early Education, 2012), and to ensure and promote children's well-being and safety.

It would be easy to think that the early years sector is a modern invention, developed over the last 20 years, following the election in 1997 of a Labour government committed to ensuring working parents had access to the childcare care provision they needed, and that this provision would be of a standard to ensure that children's early care needs and educational outcomes would be met. However, much of the groundwork for this vision had been done many years previously by early pioneers of practice to meet young children's needs. A brief overview of the early history of the sector highlights the influence of these early pioneers on the structure of the sector and the nature of early years practice today.

Early pioneers

In the late nineteenth and early twentieth centuries, pioneers of young children's education included Margaret McMillan, Frederick Froebel and Maria Montessori. All three recognised the importance of physical and mental health to development and learning, and sought to create early years provision where children's holistic development could be promoted and their understanding of the world supported and extended through play and interaction with supportive, knowledgeable adults, making full use of indoor and outdoor environments and taking into account the social and cultural influences of these children's worlds. All three called for those employed in early years provision to receive specialist training and education in how children learn and develop, reinforcing the view that valued childhood was a necessary and unique element in children's development, which could only be supported effectively by adults who were familiar with and understood a specific body of knowledge regarding children's mental and physical development.

Susan Isaacs, in attempting to understand the world of the child from the child's perspective, and advise on appropriate care and upbringing, concluded as early as 1929 that "What helps most in the long run is the ability to enter into the child's own world with informed sympathy . . . and a patient and friendly interest" (Isaacs, 1929, p. 7) and that "Children need all our affection and sympathy; but they also need all our intelligence and our patient and serious efforts to understand the ways of their mental growth" (p. 2). Thus she identified the need for knowledgeable practitioners with a clear understanding of children's mental and physical development. She argued strongly that without affectionate and sympathetic support, children's motivation and ability to explore and understand the world would be significantly limited or even impaired and that adults should have realistic expectations of the children they care for and should know their children as individuals to be able to monitor their progress and extend their development in appropriate ways. She proposed that early childhood was, in fact, the foundation for successful subsequent learning and development, and must be properly supported in ways that met the needs of the individual child if he/she was to become a socially and cognitively competent adult.

What these early pioneers had in common then was their valuing of childhood for its own sake and an understanding that children's learning was more effectively defined as their active and growing understanding of the world rather than their more passive acquisition of facts. This was coupled with an understanding of holistic development and the acceptance that mental and emotional health was not only as important as physical health but that it also supported this exploration and understanding of the world. What was required was a practitioner that understood this and could support it.

Strategy and the shaping of the sector

Table 1.1 below identifies some key points in the latter stages of the twentieth century and early twenty-first century in the development of the early years sector as we know it today. It includes key political initiatives and policies that have shaped the structure and size of the sector, significant legislation that has impacted on how early years practitioners work with others to ensure children's safety and well-being, and important development in curriculum design that have driven changes to day-to-day practice in early years settings.

Until the beginning of the twenty-first century, government-funded and -regulated nursery education could only be provided by local authority-maintained providers – nursery schools and nursery classes attached to infant and primary schools – and was not a compulsory part of education provision in the UK. The PVI sector could provide care for children from birth to 5 but this was not considered as education, nor did government fund it. As nursery education was outside the compulsory education sector, which began in infant school, this meant that in many parts of the country, nursery education was in limited supply, and many children came into infant school with no experience of education or care outside the family home.

Concerns were raised in the 1960s about the impact this was having on young children's initial experiences of settling into school and on their progress, leading to calls for provision to be put in place that would help prepare children for this significant transition in their young lives. The Plowden Report (DES, 1967), commissioned by

Table 1.1 Development of the early years sector in England

Policy or legislation	Contribution to the early years sector	Impact on the early years sector
The Plowden Report (DES, 1967) – highlights the importance of pre-school provision.	Formation of Pre-school Playgroups Association (now Pre-school Learning Alliance) 1962.	Development of voluntary pre-school provision, paid for by parents.
The Children Act 1989.	Introduces a focus on children's safety and well-being, defining children at risk and children in need; requires all providers to have suitable premises and appropriate staff.	Registration and inspection of early years day care provision by local authorities.
1997 – Labour government elected, introduces new childcare strategy – *The National Childcare Strategy: meeting the childcare challenge* (DfEE, 1998) with commitment to development of level and quality of provision, including workforce development.	Expansion of PVI sector through Neighbourhood Nursery Initiative, funding of Out of School Club provision; introduction of Early Years Development and Care Partnerships (EYDCPs) to support local providers; workforce development funding to raise number of Level 2 and 3 qualified staff; introduction of Nursery Education Grant (NEG) – funding nursery education for 3- and 4-year-olds for 12.5 hours per week.	Development of *Curriculum Guidance for the Foundation Stage* (QCA/DfEE, 2000) to support providers, and introducing stepping stones for learning outcomes – eventually to become Early Learning Goals (ELGs); Ofsted takes responsibility for national framework for inspections and registration of provision and introduces national regulation standards for different types of providers distinguished in terms of provision they offer – sessional, full day care, childminder, crèche and out of school provision; Nursery Education Funding (NEF) now extended to PVI settings, to be later expanded to 15, then 30 hours for all 3- and 4-year-olds, also available to disadvantaged 2-year-olds.
Sure Start Unit – Sure Start Local Programmes (SSLPs) in areas of greatest deprivation to meet needs of disadvantaged children and their families; later rolled out to all areas of deprivation as Children's Centres with the aim of a children's centre in every local authority ward.	Funding to tackle the impact of poverty and disadvantage on young children; development of children's centres that offered health, education and financial advice for families.	Integration of services for families and children into a single, central hub in local wards; introduction of new roles to early years sector including family support and parent outreach.
The Effective Provision of Pre-School Education (EPPE) (Sylva et al., 2004); *Researching Effective Pedagogy in the early years* (Siraj-Blatchford et al., 2002).	Key research projects, one of them ongoing, that have identified how young children learn and how this process can best be supported.	Practice focusses on shared sustained thinking, scaffolding of children's learning, parent partnership and the importance of play-based, child-led learning.

Policy or legislation	Contribution to the early years sector	Impact on the early years sector
Birth to 3 Matters: A Framework to Support Children in Their Earliest Years (Abbott, 2002).	A good practice guide for the care and development of children up to 3 years old – non-statutory but registered providers of services for very young children encouraged to follow it.	First recognition in policy terms that 0–3-year-olds had learning and development needs that went beyond health, physical development and safety.
Laming Report (2003); *Children Act* 2004; *Every Child Matters* (DfES, 2004).	Response to the Victoria Climbie case where a range of services failed to ensure the safety of the child. New legislation making it the duty of local authorities to ensure effective multi-agency working is in place.	Revised emphasis on effective multi-agency working and effective information sharing to support children's needs and outcomes; definition of positive outcomes for children – Every Child Matters.
Introduction of Early Years Foundation Stage (EYFS) (DCSF, 2008); Childcare Act 2006.	Statutory Welfare Requirements for all registered providers to follow, including all registered schools (nursery and Reception Classes) and all childminders; curriculum framework to promote good practice on supporting children's learning and development from birth to 5 years old.	Outlines principles that should underpin good practice and requires all registered providers to observe, plan and assess for all children using the setting.
2005 Introduction of Children's Workforce Development Council (CWDC).	CWDC introduced to oversee workforce reforms, including meeting the target for all settings to have graduate leadership, and to develop the criteria for this as Early Years Professional Status (EYPS).	Development of EYPS criteria and accreditation routes in partnership with Higher Education Institutions (HEIs), using sector-endorsed Foundation degrees and top-up BA Honours programmes.
Review of early years qualifications (Nutbrown, 2012); review of the EYFS (Tickell, 2011).	Review of early years qualifications and role of practitioner.	Calls for streamlining of qualifications on offer to early years practitioners to reduce confusion for employers and parents; revisions to EYFS including introduction of Characteristics of Effective Learning and the separation of prime and specific areas of learning.
More Great Childcare (DfE, 2013a).	Government introduces new titles and requirements for GCSE English and maths for practitioners; revision of EYPS to EYTS and introduction of National College for Teaching and Learning (NCTL) standards.	Early years qualifications now start to model more closely those of qualified teachers.

the government as a review of education provision in the UK, recommended nursery provision to support children's preparation for compulsory schooling. The Plowden Report also acknowledged the importance of a child-led approach to early education, with its bold statement that "at the heart of the education process lies the child" (DES, 1967, p. 7), a principle first advanced by such pioneers as Susan Isaacs and Grace Owen, and later returned to in the EYFS we use today. Early education needed to consider the unique and individual needs of the child as he/she comes to understand his or her world and required practitioners who understand how this process can be supported.

The PPA (Pre-school Playgroups Association), formed in 1962, was a parent-led organisation that aimed to set up voluntary play-based provision for children aged 3–5. The intention was to offer support to parents in their understanding of their children's development and learning, in order for them to support children's learning before they started compulsory school. This reintroduced the notion raised by the earlier pioneers of the informed adult (albeit through voluntary and unaccredited training) supporting children's early learning and development, and the need for children to learn about the world in their own way through play. However it should be noted that the emphasis of this organisation was on learning and preparation for formal education for children aged 3–5 years old, and included no provision for children under 3. The PLA and its network of affiliated pre-school groups formed the backbone of privately funded nursery education for many years, with its membership finally benefiting from government funding for its services with the expansion of nursery education funding (NEF) following the 1998 Childcare Strategy (DfEE, 1998), and from local authority support and development through the EYDCP Development Teams – see below.

The Children Act 1989

This key piece of legislation influenced how we saw the role of early years practitioners and how accountable they became in their practice. *The Children Act 1989* revised much of the existing legislation there was regarding child protection, and was the first piece of legislation to put the welfare of the child as a priority, above and beyond the rights of parents or professionals. It defined what it meant to be a child at risk or a child in need, and tasked professionals from a range of services including health, education, justice and social services to work together and share information in order to meet the best interests of a child. It was also the only legislation at that time to consider what kind of service PVI settings should be offering to children and to require that these services be delivered in appropriate and safe premises, by appropriate and safe – although not necessarily qualified – individuals. As a piece of legislation, it offered little detail about the specifics of early years practice, but was the first attempt to consider what the underlying values of practice should be, namely that children are vulnerable and require protection, and that this should not be compromised by lack of communication, adults' rights or bureaucratic processes.

Meeting the Childcare Challenge 1998

The most radical change to the early years sector began in 1998. The vision for a new national strategy set out in the green paper *Meeting the Childcare Challenge* (DfEE,

1998) – was developed by the new Labour government. This focussed on three key elements of the sector:

- Affordability of childcare
- Accessibility and availability of childcare
- Quality of childcare.

The needs of children were to some extent acknowledged:

> Our children must get the best start in life. . . . Good quality childcare can help with this. Good quality care isn't merely about caring for children, but about introducing them to the joys of imaginative play, a love of books and a diverse and exciting range of sporting activities.
>
> (DfEE, paragraphs 2, 3)

However the needs of parents and of the national economy in moving parents from state benefits to employment were considered to be equally important:

> Our economy will prosper if more skilled and capable people are able to take up job opportunities because they have access to good quality, affordable and accessible childcare.
>
> (DfEE, paragraph 5)

Affordability

Measures were put in place to support parents to pay for the substitute care they were being offered to be able to access education or employment. Tax credits and voucher systems were developed to reduce the overall cost to parents for their children's care, and early years providers were required to be competent in managing and advising on such schemes. NEF was opened up to the PVI sector, so that parents could use the same provider for their children's education and care needs, and out of school provision was developed in the PVI sector, so that older and younger children within families could use the same providers. Significant efforts were then made to make new provision accessible and user-friendly to parents, including the development of locally organised information services parents could consult, to investigate what provision was available in their locality.

Accessibility and availability

The green paper acknowledged that there were insufficient childcare places if all untrained or non-working parents were to access education or employment. Consequently, government funding was made available for the development and subsidisation of new provision – the Neighbourhood Nursery Initiatives (NNI), NEF expansion money and New Opportunities Funding (NOF) for out of school provision. Local authority support services – particularly EYDCP Development Teams – worked with potential providers to support them in setting up new provision and expanding existing services in the drive to ensure there was sufficient provision to meet demand. By

2006, 1.2 million childcare places were created nationally, with 45,000 of them being provided through the NNI, which was specifically targeted at areas of socio-economic deprivation (DfE, 2010).

Quality

New national standards were written, taking into account the different operational concerns of different types of providers, but perhaps overlooking the fact that the needs of children under 5 remain consistent wherever they are cared for. The registration and inspection of early years provision moved out of local authority control into centralised inspection provided by Ofsted – an education overseer for the compulsory education sector – who would take responsibility for ensuring children's care and learning needs were adequately met.

Two strands of regulation and support were introduced. Providers drawing down government funding for NEF places, which now included PVI provision as well as maintained schools, were obliged to meet the standards outlined formally in the Curriculum Guidance for the Foundation Stage (QCA/DfEE, 2000). For the PVI providers, these were in addition to the national inspection standards for care (DfES, 2003; for maintained schools, this was as part of their existing inspection requirements. All other providers for children aged 0–5 simply had to meet the appropriate national standards for care. Settings in the PVI sector offering NEF places were supported by local authority Early Years Consultants, previously Advisory Teachers, guiding them on the planning and implementation of learning activities to meet the Foundation Stage requirements, as were the maintained schools. PVI settings not offering NEF places were supported to meet the care National Standards by EYDCP Development Teams, whose members were required to be qualified to Level 3 advisory teams, and to have experience of developing and working in early years settings.

This divide served to widen the arbitrary gap between providers of education and providers of care, and those who offered provision for the under 3s and the over 3s. Substitute care for the children of working parents was now to be available and its quality regulated at the national level, but it was to be seen as separate from the universal provision of nursery education to prepare children for formal schooling. This was reinforced by the introduction of terminology such as 'wrap-around-care' provided by settings when the child's allotted 2.5 hours per day nursery entitlement was finished, or 'out of school care', to provide supervision for children when their educational day had ended.

Workforce development

Practitioners working with the under 3s or in non-NEF provision were first and foremost carers whose responsibility was to keep their charges safe and happy but who provided no apparent educational input for these children. There were no compulsory educational outcomes to be met or practice guidance to be followed to support these children's learning beyond generic standards of care that focussed on the appropriateness of the physical care environment and the day-to-day operation of the setting. Learning outcomes and a curriculum framework were imposed only for provision funded by government, designated as preparation for formal school when children reached 5.

However, this new strategy introduced new requirements for qualified staff to a sector that had been significantly unqualified, particularly in terms of childminders. Workers had entered from a sense of vocation – they enjoyed working with children and considered children's safety and well-being and opportunity to play to be important and worthwhile professional concerns. Even by the 1990s, practitioners entering the early years workforce had not been overburdened by the need to obtain qualifications, particularly if they worked from their own homes as childminders, nor were they encouraged to see themselves as informed specialists with a thorough, academically robust grounding in young children's holistic development. Rather, early years employment required little, if any, formal qualification, and in the case of many childminders, presented an employment opportunity they could fit around the needs of their own young family and operate from their own home.

By 2004, research into The Effective Provision of Pre-School Education (EPPE) (Sylva et al., 2004) had shown that there was a significant relationship between the quality of a pre-school centre and improved child outcomes, and that there was a positive relationship between the qualifications of staff and ratings of quality. Children made more progress where the curriculum leader was qualified at graduate level. The results of this study led the New Labour government to focus on raising qualification levels, particularly in the PVI sector. In 2006, the CWDC launched Early Years Professional Status (EYPS), a new professional status aimed primarily at the ECEC workforce in the PVI sector. CWDC (2006) set out its aim that the EYP would be a "change agent" (p. 4), tasked with improving and leading practice in settings for the full age range of children from birth to the end of the Early Years Foundation Stage (EYFS), which was age 5. The CWDC set the expectation that candidates would demonstrate that their knowledge of the EYFS would inform their practice and "their leadership of others" (CWDC, 2010, p. 99). The CWDC viewed leadership as linked to improvements in quality and outcomes for children, but said little to define the leadership role beyond stating "they exercise leadership making a positive difference to children's wellbeing, learning and development" (CWDC, 2010, p. 17). In order to meet the NCS commitment to raise quality across the sector, the government set targets to have an EYP in every children's centre by 2010 and every other PVI setting by 2015.

Services for families and children – the need to intervene

New investment in the mainstream early years sector was coupled with a recognition that early intervention in the lives of children in the most deprived of circumstances, and support for their parents in providing a good home and securing employment would lead to improved outcomes for those children. Early research into children's educational outcomes had identified that children do better in school if they have had access to good pre-school provision, and this was later supported by the Field and Allen reports (Field, 2010; Allen, 2011) both arguing that early intervention was also more cost effective in the long run. Thus, in addition to expanding free nursery education for all children, Sure Start Local Programmes (SSLPs) were established in areas of the worst socio-economic deprivation, leading on from the Family Centres of the past, and acting as the forerunners of the current Sure Start Children's Centres seen in every local authority today.

The introduction of *Every Child Matters: Change for Children* (DfES, 2004) and its five outcomes also reintroduced the discourse of intervention and remedial action to what was otherwise becoming a market place commodity to parents who could afford it. It was developed as part of the response to further failings in child protection systems (Laming, 2003), and again highlighted the need to put the rights of the child to a healthy, safe and happy childhood at the forefront of practice. The outcomes reminded practitioners that supporting children's needs was a holistic process that included their physical and emotional health, if they were to go on and be successful throughout their education.

SSLPs evolved into Children's Centres, with the aim being for every ward in every local authority to have one as a hub for integrated services for families, combining childcare provision for parents in employment or education with group and individual support for parents in meeting their children's developmental and learning needs. Children's Centres began with a designated Core Offer (DfES, 2007) to local families, who could choose to use their services or be referred for targeted help by other agencies including Health and Social Services. Core Offer became Core Purpose (DfE, 2013b), reinforcing the role of the Children's Centre in tackling the effects of poverty and poor parenting. The early years sector is now being used to address broader social issues including adequate and appropriate parenting, the instilling of values about seeking gainful and lasting employment, managing debt and finances, and health awareness.

Thinking activity

Early years policy, as set out above, has been influenced by social and cultural changes over time including:

- individualised care of children within the family
- gender division of labour
- national economic survival.

Try to identify where these factors have been significant in shaping policy and how the early years sector has changed.

Researching practice – its impact on curriculum introduction and reform

Whilst policy had focussed on developing the breadth and capacity of the early years sector and reforming the qualification base of the workforce, this was supported by research into how best children's learning could be supported and what the role of the practitioner should be. Whilst the EPPE (Sylva et al., 2004) and REPEY (Siraj-Blatchford et al., 2002) reports combined to form the basis for what good practice in the modern early years sector should be, following a child-led, play-based curriculum, with the emphasis on meeting children's individual learning needs and focussing on their interests. The *Curriculum Guidance for the Foundation Stage* (QCA/DfEE, 2000) was introduced for those delivering funded nursery education to 3 and 4 year olds and became mandatory in 2002, and this was followed by the *Birth to Three Matters: A Framework for Supporting Children in Their Earliest Years* (Abbott, 2002), the first document to officially recognise in policy terms the learning needs and capacities of the youngest age group. These documents were then combined in 2008 into the Early Years Foundation Stage (EYFS) (DCSF, 2008), which brought together all the separate care standards into a single statutory set of Welfare Requirements, for all registered practitioners to follow regardless of how they were funded. This was supplemented by good practice guidance on how to meet children's learning and development outcomes, originally set out as six areas of learning and development, and later revised (Tickell, 2011) into seven and split into Prime and Specific areas, underpinned by the Characteristics of Effective Learning. You will learn more about this framework in Chapter 7.

Thinking activity

Read the EPPE or REPEY report, and identify how the findings have been used in the EYFS in use today.

The graduate practitioner today

In 2010 when the Coalition government came to power, only a fraction of the previous funding was announced for the continuation of EYPS as a workforce development strategy and CWDC was closed. In addition the target to have a graduate leader in every PVI setting by 2015 was removed from policy. Following the publication of the revised EYFS, Nutbrown's review of early education and childcare qualifications was released (Nutbrown, 2012), which acknowledged the positive impact that EYPS programmes had on individual practitioners and on the quality of settings, whilst pointing out that the lack of parity between EYPS and QTS (Qualified Teacher Status) caused frustration in the sector. This led to a report recommendation, not to strengthen government support for EYPS, but to introduce a specialist early years route to QTS (0–7 years), with an additional conversion qualification being made available to EYPs. In 2013, Truss as Childcare Minister announced the publication of *More Great Childcare* (DfE, 2013a) as a government response to the Nutbrown review (2012). Significantly, the report announced that EYPS would be replaced with Early Years Teacher Status (EYTS) and the National College for Teaching and Leadership (NCTL) became responsible for producing the Teachers Standards (Early Years) (NCTL, 2013). *More Great Childcare* (DfE, 2013a) also identified that the quality of people working below graduate level in early years must be improved. The Level 3 Early Years Educator (EYE) was introduced and all EYEs were required to have maths and English GCSE.

> **Thinking activity**
>
> What do you think might be the advantages and disadvantages of the workforce developments outlined above? Consider talking through these developments with other students on the course, practitioners in the setting and some parents you know. Does everyone share the same opinion on workforce development?

Conclusion

There is still much debate about the level and content of qualifications required by early years practitioners today and about the parity of roles between the Key Stage 1 teacher with QTS and the early years teacher with EYTS. Those outside the sector may still think that the role of the practitioner is to keep children safe and give them space and resources for play, and that proper learning will start at school. However, research has shown us that supporting play is the basis of promoting effective early learning, giving children the best possible start in life. The early years sector will continue to be subject to change as governments and policy makers make new decisions about how best to meet children's developmental and learning needs. This means the professional education of the practitioner will likewise continue to require updating to keep pace with this change and maintain high quality provision. However, no matter how the role of the practitioner is reconstructed and defined, at the heart of it is a commitment to ensuring children learn and grow, through play, in a safe and stimulating environment.

Further research and reading

Baldock, P., Fitzgerald, D. and Kay, J. (2013) *Understanding Early Years Policy*, 3rd ed., London: Sage.

  This book provides a detailed and accessible overview of policy which has shaped the early years sector.

National College for Teaching and Leadership (NCTL) (2013) *Teachers Standards (Early Years)*, London: Crown Copyright.

Pugh, G. and Duffy, B. (2014) *Contemporary Issues in the Early Years*, 6th ed., London: Sage.

  This book presents an introduction to some of the key debates and dilemmas which prevail in the sector, and supports critical reflection on practice and provision.

References

Abbott, L. (2002) *Birth to Three Matters: A Framework to Support Children in Their Earliest Years*, London: DfES.

Allen, G. (2011) *Early Intervention: The Next Steps*, London: Cabinet Office, Crown Copyright 2011.

Children's Workforce Development Council (CWDC) (2006) *Early Years Professional Prospectus*, Leeds: CWDC.

Children's Workforce Development Council (CWDC) (2010) *On the Right Track: Guidance to the Standards for the Award of Early Years Professional Status*, Leeds: CWDC.

Department for Children Schools and Families (DCSF) (2008) *Statutory Framework for the Early Years Foundation Stage*, Nottingham: DCSF.

Department for Education (DfE) (2010) *The Independent Commission into Early Intervention*, [online] Retrieved from www.education.gov.uk/news/press-notices-new/early-intervention-opportunities (Accessed 23 September 2010).

Department for Education (DfE) (2013a) *More Great Childcare: Raising Quality and Giving Parents more Choice*, Crown Copyright.

Department for Education (DfE) (2013b) *Sure Start Children's Centres Statutory Guidance for Local Authorities, Commissioners of Health Services and Jobcentre Plus*, London: Crown Copyright 2013.

Department for Education (DfE) (2017) *Statutory Framework for the Early Years Foundation Stage (EYFS)*, London: Crown Copyright 2014.

Department for Education and Employment (DfEE) (1998) *The National Childcare Strategy: Meeting the Childcare Challenge*, London: HMSO.

Department for Education and Skills (DfES) (2003) *Full Day Care: National Standards for under 8s, Day Care and Child-Minding*, Nottingham: DfES Publications Centre.

Department for Education and Skills (DfES) (2004) *Every Child Matters: Change for Children*, London: HMSO.

Department for Education and Skills (DfES) (2007) *Governance Guidance for Sure Start Children's Centres and Extended Schools*, Nottingham: DfES Publications, Crown Copyright 2007.

Department of Education and Science (DES) (1967) *The Plowden Report: Children and Their Primary Schools*, London: HMSO.

Early Education (2012) *Development Matters in the Early Years Foundation Stage (EYFS)*, London: Early Education.

Field, F. (2010) *The Foundation Years: Preventing Poor Children Becoming Poor Adults*, London: Crown Copyright.

Isaacs, S. (1929) *The Nursery Years: The Mind of the Child from Birth to Six Years*, London: Routledge and Keegan Paul Ltd.

Laming, Lord H. (2003) *The Victoria Climbie Inquiry: Report of an Inquiry by Lord Laming*, London: HMSO.

National College for Teaching and Leadership (NCTL) (2013) *Teachers Standards (Early Years)*, London: Crown Copyright.

Nutbrown, C. (2012) *Foundations for Quality: The Independent Review of Early Education and Childcare Qualifications: Final Report*, London: Crown Copyright.

Qualifications and Curriculum Authority/Department for Education and Employment (QCA/DfEE) (2000) *Investing in Our Future: Curriculum Guidance for the Foundation Stage*, London: QCA and DfEE.

Siraj-Blatchford, I., Sylva, K., Muttock, S., Gilden, R. and Bell, D. (2002) *Researching Effective Pedagogy in the Early Years*, London: Crown Copyright.

Sylva, K., Melhuish, E., Sammons, P., Siraj-Blatchford, I. and Taggart, B. (2004) *The Effective Provision of Pre-school Provision (EPPE) Project: Final Report*, Nottingham: DfES Publications.

Tickell, C. (2011) *The Early Years: Foundations for Life, Health and Learning*, London: Crown Copyright.

Chapter 2

Placement and professional skills

Nicola Firth

Chapter aims

By the end of this chapter you will be able to:

- examine why placement is a critical aspect of learning and development
- understand how to prepare for and start placement
- consider how to make the most of placement whilst developing professional skills.

Introduction

As part of an early years degree, you are expected to spend time on placement in an early years setting or settings in order to develop the skills required to become a successful early years educator and to experience 'real-life' early years practice. Your placement is crucial not only for developing personal and professional skills, but also for essential hands-on experience of the Early Years Foundation Stage (EYFS) and Development Matters Guidance, whilst also considering the National Occupational Standards for the sector.

There are two sets of National Occupational Standards that may be linked to your course, which are: Early Years Educator (Level 3): Qualifications Criteria (NCTL, 2011) and Teachers' Standards (Early Years) (NCTL, 2013). There are many similarities between the expectations of both sets of standards, including promoting children's early education and development outcomes through effective planning and observation, safeguarding the welfare of children and considering wider professional responsibilities including working in partnership with parents and other professionals (NCTL, 2011; NCTL, 2013). The main differences between the two are that the Early Years Teacher Standards require the Early Years Teacher to be a leader within education and care (NCTL, 2013), whereas the Early Years Educator may or may not take a leading role. Nevertheless, it is expected that as an early years undergraduate you should be striving towards high quality practice and being a positive role model to others.

Evidence from the Effective Provision of Pre-School Education (EPPE) study shows that improving the quality of the early years experience is directly related to better outcomes for children and that quality is dependent on the level of qualification of staff (Sylva et al., 2004). An undergraduate early years student on their pathway to becoming a graduate early years educator must learn and develop high quality skills in order to model high quality practice to other practitioners in the sector.

Governments over the past 15 years, including the current Conservative government, therefore want an early years workforce who will be change agents to improve practice, lead the Early Years Foundation Stage, support other practitioners and model skills and behaviours that safeguard and promote good outcomes for children – in other words, staff that can deliver high quality education and care.

The importance of placement

The Nutbrown review of qualifications recommended that high quality early education and care should be led by well-qualified early years practitioners (Nutbrown, 2012). As an undergraduate student moving into a graduate role in an early years setting, you will be expected to drive forward high quality practice. In order for a graduate early years educator to be in a position to do so, it is imperative that practical and theoretical skills are gained through placement experience, as experience gained whilst on placement will allow you to link theory to practical experience (Reed and Walker, 2015). This experience is known as 'work-based learning', 'practice-based learning, or 'professional practice' and is seen as a vital element of early years higher education courses (Musgrave and Stobbs, 2015). Durrant et al. (2009) suggest that work-based learning is not only about being taught by others, but is also about being an independent learner. It involves developing a higher level of understanding in practice and crucially reflecting on practice. Throughout this chapter the term 'professional practice' will be used to refer to placement experience and other opportunities for work-based learning.

When working with young children it is crucial that early years educators are able to link child development theory and milestones to practice and an effective way of doing this is to actually experience this in the 'real world'. Babies and young children develop and learn new skills constantly and at a rapid pace through a sequence of stages, and it is important to understand what these are and be able to assess this learning and development holistically. An early years educator must have the skills and abilities to be able to understand the process of how babies and young children develop (Levine and Munsch, 2016), not only through biological aspects of development but also in terms of what influences a child's development such as upbringing, culture and experiences. Whilst on placement, you will have the opportunity to be involved in some of these, including working with parents and other professionals, being able to observe and assess children's development in order to plan appropriate playful activities, and experiencing what it is like to work with others and take responsibility not only for oneself, but also for children. The practical experience of being on placement is invaluable and can increase students' employability upon completion of their degree. Students learn valuable skills when working alongside peers including colleagues in practice. Reed and Walker (2015, p. 251) refer to this as student practitioners not only "acquiring knowledge but also constructing a purposeful knowledge base within the learning and working environment".

Preparation for and starting placement

Some students worry about starting placement, as they do not know what to expect and may lack confidence; it is completely normal for you to feel this way. Placements have different processes for accepting students, and many like to interview the student prior to starting or ask them to spend some time in the setting to observe how they interact with children. This is an excellent and valuable opportunity to get to know other educators and people working in the setting. Tutors will also offer lots of support prior to you starting and during your time on placement and if at any point you feel worried or concerned, you should contact your tutor. Normally within the first few weeks of placement, students' anxieties decrease and they have an enjoyable experience.

First impressions

First impressions matter; therefore, students must think about how they conduct themselves and about their appearance from the outset. Here is a case study from a manager of an early years setting and what she expects from students whilst on placement:

Case study: manager's expectations

Charlotte is a Pre-School Manager and offers placement to first and second year undergraduates. The setting has high expectations of students and requires students to be enthusiastic, committed and motivated whilst maintaining professional standards. Charlotte also expects students to have good communication and organisation skills, be able to use their own initiative and common sense, be a positive role model and have a smart appearance, good attendance and punctuality.

Some students Charlotte has taken on placement have not always had successful outcomes, and she says "you feel like you put your time and effort into students . . . I am investing my time and not seeing any results. . . . It then puts you off having more students as you question their commitment to placement." Charlotte recalls a particular student who started off well on placement, but as time progressed she began to show an immature attitude, became unreliable and started to lack interest; she said "their social life became their priority, which is unacceptable when working with young children." The student also started to raise her voice at children and took no pride in her appearance so Charlotte felt she had no option but to contact the student's personal tutor. Fortunately for the student this was towards the end of her placement; however, Charlotte would have terminated the placement had this happened earlier on.

Nevertheless, Charlotte has generally had successful students on placement, and an example she recalls is of a very affable first year student who had a good understanding of children's development. Charlotte said "she was like one of the staff, part of the team, who consistently showed high quality and inspiring practice. She had a good understanding of the EYFS and knowledge of policies and procedures, including safeguarding protocols." The student would plan her own activities and participated in supporting the key person approach whilst working alongside a member of staff. She was able to take constructive criticism and would ask for advice. This student had a very productive and positive time on placement, and Charlotte expects all undergraduate students to develop and evidence such skills in order for them to be successful.

Thinking activity

Write a list of the skills and attributes you need to have in order to be success-ful on placement. Identify those which are your strengths and those that you need to develop. Think about how you can develop these skills by writing an action plan.

Your initial communication with placement is key, and you need to think about the best method to use, for example e-mail or telephone. It is recommended that you do not go directly to the placement prior to initial contact, as early years settings are very busy places. You must adopt a professional approach; therefore, practise beforehand what you want to say, or write a draft e-mail and proofread it carefully. It is useful to ask for support from a more experienced person such as a tutor or member of the family.

Thinking activity

Plan your initial contact with placement by writing answers to the points below:

- introduce who you are, what you are studying and where
- explain why you need a placement and why you would like to go there
- tell them the start date and days of the week you would like to attend – you will need to negotiate hours depending on how many your course expects you to complete
- be ready to answer questions they may ask you – be prepared and do some research about the setting you are contacting.

When looking for a suitable placement, it is important to find out the Ofsted rat-ing of the setting. Many universities will only allow students to be placed at Ofsted rated 'good' or 'outstanding' settings, therefore the student must check this with the university prior to approaching a placement. Nutbrown (2012) recommended that students need to observe high quality practice with high quality practitioners; there-fore, only 'good' or 'outstanding' settings should take students on placement. It is also a good idea to think about your possible career path, and approach the type of setting you want to work in when qualified. Some students think they know what career path they are following, but after time spent on placement, they realise it is not what they expected. An example of this is when students thinks they want to be a primary school teacher so they undertake placement in a Reception or Year 1 class, but they do not enjoy the experience; this however, should not be viewed as a negative experience. The student may then do another placement with younger children in a different type of early years setting and realise this is the job for them. Therefore, as a student, be open to new experiences and to the possibility that you might change your mind.

Some examples of placement settings are:

- Private Day Nursery
- Charitable Pre-school
- School Nursery or Reception Class
- Childminder
- Children's Centre.

It is also worth considering other practical aspects when organising your placement; for example:

- How far away is the placement from home?
- Is public transport easily accessible?
- What hours will the placement expect me to do?

Punctuality and reliability are key when working with young children, and placement will expect you to be on time and reliable; therefore, you must think very seriously about how long it will take you to get there, and how easy it is to reach. Children need consistency, and an unreliable student can impact negatively on their time in the setting. If for any reason you are going to be late or cannot attend placement, you must contact them as soon as possible so they can plan for your absence and limit the negative impact on the children's learning and development.

Your induction to the placement should be carried out by a manager or supervisor on the first day, and you should be made aware of the following policies and procedures: safeguarding, health and safety including fire drills, and confidentiality. It is important to start developing professional relationships with the staff team and children from the outset; therefore, you must take time to speak to and interact with them. It is likely that at the beginning of placement you will be given tasks which may include working with the children and other jobs such as cleaning floors and washing paint pots. These tasks are part of the job of the early years educator but should only be a small part of your role. Once you are settled you are expected to use your own initiative to identify tasks you need to complete as part of your studies. It is important to ensure that you take a proactive approach in planning what you need to do and that you communicate this to your supervisor on placement. Please read Chapter 3 for more on communication and teamwork.

You will be allocated a supervisor whilst on placement in order to support your professional development, and it is important to build a good relationship with them. Regular meetings are a part of the supervisor's role, as these will allow for dialogue and reflection to take place about what you are doing well, but also areas for development. The supervisor should be a qualified professional who has the skills and abilities to support you, and this will allow for you to learn and understand from their experiences. Nevertheless, sometimes supervisors have very busy job roles and may find it difficult to find time to sit and have productive dialogue with you. Therefore, it is useful right at the beginning of placement to negotiate professional ground rules, and ask when a good time to meet on a regular basis would be. A word of caution though: do not expect the supervisor to be able to meet at the same time every single week, as other duties may need to prioritised, so you need to be understanding and flexible.

Skills for a successful placement

Professionalism

As previously discussed, it is important to build professional working relationships with children and staff, and these will develop over time. Professionalism within the early years workforce is a relatively contemporary phenomenon, and it is not until recently that the UK government have started to listen to the early years educators' voice, in order to address early years policy and practice (Brock, 2012). This is a view supported by Osgood (2010) who agrees that professionalism within the early years' sector has become of central concern to policy makers, early years educators, parents and others who are working with children. This is positive and exciting news for you moving into a career in the early years sector. Brock (2015) argues that there has never been a more important time for early years educators to consider how they develop their own professionalism; therefore, this is also an important point for you to consider and think about.

A model of professionalism for early years educators developed by Brock includes seven dimensions (see Table 2.1).

As a student this model can be used to consider how the dimensions can be developed whilst studying for the degree and being on placement, so the professional nature of the early years educator will begin to be established.

Thinking activity

Think about the professional skills you already possess and how you might develop professional attributes linking to the seven dimensions featured in the table above. Write them in a table and revisit them whilst on placement to reflect on your emerging professional skills.

Table 2.1 Model of professionalism, adapted from Brock (2015)

1. Knowledge	What you need to know. *Specialist knowledge, unique expertise, experience.*
2. Education and training	How you have achieved knowledge and expertise. *Higher education, qualifications, practical experience.*
3. Skills	What you need to do. *Competence and efficacy, task complexity, communication, judgement.*
4. Autonomy	Your voice and advocacy – being allowed to do the job. *Entry requirement, self-regulation and standards, voice in public policy, discretionary judgement.*
5. Values	What informs and sustains you? *Ideology, altruism, dedication, service to clients.*
6. Ethics	What are your moral guidelines and codes? *Codes of conduct, moral integrity, confidentiality, trustworthiness, responsibility.*
7. Reward	Why you do the job. *Influence, social status, power, vocation.*

Nutbrown (2012) recommends that early years educators should take professional pride in their work, ensuring that their skills and pedagogical approaches are current. Both classical and contemporary theories of child development and pedagogical approaches will be learned whilst at university, and you must learn how to apply these in your practice. It is important, however, to remember that practice in the setting may not always reflect exactly what is taught to you in university, and you may have to draw on your own values and knowledge if practice is weak. The case study below outlines the experience of a student who experienced poor practice in the placement, and how she dealt with this:

Case study: problems on placement

Katherine was a second year early years undergraduate student and went on placement to a school where she was based in Reception Class and Year 1. During Katherine's first placement in Year 1 at university, she had enjoyed a positive placement experience and really found her time in the setting extremely valuable; unfortunately, this was not the case in her second year placement. During Katherine's first few weeks, she started questioning the teacher's practice in the setting, and what she observed and experienced in the classroom on placement was different than what she was learning about at university; Katherine referred to this as 'old school practice'. This made Katherine feel uncomfortable with the practice she was experiencing, and after taking time to reflect, she spoke to a tutor at university to seek advice.

After advice was given, she attempted to discuss her concerns with a senior member of staff in the setting who did listen to her concerns; however, Katherine felt that nothing was changing. Katherine persisted at placement but as she was feeling very unhappy and uncomfortable with practice, she decided to ask her tutor if she could move to another setting. Katherine felt that she was not learning from the experience or developing her professional practice. At this point Katherine was helped to secure another placement, which she did and she went on to have a positive experience.

Through reflection on practice and seeking advice from experienced tutors at university, Katherine found a solution to the problem. However, it does not always mean that leaving the setting is the only solution; often, students, and those they are working with, can resolve problems through discussion or through the intervention of a tutor to assist in resolving the concern.

Thinking activity

Imagine you experienced or saw what you deemed to be poor practice such as a child being shouted at or a member of staff talking in a derogatory way about another member of staff or a child. What action would you take and who would you report it to? Also consider if you were not enjoying placement and did not feel valued or supported, who might you report that to?

Confidentiality, honesty and integrity

Confidentiality is a key skill within professional practice and you must adhere to confidential and ethical practice at all times. It is imperative that you do not discuss any information about children and their families outside of the placement, and if there are any concerns you have then they must be reported to the appropriate person. An example of this may be that you have observed a child role playing aggressive behaviour, and the child may imply or disclose they have seen this type of behaviour at home. This would then need to be documented and reported to the settings safeguarding officer. The safeguarding officer would then support and guide you through the safeguarding policy and procedures. Confidential practice includes not using names of children in assessed pieces of work and not sharing any of their personal details outside of the setting. Normally the use of mobile phones with cameras are not permitted in the children's care and learning environment, and in some cases they are locked away and can only be used in staff-only areas; this is to protect children's identities and safeguard them from harm such as indecent images being taken.

Honesty, integrity and trustworthiness are expectations when working with children and the examples above are where these skills are needed.

Your aim is to be respected by others working in the setting and through showing them that you are honest and trustworthy, respect will begin to develop whilst relationships are being formed. Always be honest about issues or events rather than being dishonest. Examples of dishonesty include students asking for time off or to finish early but not stating real reasons for the request, or phoning in sick when in fact they are out shopping with friends. Once the trust is broken, it is difficult to regain. It is easy to also get caught up in conversations with others and these may not be of a professional nature; if this is the case, be professional and move away so there are no repercussions. It is important for you to take time to think about and reflect upon honesty and integrity and how you can maintain these professional skills not only within placement, but also other aspects of your life.

Initiative and developing confidence

Using initiative is a professional skill that you must develop whilst being on placement, and this is something the setting and university will be looking to develop and assess. When working with children you must be able to show that you can use your initiative, as young children are unpredictable and do things very much on the 'spur of the moment'. You need to show you can deal with things children do that you may not be expecting; for example, not wanting to carry out a planned activity, or sit for story time (which takes patience and understanding). In order to develop this skill the setting will advise on how they manage unwanted behaviour, and you can also observe how the early years educators or teachers deal with situations on a daily basis. The setting will also have policies and procedures in place that you can refer to. Using initiative is also about having ideas for planning activities and carrying them out with children, offering to help with mealtimes and hygiene routines, being willing to help on playground duty and much more. By developing and showing your initiative, you will gain confidence.

The following case study is an example of feedback received from a student's supervisor showing how she used her initiative, professionalism and knowledge developed through study and placement practice. The student was in the first year of her early years degree, and this shows that if students put time and effort into their placement and studies, they can succeed at very early stages of their undergraduate course:

Case study: positive feedback from placement

I wanted to let you know what an asset Sarah has been to us during her placement. Her commitment to her course and the children's learning has been outstanding. She has made many astute observations and has created activities which have supported and extended children's learning according to their needs. She has shown a great understanding of a range of theories and has researched to find further evidence and has put what she has found out into practice, supporting learning within the class. We have been able to have many professional discussions around Sarah's reading, research and observations which has enabled us both to reflect on our practice. It has been a pleasure for us all to have had Sarah work with us, and we are really pleased she has volunteered to stay with us, one day a week, for the next half term. We wish her all the best in her future studies and I know she will be a real asset in her next placement.

Here is a snippet of Sarah's weekly reflection of placement where she can be seen putting some of these skills into practice:

The activity involved 4 children working in pairs to construct a paper boat using only sheets of A4 paper and masking tape that could carry as many Lego characters as possible when placed in a water tray; the pairs were in competition against each other. I was seeking to observe not only paired working skills but also Characteristics of Effective Learning as detailed in Development Matters (Early Education, 2012). Two children that had worked together last week showed a clear division of labour between Child W the 'leader' and initiator and Child J the 'follower' and assistor; I was interested to pair these two children with different partners to see how the dynamic altered when they were in competition rather than in cooperation.

Sarah can be seen here observing and planning for children's individual needs using what she had observed in practice the previous week. Sarah had taken time to plan an appropriate activity for the children, whilst also taking into consideration appropriate non-statutory guidance from Development Matters. For more information on Development Matters, please read Chapter 7. From the feedback received from her supervisor and this small snippet of reflection from Sarah, many skills can be seen developing both in placement and at university. As a placement student you should aim to take a similar approach, using your university learning to inform and improve your practice.

Confidence matters when working with babies and young children and Sarah certainly grew in confidence, not only through support from her supervisor and others in placement, but also through her own sheer determination. At the beginning of placement you may lack confidence, as new experiences are always a little daunting. Expectations of placement and those you will be working with will be unknown and this can be worrying. Nevertheless, in time confidence should increase as their expectations of you become clear. You will be expected to work with small groups of children, and sometimes the whole class, for example reading stories or singing with children, and this may be worrying when you have never done this before; watch how the early years educators and teachers carry out these activities and follow their lead. You may feel embarrassed and scared about making a mistake. Remember we all learn by making mistakes, and it is more than likely that the children will not realise that you have made a mistake if they are having fun.

Roles within the setting

In placement, students will work with a range of practitioners qualified at different levels including:

- Level 2: nursery assistant or teaching assistant
- Level 3: early years educator
- Level 4: higher level teaching assistant
- Level 6: graduate early years educator or if the person has completed Early Years Teacher Status, they will be known as an early years teacher.

It is important to understand the different job roles people hold, so you are aware of who to turn to for support. There will also be additional roles that people hold, including safeguarding officer, special educational needs coordinator and first aider, so you need to be aware of these for reporting purposes, and to adhere to confidentiality. An example of this would be if you witnessed a child have an accident, you would need to immediately report the accident to the first aider on duty.

Emotional involvement and the professional role

As you can probably imagine, working with young children and their families can be emotionally challenging. Schutz et al. (2006) suggest that emotions should not be ignored but used to empower professionals working with children; when the practitioner becomes emotionally involved with children and their families, the key is to maintain a professional approach. As you develop relationships with children and some families, it is important to consider the emotional dimension of the work, and it is suggested to use the 'heart' and 'head' in tandem (Moyles, 2001), and not allow the 'heart' to take over but use it for empathy and compassion. This leads to emotional intelligence, which can be defined as the ability to identify and manage our own emotions and the emotions of others. Emotional intelligence comprises self-awareness, self-regulation, motivation, empathy and social skills (Goleman, 1995). These skills and qualities tend to develop over time, but you need to be aware of the importance of understanding not only your own emotions but also the emotions of others. Emotional intelligence will be further explored in Chapter 3 – Communication and teamwork.

Conclusion

As can be seen throughout this chapter, professional skills and attributes are a key concept that the early years undergraduate student needs to be thinking about, even before they start placement. From the moment contact is made with placement, you will be judged on your professionalism. Therefore, it is imperative that you are well prepared for that initial contact and present yourself with a professional and organised attitude. You need to show the placement supervisor that you will be an asset to their setting whilst on placement. Consideration of the Seven Dimensions of Early Years Professionalism (Brock, 2015) will assist you in further developing your professional skills. Your placement experience should be enjoyable and invaluable in supporting your professional development. You share the responsibility with your setting to ensure that your placement is a success; therefore, it is imperative that you show commitment, enthusiasm and initiative right from the start.

Reflection point and thinking activity

Considering what has been discussed in this chapter, produce an action plan of your approach to placement. Think about the skills you need to develop and how you will improve them.

Further reading and research

The *Nutbrown Review: Foundations for Quality: The Independent Review of Early Education and Childcare Qualifications Final Report* is a valuable read and offers an insight into recommendations for a highly skilled and professional early years workforce. The final report is available from: www.gov.uk/government/uploads/system/uploads/attachment_data/file/175463/Nutbrown-Review.pdf.

The National Occupational Standards that may be linked to the course will be a useful resource and available from: Early Years Educator (Level 3): Qualifications Criteria www.gov.uk/government/uploads/system/uploads/attachment_data/file/211644/Early_Years_Educator_Criteria.pdf.

Teachers' Standards (Early Years) www.gov.uk/government/publications/early-years-teachers-standards.

References

Brock, A. (2012) Building a model of early years professionalism from practitioners' perspectives, *Journal of Early Childhood Research*, 11(1): pp 27–44.
Brock, A. (2015) *The Early Years Reflective Practice Handbook*, Oxon: Routledge.
Durrant, A., Rhodes, G. and Young, D. (2009) *Getting Started with University-Level Work Based Learning*, Middlesex: Middlesex University Press.
Early Education (2012) *Development Matters in the Early Years Foundation Stage (EYFS)*, London: Department of Education.
Goleman, D. (1995) *Emotional Intelligence*, New York: Bantam.
Levine, L. and Munsch, J. (2016) *Child Development from Infancy to Adolescence*, London: Sage.

Moyles, J. (2001) Passion, paradox and professionalism in early years education, *Early Years: Journal of International Research and Development*, 21(2): pp 81–95.

Musgrave, J. and Stobbs, N. (2015) *Early Years Placements: A Critical Guide to Outstanding Work-Based Learning*, Northwich: Critical Publishing.

National College for Teaching and Leadership (NCTL) (2011) *Early Years Educator (Level 3): Qualifications Criteria*, London: NCTL.

National College for Teaching and Leadership (NCTL) (2013) *Teachers' Standards (Early Years)*, London: NCTL.

Nutbrown, C. (2012) *Foundation for Quality: The Independent Review of Early Education and Childcare Qualifications*, London: Department for Education.

Osgood, J. (2010) Reconstructing professionalism in ECEC: The case for the 'critically reflective emotional professional', *Early Years*, 30(2): pp 119–133.

Reed, M. and Walker, R. (2015) *A Critical Companion to Early Childhood*, London: Sage.

Schutz, P., Hong, I., Cross, D. and Obson, J. (2006) Reflections on investigating emotion in educational activity settings, *Educational Psychology Review*, 18(4): pp 343–360.

Sylva, K., Melhuish, E., Sammons, P., Siraj-Blatchford, I. and Taggart, B. (2004) *The Effective Provision of Pre-School Education (EPPE) Project: Final Report*, London: DfES.

Chapter 3

Communication and teamwork

Nicola Firth

Chapter aims

By the end of this chapter you will be able to:

- consider why communication and teamwork are important factors for the early years undergraduate student
- understand why teamwork is essential and examine theories that link theory to practice
- develop skills and techniques for written and verbal communication.

Introduction

When working with children, it is recognised that it is not only the children that professionals need to develop relationships with but also other people they are working with (Rodd, 2013). These are known as interpersonal relationships. "Morale, commitment and performance levels are affected by attitudes to and expectations about relationships in the workplace" and these relationships influence teams working together to do so in a "caring, respectful and constructive manner" (Rodd, 2013, p. 67). Therefore when working with others both at university and in placement, the undergraduate early years student must consider other people's points of views, attitudes and beliefs. Sometimes however, people will have different points of view and the team needs to work together and communicate clearly in order to understand each other's viewpoints, and deliberation and debate will take place within this process. There will also be a leader within a team of people working together when in the workplace, and this individual's role will be to ensure the team comes to an amicable and desirable decision.

There are various theories and strategies that will be explored in this chapter that assist early years undergraduate students in developing their knowledge and understanding of teamwork and effective communication. Whilst reading this chapter, it is important to consider how the theory and strategies discussed link to the students developing skills and qualities, and how the theory relates to practice. Some of the theories and concepts explored include group formation and group dynamics, different roles people play within a team, emotional intelligence and how to manage one's own emotions and the emotions of others, and how to communicate and listen in an effective and active manner.

Why are communication and teamwork important factors for the early years undergraduate student?

Early years educators are expected to work as part of a team, and within this team clear communication is vital. At times the early years educator will work individually, particularly depending on their job role, but much of their time will be spent working with others. This will not only include those they work directly with but also other professionals such as social workers, health visitors, speech and language therapists, advisors from local authorities and Ofsted, to name a few. Within these teams clear communication is needed, both verbal and written; otherwise, the child or children may not receive the support required. This could have disastrous consequences for the child and his or her family for the rest of their lives if it is something that is vital to their needs. Due to teamwork and communication playing such a large part in the role of the early years educator, it is imperative for early years undergraduate students to practise and develop these skills throughout their studies and time on placement; these skills will nonetheless continually develop throughout life and do not just stop when the student qualifies.

Working in a team can involve working with one other person or a large number of people. The size and who is in the team will determine the type of communication that is necessary. For example, if the early years educators are working with those directly in their organisation, then verbal communication may be the chosen method; however, if they are working in a team that involves those outside the organisation, then it is likely that both verbal and written communication will be necessary. Relationships within the teams will also differ, and the early years educators will take on different roles depending on who they are working with and why they are working with them. Working in a team within the organisation may be less formal due to the day-to-day personal and professional relationships that are built, whereas working in a team with other professionals outside the organisation will have a much more formal approach with a professional attitude being required and appropriate.

At the start of placement, the early years undergraduate student will develop professional relationships with others nevertheless, due to the nature of the role and working as part of a team. As relationships are formed, more personal relationships may develop. It is, however, important to remain professional within these relationships and not allow personal feelings to become involved with professionalism. Relationships in teams and with others can be challenging, as they are sometimes with family and friends. Sometimes personalities will clash and sometimes there will be disagreements between team members and factions can form. In terms of disagreements, this is not always adverse and it allows for debate to take place and a sound decision to be made. The problem arises when no agreement can be reached; therefore, whatever final decision is made might not be agreed by all. This can leave people feeling devalued and undermined, so it is important to explain and communicate clearly just why particular decisions are made.

We all have different personality traits, and the undergraduate early years student must bear this in mind not only when working with other professionals but also with children and their families. Personality trait theory is known as the study of human personality and is generally defined as a person's behaviour, their thoughts and their emotions. A person's personality is defined by genetics, physiology, learning and social factors (Matthews et al., 2009), and all of these influence how the person behaves, thinks and deals with their own emotions and the emotions of others (emotional intelligence – links to this will be explored in the next section of this chapter). It is suggested that people with similar personality dispositions will generally get along (Matthews et al., 2009), so does this mean that people with different personality traits will not get along? This is not generally the case and often people with very different personalities will get along and develop relationships; however, they may need to work a little harder to understand each other's behavioural patterns and thoughts. An example of a difference in personality traits is one person having an extrovert personality – being very outgoing, possibly loud and pushing forward their own opinions – and another person being an introvert where they are quiet and shy.

Thinking activity

Think of a time when you have met someone who has a different personality to that of your own. What were your initial thoughts about this person? Did you like them or were you wary of them? Now reflect on how you got to know this person. Did your differences in personality type affect your relationship with them?

Whilst you are studying at university and on placement, it will become apparent that everyone has different personalities and some will be similar to your own, whilst others are very different. As an early years undergraduate student, it is important to consider how personality traits impact on the team but also how they can complement each other. The next part of this chapter will further explore working as a team and linking this concept to theory and practice.

Working as a team: theory and practice

Group formation and dynamics

When groups of people come to work together, there are theories of team development that support the group in its formation. Bruce Tuckman's theory is commonly referred to when teams are developing. Tuckman (1965) considers four stages of team development, these being:

1   Forming: at this initial stage when the team comes together, team members tend to be polite and positive. There may also be some anxiety about the task ahead.
2   Storming: conflict commonly arises during this period due to different working styles with individuals in the team. Team members become frustrated and little is often achieved.

3   Norming: the team starts to resolve their differences and starts to work together, whilst individual team members begin to see the different styles of working as strengths.

4   Performing: the team works harmoniously together and goals are achieved.

A fifth stage of 'adjourning' was also developed in 1977 when Tuckman worked with Mary Jensen, and this is when the team disbands (Tuckman and Jensen, 1977). However, this will generally only be the case when working with professionals outside of the organisation; for example, when working on projects or resolving a child protection case. The undergraduate student may enter the team at any of these points, and sometimes the stages can overlap; therefore, they are worth considering when starting and throughout your time on placement. It will also be the case that students go through these stages when working together at university such as whilst working as a team to produce group presentations; therefore, be ready for some disagreement, as it is rare that a team will work in harmony all of the time.

Group dynamics also form whilst teams are working together, and Forsyth (2006, p. 2) defines a group as "connections linking the individual members". Groups of people can range from families and friends known as primary groups to colleagues and people you work with known as secondary groups (Forsyth, 2006). These groups are all unique and dynamics within them will differ depending on the relationships and personality types. This is where dynamics are formed, and when considering dynamics of groups of people who work together, individuals will bring with them their own personality style and strengths and weaknesses. When linking to the life of the undergraduate student, we will think here about group dynamics, the formation of groups with other students at university and of teams whilst in placement, therefore, primarily secondary groups.

Thinking activity

Give some thought to how the dynamics between family and/or friends differ to those when teams of professionals work together. What are the differences and similarities?

Within secondary groups, other types of groups will emerge, and these may be 'planned' and 'emergent' group types. A planned group is one that is deliberately formed by its members or an external authority, whereas an emergent group comes together over time and interacts with the same set of individuals. Therefore planned groups are 'founded' and emergent groups 'find' one another (Forsyth, 2006). Considering these types of groups, the emergent group also links to primary groups, so consequently in placement/work settings the planned group will be the most common. Nevertheless some groups may then lead to emergent groups; for example, if some of the members become friends and socialise together outside of the planned group.

No matter what type of group the person is working in or choosing to socialise with, as stated earlier in the chapter, there will be personality clashes, and at times learning to deal with differences in personality can be frustrating. Everyone has different values, beliefs and personalities due to their upbringing and background, and these will form part of the group dynamics. It is important to try to understand other people's values and beliefs, and you can do this by talking to them and developing professional relationships. As discussed previously, personality types will differ between group members, and some people may be loud and outspoken whereas others may be quiet and stand back. The different personality types are needed though, and this is where leaders and followers tend to emerge; and every team does need at least one leader to keep them on task. This does not mean that the loud and outspoken person should be the leader though, and it may be the person that stands back and observes what is going on around them that makes a more effective leader.

Reflection point

Reflect on a time you have been part of a group, and think about the people in the group and their different values, beliefs and personality types. Ask yourself: What types of differences in personality were there? What and why did people in the group have different values and beliefs? How were the differing values, beliefs and personalities managed in order to make an effective team?

Teamwork and leadership

Whilst considering leadership, John Adair developed a three circle model of "task, team and individual", which refers to the importance of interaction with each other (Adair, 2009). The leader must be aware of these three factors in order to develop the team. However, it is important here not to just consider this model for the leader but also members of the team who are working together, in order for them to work together effectively. Adair (2009, p. 8) also discusses some of the qualities of a leader and includes: "enthusiasm, integrity, toughness or demandingness and fairness, warmth and humanity and humility". Again these qualities need to be considered by those working in the team; therefore, the early years undergraduate student must develop these qualities. It is imperative that those working with babies and young children are:

1   Enthusiastic – Children need enthusiasm in order to develop and thrive. The team around the child needs to maintain this approach in order to be effective in everything they do when working with children and their families.
2   Integrity – This will build trust from others. When working in a team and with children and their families, trust is key to effective relationships.
3   Toughness or demandingness and fairness – Working in a team is demanding and brings demands from others; therefore, there will be times when the early years educator needs to be firm (tough) but fair.
4   Warmth and humanity – Warmth towards others is a key quality, and showing the human side of personality is required in order to demonstrate the caring and nurturing disposition of the early years educator.

5   Humility – Remain open-minded and do not be arrogant towards others; understand the values, beliefs, views and opinions of others.

Thinking activity

Do you have all of these qualities? How can you further develop them and which are your strongest and weakest? Write an action plan of how you can start to further develop your qualities and also include any other qualities you think are needed when working in a team.

Emotional intelligence

Our own emotional intelligence is a strong influence when working with others. In Chapter 1, emotional intelligence was defined as "the ability to identify and manage our own emotions and the emotions of others" and Goleman (1995) relates emotional intelligence to self-awareness, self-regulation, motivation, empathy and social skills. It is considered by socio-biologists that emotional intelligence is more important than a person's IQ and it is our emotions that guide us through dilemmas and tasks rather than intellect on its own (Goleman, 1996). Emotional intelligence is innate but also shaped by life experiences and culture; therefore, everyone will have different levels of emotional intelligence and some people will be better than others in showing these qualities and skills. In the table below is a brief guide of the qualities that may be seen:

Table 3.1 Emotional intelligence: qualities and skills

Self-awareness	Knowing and understanding own emotions, strengths and weaknesses and being able to recognise when these may impact on others.
Self-regulation	Being able to regulate own emotions and manage them when they may be negative towards a situation or others.
Motivation	Ability to motivate oneself.
Empathy	Understanding other people's feelings and recognising when decisions are made how the person may feel and/or react.
Social skills	Being able to manage others and relationships and inspire them.

As can be seen from the examples above, it is essential to maintain a positive outlook; at times we all get a little down and feel fed-up, so this is when a person may rely on someone else in the team to use their emotional intelligence and support someone who is feeling this way. "Each emotion offers a distinctive readiness to act: each points us in a direction that has worked well to handle the recurring challenges of human life" (Goleman, 1996, p. 4). If we use our emotions wisely to guide ourselves and others, combined with intelligence, then working with others will be made easier with a better understanding of each other.

Team roles

Within teams attention needs to be given to the roles that people play, and Meredith Belbin refers to nine particular roles that became apparent during research undertaken in 1969, that are still used widely in organisations. Belbin (2015) says,

> A team is not a bunch of people with job titles, but a congregation of individuals, each of whom has a role which is understood by other members. Members of a team seek out certain roles and they perform most effectively in the ones that are most natural to them.

The key here is the term 'natural', meaning that people generally fall naturally into one or more of the roles Belbin refers to. The roles are:

Table 3.2 Belbin's team role descriptors, adapted from Belbin (2016)

Role	Description
Resource Investigator	Outgoing, enthusiastic, explores opportunities and develops contacts.
Teamworker	Cooperative, perceptive, diplomatic, listens and averts friction.
Coordinator	Mature, confident, identifies talent, clarifies goals and delegates effectively.
Plant	Creative, imaginative, free-thinking, generates ideas and solves difficult problems.
Monitor Evaluator	Strategic, discerning, sees all options and judges accurately.
Specialist	Single-minded, self-starting, dedicated and provides specialist knowledge and skills.
Shaper	Challenging, dynamic, thrives on pressure and has the drive and courage to overcome obstacles.
Implementer	Practical, reliable, efficient, turns ideas into actions and organises work that needs to be done.
Completer Finisher	Painstaking, conscientious, anxious, searches out errors and polishes and perfects.

The roles above are all strengths the person within the team brings with them, but there are also weaknesses. An example is the Teamworker who is cooperative, listens and averts friction; however, a weakness they bring with them is they can be indecisive and tend to avoid confrontation, due to their desire to avert friction. Belbin claims that to have a balanced group all nine roles need to be present within the team; nevertheless, it is argued that the validity of this claim is not conclusive (Meslec and Curseu, 2015). Therefore, it may be that not all roles need to be present as long as there is a good balance of strengths within the team.

Thinking activity

What role or roles do you believe you play within a team? Can you see some of the predispositions and roles in others you have worked with? Do you think all roles are needed for a team to work harmoniously together?

As it is clear to see, there are various theories to consider when working as a team and these cannot be ignored if the team is to work well together in order to achieve high quality care and outcomes for children and their families. Take time to observe how teams are formed both at university and whilst on placement, and take time to think about how problems can be resolved when they arise and how support from others is an essential part of working in a team in an early years setting.

Verbal and written communication

Communication takes place in a variety of ways, and these are defined by Manning et al. (1996) as written, oral, verbal and non-verbal. As human beings we constantly communicate through a range of means including verbal conversation, which might be face-to face or at a distance by telephone. Social media plays an increasingly important role in how we communicate and will be explored further in this section. Siraj-Blatchford and Manni (2006) suggest the following multi-functional and multi-directional skills are required in order to communicate effectively and involve:

1 Speaking
2 Listening
3 Encouraging
4 Reflection
5 Translating
6 Interpreting
7 Consulting
8 Debating
9 Summarising
10 Understanding
11 Acknowledging
12 Verifying.

There are many considerations here for communicating, and point number 2 is key; **listening attentively** to what others are actually saying, which is known as 'active listening' (Manning et al., 1996). There are times when we are having conversations with someone else and our minds start to wander and we stop listening to what the other person is saying but still 'pretend' we are listening to them by acknowledging them (point 11 above). Nevertheless during or at the end of the conversation we realise we do not actually know or remember fully what was stated. If this is the case during an important conversation and something needs to be actioned, the person who was not listening actively but was listening in a passive manner will not be able to do so; the consequence of this could be disastrous, particularly if it concerned the care of a child. Communication breakdown is generally due to poor listening skills, and many of the points raised by Siraj-Blatchford and Manni (2006) would not be put into action if active listening was not taking place; therefore the multi-functional and multi-directional skills of communication would not be deployed.

Verbal communication

Albert Mehrabian developed a rule of communication and interpretation that suggests 7 per cent of what is said derives from spoken words (what is actually being said), 38 per cent from voice (how something is said) and 55 per cent by expression (facial and body language), known as the "7–38–55 rule" (Clayton, 2007). This rule, however, can only be applied when there is face-to-face contact, as expression cannot be seen with any other type of communication; the voice and words can be heard, but according to Mehrabian this would only equate to 45 per cent of interpretation. Therefore looking back at expression, this is generally a concept that can be seen and observed, and a person's expression can convey much more than words. Signs to look out for when observing a person's non-verbal communication include facial expression and body language; does the person look happy, worried or confused? How is the person holding their body? Is the individual standing upright and confident or slouching with the head down? These are signs that cannot be dismissed when communicating with others and often tell us important information about how the person is feeling and communicating their message. This would also relate to our emotional intelligence, including empathy and social skills.

Misinterpretation and misunderstanding can also be a problem with verbal communication, and this is known as the 'Arc of Distortion'. This is where two people are having a conversation and person A communicates/states their point but person B hears what they are saying differently, and this is sometimes where misunderstanding takes place (Manning et al., 1996), with the wrong message being received. Manning et al. (1996) raises six key points in order to overcome a passive listening approach, including:

1   Look at the person who is talking
2   Ask questions in order to ensure understanding is present
3   Do not interrupt
4   Do not distract
5   Establish a trusting relationship
6   Respond in a clear manner.

If these strategies are deployed, then the person receiving the message will be taking an active listening approach and understanding should be clear.

When communicating verbally with others, language barriers can become a problem, and not only should we consider people with English as a second language but also terminology that may be used between the early years educators (EYE) and the person they are having a conversation with, for example a parent. Terminology within the Early Years Foundation Stage should be understood by the EYE, but this does not mean the parent will understand the true meaning of the words used. There are various examples we could look at here, but let's take the word 'key person'. The EYE will understand the terminology and what the 'key person' is and does, but this does not mean the parent will; therefore, clear explanation must be provided for specific key terminology. Not only must the EYE bear this in mind but also the undergraduate early years student. Students may also find themselves in a position of not understanding key terminology, so they must ask what such terms mean or read/research in order to find out.

English as a second language can be a huge barrier for parents, children and EYEs. As society becomes more diverse, there are many more different languages used in schools. Some of the most common are languages are from Asia and the Middle East such as Urdu, Arabic (Arabiyya) and Mandarin but also various European languages are becoming more common, including Polish and Russian. The EYE is not expected to learn new languages, but they must be able to communicate with the children and parents; therefore, as the undergraduate early years student, it is imperative that observation is undertaken to ascertain how EYE's communicate and break down the language barriers. They will use strategies such as signs, pictures and use of simple words/language. These strategies may also be used with people who may have hearing difficulties or may be deaf, but in this case the use of written language may also be a useful approach. It is also imperative that an active listening approach is taken at all times.

Written communication

Practising writing skills will become part of the students' everyday life and they will find themselves writing for different purposes: essays for assessment, written tests, e-mails, personal statements and CVs. Written communication is also fundamental to early years practice, and the undergraduate early years students will find themselves not only writing observations regularly but also writing up planned activities whilst on placement. The observations may form part of a child's learning journey so writing must be to a very good standard with no spelling mistakes or grammar errors, as learning journeys form part of children's assessment and are seen by parents and other relevant professionals. This is also the case when writing for assessment, and spelling, punctuation and grammar must be to a high standard or students can lose valuable marks.

It is important to get out of bad habits when writing, and an example of this is using text speak. If a student e-mails a tutor or placement supervisor using text speak, this does not give a good impression and the person receiving the message may not understand the meaning of the text speak so cannot answer the e-mail. This will frustrate the tutor/supervisor, as they have to spend time e-mailing the student back and asking for clarification of meaning, and this is not acceptable. It is quite acceptable for a student to use text speak between friends, but never use this type of written language when communicating with a professional. Think about how unprofessional it looks, and it can also be construed as a very lazy approach. Get into the habit of using full and correct words/terminology and correct punctuation and grammar; this will then become part of everyday written communication, and this style of professional writing will become more natural.

Most of the time the use of mixed written and verbal communication is adopted, particularly in everyday aspects of life; below is a case study of this type of communication working effectively:

Case study: clear communication

Whilst Suzanne was on placement, she regularly met with her supervisor so they could reflect on her learning together and plan for future development. Suzanne would then write a reflection and pass this onto her supervisor to comment. Here is an example of clear written communication by the supervisor to Suzanne, after a face-to-face meeting:

"Be confident Suzanne – you have every reason to be! You've learned a lot this half term – not only regarding how children learn, but a lot about yourself and how to develop your own skills! The way you have planned and carried out activities to support your understanding of child development and social interaction have been thoughtful, well managed and, from our discussions, useful – even when they haven't gone quite as hoped! You are using what you are finding out to lead you on to further learning. Continue to be more assertive – say what you are thinking/feeling about what you have learned/been asked to do/ what you have observed. We can all learn from each other!!"

In the case study it is apparent that both Suzanne and the supervisor not only communicate effectively but they also have a professional and open manner with each other, with two-way communication taking place. Suzanne is encouraged and supported to further develop her skills and the supervisor ends by stating, "we can all learn from each other!!". This is undoubtedly encouraging Suzanne to continue to keep clear channels of communication open, as she will be developing confidence from seeing such motivational words written down.

Social media

Social media has become a way of communicating in everyday life such as Facebook, Twitter, Yammer and Snapchat to name a few. These are useful ways for keeping in contact with friends and in some cases colleagues but they must be used with caution. There have been cases of professional misconduct and cyber-bullying; for example, *The Guardian* (2012) reported a number of teachers being struck-off and given prohibition orders because they had befriended pupils on Facebook in an unprofessional manner (Vasagar and Williams, 2012). Even the police force had to launch an investigation when a secret online Facebook page was discovered full of abusive comments about 'Gypsies and Travellers' that police officers had allegedly written (Green, 2015). These examples show how easy it is to be able to hack into what others are saying or people reporting others for unprofessional conduct.

Within early years education one of the most common misuses of communicating on Facebook tends to be matters of confidentiality such as naming children, settings and other professionals and also putting photographs of children and settings on Facebook pages. This may be done naively; however, it is completely unnecessary and would be a breach of confidentiality procedures both within the setting and for the university. This could result in the early years undergraduate student being suspended from placement and university whilst an investigation takes place under the Fitness to Practise policy, which in turn may result in the student losing their place on their early years degree course. Therefore the student must ensure they use Facebook and other social media applications in a professional manner and always think about what they are writing and commenting on, as an unprofessional comment or image could jeopardise their future career!

Conclusion

There are many factors for the undergraduate early years student to consider and think about when working as a team, and as can be seen throughout this chapter, communication is key for effective working relationships. The student must take time to develop relationships with children but as important are staff teams they are working with on placement, tutors at university and also their peers at university. There will be times both in placement and university where the student may have to work with colleagues and peers they may prefer not to due to different personality traits or views and opinions. Nevertheless, working with others outside of 'friendship' groups can be beneficial to learning; as new and varied views and experiences of others become apparent, new knowledge and understanding can be developed.

The theories explored in this chapter will support the undergraduate early years student in developing teamwork skills. It is imperative that whilst on placement the student observes teamwork practices and also considers how matters such as communication breakdown and poor group dynamics are dealt with and resolved, often by leaders in the setting. Consideration of Tuckman's Group Formation will assist the student in seeing at what stage a group is at, and this theory can then support the team in developing and moving onto other stages. For example, a team that is in the 'Storming' stage where conflict arises really needs to move onto the 'Norming' and 'Performing' stage as quickly as possible, in order to have a better working and efficient team. Also understanding Belbin's Team Roles will support the student, and they can think about the role they can adopt, so that they have a role to play within the team.

It is imperative that the early years undergraduate student attempts to fit in with the team they are working with as soon as is possible, but in a way that is not intrusive. In order for the student to do so they need to ensure that they have a friendly but professional manner, use initiative, communicate clearly with others and ask questions. The student can think about the skills that were discussed in the Placement and professional skills chapter in order to fit in with the team the student is working with and to develop strong professional relationships with others.

Further reading and research

For further detail and explanation of Belbin's Team Roles, the following link will provide an overview. This will be useful in order to consider the roles played by others and the role that suits your skills and qualities: www.belbin.com/media/1486/team-role-summary-descriptions-2016.pdf.

Infed.org is a useful website for further researching theory that supports teamwork. The website aims to specialise in the theory and practice of informal education, social pedagogy, lifelong learning, social action, and community learning and development. It is a simple site to use and has a specific search button that uses keywords to find what you are looking for. Follow this link will take you to their search page: http://infed.org/mobi/welcome/.

References

Adair, J. (2009) *Effective Leadership: How to be a Successful Leader*, new rev. edn., London: Pan Macmillan.

Belbin, M. (2015) *Belbin: History and Research*, Retrieved from www.belbin.com/about/history-and-research

Belbin, M. (2016) *Belbin Team Roles Summary Descriptions*, Retrieved from www.belbin.com/media/1486/team-role-summary-descriptions-2016.pdf

Clayton, I. (2007) Super models: In a series of articles examining learning models, *Training Journal*, 62.

Forsyth, D. (2006) *Group Dynamics*, 4th edn., London: Thomson Learning.

Goleman, D. (1995) *Emotional Intelligence*, New York: Bantam.

Goleman, D. (1996) *Emotional Intelligence: Why It Can Matter more than IQ*, London: Bloomsbury Publishing.

Green, C. (2015) Met police to face racism probe after secret online Facebook page filled with abusive comments discovered, *The Independent*, Retrieved from: www.independent.co.uk/news/uk/home-news/met-police-to-face-racism-probe-after-secret-online-facebook-page-filled-with-abusive-comments-10399244.html

Manning, G., Cutis, K. and McMillen, S. (1996) *Building the Human Side of Work Community*, Duluth: Whole Pearson Associates Ltd.

Matthews, G., Deary, I. and Whiteman, M. (2009) *Personality Traits*, 3rd edn., Cambridge: Cambridge University Press.

Meslec, N. and Curseu, P. L. (2015) Are balanced groups better? Belbin roles in collaborative learning groups, *Learning and Individual Differences*, 39: pp 81–88.

Rodd, J. (2013) *Leadership in Early Childhood: The Pathway to Professionalism*, 4th edn., United Kingdom: Open University Press.

Siraj-Blatchford, I. and Manni, L. (2006) *Effective Leadership in the Early Years Sector (ELEYS) Study*, London: Institute of Education.

Tuckman, B. (1965) Development sequence in small groups, *Psychological Bulletin*, 63(6): pp 384–399.

Tuckman, B. and Jensen, M. (1977) Stages of small group development revisited, *Group and Organizational Studies*, 2: pp 419–427.

Vasagar, J. and Williams, M. (23 January, 2012) Teachers warned over befriending pupils on Facebook, *The Guardian*, Retrieved from: www.theguardian.com/education/2012/jan/23/teacher-misconduct-cases-facebook

Chapter 4

Being a reflective practitioner

Mary Dyer and Nicola Firth

Chapter aims

By the end of this chapter you will be able to:

- identify what reflective practice is
- understand its importance in the development of professional expertise through a transformational approach to professional education
- explain a range of different approaches you might want to use to structure your own reflection
- demonstrate how critical reflection can be applied to your own early years practice.

Introduction

This chapter explores what reflective practice is and how you can use it support your professional education and development as an early years practitioner. Early years practice focusses on the unique needs of individual young children, and as such presents practitioners with challenges on a daily basis, so that it can never become a matter of routine to follow set procedures and policies (Nutbrown, 2012). Instead, as a practitioner you will need to consider the individual needs presented to you by different children, and how to address these using your professional education and past experience to guide you. Moss (2006) argues strongly that early years practitioners need to be creative, independent, reflective thinkers rather than well-educated technicians applying routine practices to far from routine situations, and to achieve this you need to understand and apply the processes of critical reflection.

What is reflective practice?

For most people, reflection is a process of evaluating our actions, whether that is in the workplace, the education or training setting, or in our personal lives. Most of us would define it as thinking about what we have done and whether or not it produced the results we wanted. Reflective practice brings this process into the workplace, and offers the opportunity to consider the impact of our actions on the children we work with, their families, our colleagues, our setting, even colleagues within different agencies and organisation. Anything we do in early years practice can affect so many people around us, so it is important to consider why and how we do things to ensure that our practice is of the highest possible quality and we maintain an ethical stance in our work.

Moon (1999) argues that reflection is a difficult process to define succinctly, although a number of different processes appear to contribute to it, including thinking, reasoning and problem solving. It begins with the act of noticing, i.e. having our attention drawn to a particular event or activity, especially if it surprises us in some way (Jaworski, 1993), so that we question what has happened, how it has come about and what its impact might be.

Johns (2004) identifies reflection as a process for analysing and understanding our own practice, and equally importantly, the values that underpin it, more clearly, so that future practice is made more effective, and our confidence in the ethical quality of our actions is made more secure. Not only should you consider how effective your practice was in meeting your intended outcomes and objectives, but there is also the need to consider what those outcomes are and if they do represent the best of outcomes for the children with whom you are working. Whilst this may seem like a daunting challenge, and not something you feel you have the experience to take on as you begin your early years career, you will soon start to hear colleagues question if specific goals are appropriate to individual children's developmental progress; or you might come to question if local or national priorities for young children's learning truly match the priorities you have identified for key children in your care, whose personal and family circumstances may be significantly different from the typical norm. You may feel at this point that you do not agree with national or local policy and are being asked to practise in ways that do not sit comfortably with your own views on early years practice.

Reflection can involve a level of discomfort, particularly for the beginner who often finds reflection to be a process for discovering what they did wrong. However, if you are using reflection properly, such negativity should not be the main focus of your self-evaluation – it is equally important to know why successful practice has worked, especially if you are one day going to lead and support other new practitioners. Effective practice is not simply a matter of luck or intuition, but is arrived at by a clear understanding, not only of what does not work, but also of the factors that contribute to good practice – what to take into account about individual children, what to know about resources you intend to use, what contingency planning might be useful, what theory and research can be used to inform your planning and decision making – so that effective practice becomes the norm of your working life rather than the exception.

Reflection requires you to have your own idea of what you consider good or effective practice to be, and to have the confidence to question your practice, your values and your motivations objectively and honestly. As you become more practised in reflection, then the deeper your reflection should be, giving you a stronger base from which to determine not only the practical effectiveness of what you do in the workplace but also the personal, ethical values you apply to your work. Goodman (1984, cited in Jasper, 2013, p. 8) identified three levels of reflection, progressing from a simple evaluation of deciding if something worked the way it was intended to, to considering the ethics of practice and the 'rightness' of a particular course of action or event, which as you become more practised in the process you should find yourself moving through.

Table 4.1 identifies these levels and demonstrates how they might be applied to your own practice within an early years setting when planning an outdoor activity to promote physical development for 3-year-olds:

Table 4.1 Levels of reflection

Outdoor activity to promote physical development		
Level 1 Reflection	*Level 2 Reflection*	*Level 3 Reflection*
Reaching given objectives	Considering the rationale for practice, the implications and consequences of actions	Emancipation, social justice, empowerment
Were Development Matters statements for physical development achieved by all/any of the children?	What else could you have done to achieve the same outcomes; would these different approaches have been more appropriate to the individual needs of different children?	Why is it important to promote and support such development and learning? Does this apply to all children?
Was there opportunity for children to practise gross and fine motor skills and develop new skills?	Did your activity take full account of children's learning needs, their individuality, their rights and their voice – how do you know you achieved this, or what else could you have done?	Consider questioning the content of the curriculum framework you are following and how that meets the needs of the children for whom it is used.
Was the activity a safe and effective use of resources?	How did your practice meet the requirements for supporting the characteristics of effective learning?	
Did it take account of individual children's needs?		

Level 1 is a very outcome-focussed approach to evaluating practice, one used by novice practitioners whose practice is guided and supervised by more experienced colleagues. However, reflection should not stop at this point, but eventually go on to consider how else such outcomes might be achieved, what Goodman refers to as Level 2, where the impact of practice on the children you are working with needs to be considered in a range of different contexts. Finally, reflection should move on to Level 3, considering why it is important to promote and support such development and learning, and if this is the case for the children and families you are working with. This is the deepest level, considering issues of social justice, and where true empowerment and emancipation for you as a practitioner can be found. By reflecting at Levels 2 and 3 you have the opportunity to consider a broader approach to defining effective practice and contributing to knowledge and understanding of good practice within your setting and perhaps across the wider early years sector.

Reflection and the development of expertise

When considering the purpose of reflection for the early years practitioner, we first need to think about what it is the role requires and the breadth and depth of understanding that is necessary to underpin the complex day-to-day decision making it involves. For reflection to have value for you as an early years practitioner, you need to understand how it can support your development of expertise within this field, and how it can empower you to contribute to the creation of knowledge about the most effective ways of meeting the individual and unique needs of young children. Strandgaard (1981, cited in Megginson and Whittaker, 2007) and Dreyfus and Dreyfus (1986) offer us different ways of charting the development of a novice worker from the start of their professional learning to the eventual achievement of expertise on their field (see Table 4.2). Similarly, Johns (2004) likens this process to the development of the voice of the practitioner, from being silent and under the control of others and their expertise (hence the characterisation of this as a victimic stance), to the more agentic position of being able to combine the knowledge of others (from colleagues, research sources, additional training) with their own experience, and through critical analysis and evaluation, arrive at their own understanding of how situations should be addressed, making their own contribution to the professional knowledge of their sector.

When viewed together and applied to the early years sector (see Table 4.2), the three different theories show a similar pathway from the silent, unknowing novice to the articulate and confident expert who applies a combination of knowledge and experience to her or his own practice and to leading and supporting the practice of others. This is achieved through a process of learning from others and from experience, to a position of being able to operate almost intuitively in applying past experience and knowledge to ever-changing situations in the workplace, supported throughout by the use of critical reflection on one's own practice.

How then does reflection support this development of expertise and the confidence to contribute to professional knowledge based on personal experience? There are different models of reflection (See 'Different Approaches to Reflection' below) that can be used to support you in this progression from novice to expert, which offer you not only the opportunity to consider how effective your practice is at an operational level (a "have I done what I was supposed to do?" kind of level) but also at a deeper, more empowering level, considering broader questions of social justice and impact of practice on individuals (an "is our practice right for these children, is this what we should be focussing on in early learning and development?" kind of approach).

Reflection is not simply a process of measuring efficiency of practice and effective use of resources, but eventually one where we question what we mean by terms such as efficiency and effectiveness, and consider wider questions of who we are accountable to as practitioners – the children, their parents, Ofsted, funders, society. And whose needs or agenda are more important? The work of Goodman (1984, cited in Jasper, 2013) and King and Kitchener (1994) demonstrate how different levels and types of reflective thinking can be associated with the different stages in the development of professional expertise (see Table 4.3) and present a clear argument for how higher levels of expertise may not be reached without a change in the quality and depth of your reflective thinking. To be a true expert, it is not enough simply to consider how efficiently, cost-effectively, or skilfully individual tasks were done by ourselves or others, but we must also consider why those tasks were done, the impact of them on a wider range of people, and whether or not they should be done in that manner, or even done at all. This is a lot to ask of a beginner, and explains why it takes confidence, knowledge and experience to be able to reflect at the deeper levels, but it is something you should keep in mind as you begin to use reflective thinking to support and develop your own practice.

Table 4.2 Developing expertise

Strandgaard (1981)	**Unconscious incompetence** Being unaware of how much we do not actually know; even being unaware of how much there actually is to know.	**Conscious incompetence** Becoming aware of how little we do know and how much we have to learn; understanding what our areas for development are.	**Conscious competence** Developing knowledge by learning from others, through our own research and experience; developing skill and understanding in relation to day-to-day tasks and challenges; feeling confident in working without supervision.		**Unconscious competence** Drawing on experience almost intuitively to meet challenges and overcome new problems; able to support others in the development of skill and understanding.
Dreyfus and Dreyfus (1986)	**Novice** Follows rules – identifies objective facts and key elements within situations.	**Advanced beginner** Flexible responses, learning to cope with the unpredictable – adapts rules to take account of situational elements when encountering real-life situations with unexpected elements.	**Competence** Decision-making skills with feeling of ownership/responsibility – accumulates wealth of context-free and situational knowledge, and needs to learn to prioritise and identify which elements can be used to formulate an action plan.	**Proficiency** Combination of intuition and analysis – deep involvement with task; identification of salient features of a situation and can change these as a situation unfolds – application of memory and experience to current situation,	**Expertise** Critical reflection on intuition, fluid performance – unconscious application of skills, doing what normally works and deliberating/decision making where appropriate.
Johns (2004)	**Silence/received knowing (victimic)** A subordinate role – speaking with voice of others.	**Subjective knowing** A tentative, vulnerable, uncertain voice, one which requires nurturing.	**Procedural knowing – connected** The development of empathy and moral responsibility – the consideration of what others experience, how they give meaning to their experience.	**Procedural knowing – separate** Challenging received knowledge, the development of critique and reasoning.	**Constructed knowing (agentic)** The informed, passionate and assertive combination of connected and separate knowing; the valuing of objective and subjective knowledge, leading to a contribution to the creation of knowledge.

Table 4.3 Reflection and the development of expertise

	Unconscious incompetence	Conscious incompetence	Conscious competence		Unconscious competence
Strandgaard (1981)	Unconscious incompetence	Conscious incompetence	Conscious competence		Unconscious competence
Dreyfus and Dreyfus (1986)	Novice	Advanced beginner	Competence	Proficiency	Expertise
Johns (2004)	Silence/received knowing (victimic)	Subjective knowing	Procedural knowing – connected	Procedural knowing – separate	Constructed knowing (agentic)
Goodman (1984)	Level I Reflection Reaching given objectives.		Level 2 Reflection Considering the rationale for practice, the implications and consequences of actions.		Level 3 Reflection Emancipation
King and Kitchener (1994)	Levels I–3 *Pre-reflective reasoning* Knowledge is certain and stable.	Levels 4–5 *Quasi-reflective reasoning* Knowledge contains elements of uncertainty – you cannot prove everything; you can use evidence to support a conclusion, but you may be unsure about how the evidence leads to this conclusion so that your conclusions may be regarded as idiosyncratic.	Levels 6–7 *Reflective reasoning* Knowledge is uncertain and there may be no right answers. The key thing in decision making and reaching conclusions is the validity and strength of the argument or the thinking.		
Schon (1983)	Knowing in action Getting a feel for the situation, the role, the context.		Knowledge in action Developing concepts and understanding about situations.	Knowing in practice Tacit, spontaneous, automatic response to a situation.	

Different approaches to reflection

Reflection as a process is relatively simple and straightforward, and is usually triggered by a 'critical incident', i.e. something happens that takes you by surprise. It may be that what you had considered to be a routine act or well-planned event does not go as you had expected, or equally, it could be that something you were concerned about, for lack of experience, or lack of certainty over how to proceed, goes much better than expected. Critical incidents may seem small, and might only be of interest to you as an individual, but to critically evaluate and develop your practice, you need to start with what catches your attention, no matter what it is. The key to reflection is not what you reflect on, or even how you structure and manage the process, but actually the depth and detail and the criticality of your analysis, and what you learn from it to develop your practice.

There are many different models and approaches, all designed to support you in structuring your thoughts and considering your actions in some depth. Some are more detailed than others, some ask more specific questions than others. Which one you choose is a matter of personal preference, and no single model suits all people or even all occasions. For many beginners, following a specific model is very helpful and allows them to build up confidence in knowing what to focus on and how to analyse and evaluate their actions, values and motivations so that they can judge objectively how successful they think their actions have been. For others (beginners included), a model with a series of questions or thought-provoking headings can seem too restrictive, or too formulaic, so that reflection either becomes stilted or a meaningless process of completing the model rather than thinking critically about what happened in the event that has taken them by surprise.

For that reason, we will focus here on only four approaches out of many, which have been used by early years undergraduates, to give a flavour of how you might approach your own reflections. It remains up to you to use the one that suits you best or to read further to find a model that you find more appropriate. The first two of these encourage you to consider the impact of your actions on others, and what theoretical knowledge can be used to develop and underpin your practice.

Brookfield's Lenses (Brookfield, 2002) asks you to consider the impact of your practice from a range of different points of view:

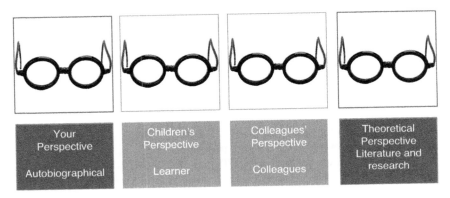

Figure 4.1 Brookfield's lenses, adapted from Brookfield, 2002

What is helpful about this model is that it specifically requires you to identify the relevant people who might have a perspective on what has happened. In the example above, children and colleagues within the setting have been identified, but they could just as legitimately be replaced, or added to, with parents/carers as service users, colleagues from other agencies, managers and supervisors, your own family and so on. What matters is that you consider the wider impact of your actions and practice and also draw on research and theory to understand not only what happened and why but also how you can either address something that requires improvement, or repeat, share or justify something reliably that worked very well. There is no set format for writing the reflection that this model supports, but many students and practitioners find it helpful to use the columns as simple subheadings for a series of paragraphs. This report should then be concluded with an action plan detailing how the learning gained from the process will be applied to practice in future.

De Bono's model (De Bono, 2000) encourages you to consider a situation from a range of perspectives, each represented by a different coloured hat:

Table 4.4 De Bono's thinking hats

White hat	Information	What do we know, what information is missing?
Red hat	Feelings intuition and emotions	What do you feel about the situation?
Black hat	Caution	What are the risks in this situation or associated with this action? Why might something not work?
Green hat	Growth, energy and life creativity	Put forward proposals, suggestions, ideas and alternatives, possibilities.
Blue hat	The thinking process	Defining the situation/problem and deciding what we need to consider in what order – which hat to wear to begin with. Action planning and strategy.
Yellow hat	Sunshine and optimism	Find the values and benefits in a suggestion or proposal – what is good about this, what are the different values?

De Bono's hats can be worn in any order, although the blue hat is a useful one to start with as this is when you consider the overall approach to tackling a situation or reflecting on an incident. For example, some situations require an initial examination of knowledge, whilst at other times, it is people's emotional responses that need to be addressed first. What the model does overall is ask you to consider why something happened, taking into account a range of factors rather than simply your own perspective. By using a multi-factored approach like this, you are more likely to present an objective reflection and evaluation, and to consider a wider range of strategies for addressing and developing your practice.

Alternatively, Rolfe et al. (2001, cited in Jasper, 2013, p. 102) present a model based on Borton's framework (Borton, 1970, cited in Jasper, 2013, pp. 99–100) which requires you to question the content and purpose of your practice in some depth by using three key questions, which seem to be very simple and straightforward. Many undergraduates like this approach and may be misled by its initial simplicity, but

- What:
  - o is the situation
  - o am I trying to achieve
  - o actions did I take
  - o was the response of others
  - o were the consequences

- So what:
  - o does this teach me
  - o was I thinking and feeling
  - o other knowledge can I bring to the situation
  - o is my new understanding of the situation

- Now what:
  - o do I need to do to improve things
  - o broader issues need to be considered if this action is to be successful
  - o might I do differently in future
  - o might be the consequences of this action

Figure 4.2 Rolfe et al. (2001) 'what' questions

Rolfe et al. then break these opening questions down into a series of sub-questions, to encourage deeper consideration of your answers (see Figure 4.2).

Again there is no set format for the writing of this reflection, but the questions and sub-questions themselves provide a useful series of headings to be addressed. You can see that the perceptions of others and their responses are important in the description of the incident, and the use of research and theory to explain and address the incident are a key part of the second question: 'So what?' What this model also highlights is the role emotional responses can lay in our own actions and the responses of others so they should not be overlooked. The model also draws attention to the notion of reflection as continuous process in the final question 'Now what?' by asking you to consider the consequences of changing your practice.

For practitioners who prefer a journal writing approach, Russell (2005) advises that reflection should start with telling the story – a much more free-hand approach to describing critical incidents you have experienced, and then considering what you may have learned from it. There are no specific questions that Russell advises students to use, but his emphasis on how much detail you include in the narrative you write about the incident can be helpful in getting you to consider the finer points of what went on, even the things you might have dismissed as insignificant. This approach has worked well with some undergraduates when used as a way of compiling a placement journal of evidence of their practice, which is then used to answer a series of questions posed at regular intervals to measure their progress and professional learning (see Table 4.5). By having a detailed journal of placement experience, students have found they can discuss the development of their practice with more confidence and greater objectivity and detail, so that they start to see how they are developing their skills and knowledge.

Table 4.5 Reflective questions

Pre-placement questions	What do I bring to this placement – skills, knowledge, previous experience? What do I want from this placement? What am I unsure about as I begin this placement?
Initial on-placement questions	How do I feel about this placement now? What have I learned that is new and how is this going? Have I encountered success or failure and how has this made me feel? How am I managing my own learning and development? If I had to improve this placement in some way, what would I change?
Later-on placement questions	Use some of the questions above, but also consider: What am I doing well and how do I know this? How have I dealt with any failure and how do I feel about this? Will I look back on this placement as a success when I leave and why?
End-of-placement questions	How do I feel about my placement now? What are my overall strengths and how do I know this? Do I still have weaknesses or gaps in my knowledge and how can I address these? Has this placement been a success – why do I feel this?

These models represent just a few of the many and varied ways you might use to reflect on your practice. Other models early years students have included Gibbs' cycle (Gibbs, 1988), reminding us that from reflection comes change to practice, which itself requires further reflection, which may lead to further change and so on. Johns (2004) presents a model (aimed initially at the nursing profession) using 17 questions, considering in some depth the values, ethics and aesthetics that support practitioners in understanding what they hope to achieve in their practice and how this impacts on their service users. Whilst 17 questions may seem a challenging model, early years students have used this effectively by selecting the questions most useful to themselves and focussing on these to evaluate their practice. What these models all have in common is an approach that encourages the user to see that reflection is not a particularly complicated, mysterious or frightening process, but one which with the right supporting structure can help even the least experienced of practitioners to understand what has happened in a critical incident, how this has affected them and the people around them and how it can be addressed and developed in the future. By taking a systematic approach to evaluating your practice, you will come to recognise your strengths and weaknesses, and to understand why some things work and why others do not so that you can contribute to the development of expertise in your own practice, practice within your setting and practice across the early years sector as a whole.

It is up to you to find a model that suits you and your experience, bearing in mind that to develop your practice and your professional understanding, and to develop your expertise, you need to do much more than simply follow the instructions of others and the requirements of an academic curriculum. Reflection is the process through which you come to consider and judge the usefulness of what you read, see and hear, and become the knowledgeable, critical and sensitive practitioner young children need you to be to support their learning and development.

Applying critical reflection to your own early years practice

We have explored various models and theories of reflection so far in this chapter, and now we must consider how you can put these to use in your everyday practice. We will start by thinking in a realistic manner and with sheer honesty; you cannot reflect on every single thing that happens in both everyday life and professional practice. If this was the case you would actually spend your whole life in a reflective state and not moving forward, as time would not allow. It is important to think about what you need to take time to reflect on and these tend to be what are called 'critical incidents'; they are not always everyday occurrences and normal issues and/or situations that occur and may be out of the ordinary. Some examples could be: a child having a serious accident at nursery, witnessing a child protection issue, a parent complaining or staff members not acting professionally. There are, however, some things that should be reflected on a daily basis and these include evaluation and reflection of activities that have been carried out and observations and assessments of children; these are both key elements of everyday practice in high quality settings.

Critical reflection is defined by Mezirow (1990, p. xvi) as an "assessment of the validity of the presuppositions of one's meaning, perspectives and examination of their sources and consequences", and Mezirow links this to transformative learning, where meaning allows a more inclusive approach to understanding your own experiences. To put this into basic terms, you need to be able to make sense of the experiences you encounter and be able to interpret these in order to learn from the situation and action plan to move forward. As an undergraduate early years student, you will experience many new phenomena and use critical reflection as a guide to make sense of new situations and experiences. Some of the new experiences may make you feel a little uncomfortable, as it is fear of the unknown; however, reflecting on the experience and making sense of it will allow you to deal with that situation better if it occurs again.

When engaging in critical reflection, it is imperative that you are honest and open-minded and understand not only your own values and beliefs but also the values and beliefs of others. The ability to be able to look at yourself in a constructive critical manner will assist and guide you through the reflective process.

Sometimes you will find yourself reflecting whilst the event is taking place, known as "reflection-in-action", and at other times you will "reflect-on-action" after the event has taken place (Schon, 1983). When reflecting-in-action, you will be thinking about the immediate situation that is taking place and how you can deal with it at that moment in time, so decisions are made quickly; therefore, it is imperative that you take time to reflect-on-action after the event has taken place, and this is when critical reflection will happen. Time must be set aside for critical reflection to take place. Reflection is a core value for those working with babies and children and must be taken seriously.

There are various ways in which the undergraduate early years educator can reflect, including:

1   Written reflective log/journal
2   Individual written reflective accounts
3   Recording reflections verbally
4   Discussions with placement supervisors, university lecturers/personal tutors, peers and colleagues.

A written or recorded reflective account will assist you in keeping a record of the event and you can return to this at anytime, whereas reflective discussions are not generally recorded and therefore cannot be as easily revisited. Nevertheless, this does not mean that reflective discussions are not valuable; they are just as valuable or sometimes more valuable than your own written account, as you will be allowing for other people's thoughts and opinions to come into the reflective process. In Chapter 2 we looked at a case study from a placement supervisor about Sarah, and in an e-mail the supervisor specifically relates to reflective practice and states:

> We have been able to have many professional discussions around Sarah's reading, research and observations which has enabled us both to reflect on our practice.

This is a good example of two-way reflection taking place through critical reflective discussion and not only enabling the student to consider reflection but also the professional. The student, Sarah, had some very useful reflective discussions with her supervisor, but she also kept a weekly reflective log of her time in placement. Here is an example of critical reflection taking place on week 18 of placement:

Reflective log

Child C (see week 12 and appendix T2) had previously seemed to struggle with all the collaborative working activities and I tentatively concluded that she was lacking skills in being able to commentate on what she was doing in order to initiate another child's interest in her endeavours. During the marshmallow activity, however, Child C demonstrated a great willingness to commentate on what she was doing and gave some excellent instructions so that I could make a snail as well. Her levels of interest and engagement surprised me as in previous activities she had appeared to exhibit limited attention. C's interest in the activity seemed to be entirely driven by the role-play possibilities it created; she was keen to create new characters so that they could be included in the role play. C's interest in role play could be interpreted as suggesting that the previous problem-solving and collaborative activities had not sustained her interest due to a lack of role-play opportunities.

We can see critical reflection taking place at key points in this snippet of the full reflective account. Immediately Sarah makes reference to an activity the child had 'struggled' with at week 12 of placement, and this was 4 weeks later. She then goes on to reflect just how the child's interest in another area of provision had started to support the child's learning and development.

Thinking activity

Highlight the parts in the reflection above where critical reflection is taking place then have a go at writing a reflective account of an event or situation you have found yourself in where learning and development took place for you.

Upon completion of critical reflection, the next point to consider is how to move forward, and you can do this by evaluating the key issues and developing an action plan. Illeris (2008) states that reflective practice should flow together as a process of action, experience and reflection, and at this point you have reflected on the experience and it is now time to put some actions in place. Developing an action plan will help in ensuring goals are met, and the following points need to be considered:

1   What **goal** do you want to achieve?
2   What **actions** do you need to take in order to achieve the goal?
3   What **timescale** do you need to achieve the actions and goal?
4   How will you **evidence** that you have achieved your actions and goal?

You can remember these four points for action planning by thinking GATE:

Goal
Actions
Timescale
Evidence of actions and goals met

The following table shows an example of an action plan:

Table 4.6 Action plan

Goal	Actions	Timescale	Evidence of achievement
1. Meet placement supervisor on a weekly basis for feedback	1. Agree date and time in the diary to meet supervisor. 2. Make notes of meeting. 3. Action development points.	10th October	1. Dates agreed and in diary. 2. Notes written and reflected upon. 3. Action plan created and using as a working document.

Thinking activity

Produce your own action plan of what you need to do in order to successfully complete your Undergraduate Early Years Degree. You can also produce an action plan for placement and consider personal and professional skills.

Conclusion

Throughout this chapter various approaches to reflective practice and theories have been considered. As an undergraduate early years student practising your developing skills in placement, it is now the perfect opportunity to start reflecting in a critical manner. You can use various cycles and models to support the reflective process such as those written about in this chapter, including De Bono's hats, Brookfield's lenses or Rolfe et al.'s 'what', 'so what', 'now what'. You must use these models in a critical manner and reflect at a deep level of thought and not just only at a surface level. The art of reflection is one that is powerful and can guide and support you through life, and it is imperative that this art is practised and refined so that when you are working with children and their families they will benefit from your open-minded and reflective approach. The more you practise and become accustomed to reflecting critically the easier it becomes, and it will start to be a normal part of your everyday life. It is not a difficult process as long as you embrace the outcomes of your reflections and change what needs changing, but that will not be everything; sometimes even the small changes make a big difference.

Further reading and research

Brock, A. (ed.) (2014) *The Early Years Reflective Practice Handbook*, Abingdon: Routledge.
Jasper, M. (2013) *Beginning Reflective Practice*, 2nd ed., Andover: Cengage Learning, Cengage Learning MUA.

References

Borton. T. (1970) *Reach, Touch and Teach*, London: Hutchinson.
Brookfield, S. D. (2002) Using the lenses of critically reflective teaching in the community college classroom, *New Directions for Community Colleges*, 2002(118): pp 31–38, doi:10.1002/cc.61.
De Bono, E. (2000) *Six Thinking Hats*, London: Penguin.
Dreyfus, H. L. and Dreyfus, S. E. (1986) *Mind over Machine: The Power of Human Intuition and Expertise in the Era of the Computer*, Oxford: Blackwell.
Gibbs, G. (1988) *Learning by Doing*, London: FEU.
Goodman. J. (1984) Reflection and Teacher Education: A Case Study and Theoretical Analysis, *Interchanges*, 15, 9–26.
Illeris, K. (2008) *How we Learn*, Abingdon, Oxon: Routledge.
Jasper, M. (2013) *Beginning Reflective Practice*, 2nd edn., Andover: Cengage Learning, Cengage Learning MUA.
Jaworski, B. (1993) The professional development of teachers: The potential of critical reflection, *Professional Development in Education*, 19(3): pp 37–42.
Johns, C. (2004) *Becoming a Reflective Practitioner*, 2nd edn., Oxford: Blackwell Publishing.
King, P. M. and Kitchener, K. S. (1994) *Developing Reflective Judgement: Understanding and Promoting Intellectual Growth and Critical Thinking in Adolescents and Adults*, San Francisco: Jossey-Bass Publishers.
Megginson, D. and Whittaker, V. (2007) *Continuing Professional Development*, London: CIPD.
Mezirow, J. (1990) *Fostering Critical Reflection: A Guide to Transformative and Emancipatory Learning*, San Francisco: Jossey Bass Publishers.
Moon, J.A. (1999) *Reflection in Learning and Professional Development*, Abingdon: Routledge Farmer.
Moss, P. (2006) Structures, understanding and discourses: Possibilities for re-envisioning the early childhood worker, *Contemporary Issues in Early Childhood*, 7(1): pp 30–41.
Nutbrown, C. (2012) *Foundations for Quality: The Independent Review of Early Education and Childcare Qualifications: Final Report*, London: Crown Copyright.
Rolfe, G., Freshwater, D. and Jasper, M. (2001) *Critical Reflection for Nursing and the Helping Professions*, Basingstoke: Palgrave.
Russell, T. (2005) Can reflective practice be taught? *Reflective Practice*, 6(2): pp 199–204.
Schon, D. (1983) *The Reflective Practitioner: How Professionals Think in Action*, New York: Basic Books.
Strandgaard, F. (1981) *NLP Made Visual*, Copenhagen: Connector.

Chapter 5

Early years curriculum

Jo McEvoy

Chapter aims

By the end of this chapter you will:

- be familiar with the Early Years Foundation Stage (EYFS) statutory framework so that you can locate information you may need as a student on placement
- understand the principles of the EYFS and be able to apply these to practice
- understand the importance of the Characteristics of Effective Learning in supporting how young children learn
- appreciate the importance of child-initiated, play-based learning and be able to apply this approach to practice.

Introduction

Many parents have commented that when they collect their child from nursery, they are anxious to know how they have spent their time. It is often the case, though, that an excited parent, having waited in anticipation to pick up their child, asks the question, "What did you do in nursery today?" only to be given the standard answer, "Nothing, I just played." So, what are the children learning in nursery? Are they 'just playing'? What is the curriculum that underpins their development and learning?

There is actually no set curriculum that dictates *what* children should be taught in early years settings. There is, however, a statutory document that sets out the standards for care and education that is required by law of all Ofsted-registered early years settings in England. This document is called 'Statutory Framework for the Early Years Foundation Stage' (DfE, 2017), often referred to as the 'EYFS'. In addition to the statutory framework, there is also a non-statutory guidance document, 'Development Matters in the Early Years Foundation Stage' (Early Education, 2012). This document supports practitioners to apply the statutory requirements of the EYFS to practice.

Rather than outlining programmes of study that stipulate *what* children should learn, the EYFS outlines four key principles, upon which each setting should build a curriculum tailored to the needs of their particular children, and it provides guidance on *how* children typically learn. It describes what effective learning looks like, and promotes a holistic play-based pedagogy incorporating seven areas of learning and development.

'Statutory Framework for the Early Years Foundation Stage'

'Statutory Framework for the Early Years Foundation Stage' (DfE, 2017) outlines all the legal requirements for the care and education of children from 0–5 years (till the end of the reception year in school). It covers expectations for learning and development, assessment processes and the requirements for the safeguarding and welfare of young children.

The statutory framework requires providers to plan their EYFS curriculum around seven areas of learning and development:

- personal, social, emotional development
- communication and language
- physical development
- literacy
- mathematics
- understanding the world
- expressive arts and design.

The first three areas are referred to as the prime areas of learning and development. They are described as 'prime' because they are the foundation for all future learning. They support children to acquire the skills needed to learn and develop in the other four areas. These four are referred to as the 'specific' areas of learning and development. All seven areas of learning and development must be included in each setting's EYFS curriculum regardless of the age of the children. There is an understanding that the prime areas should be predominantly, but not exclusively, focussed on for babies and toddlers, because these are the starting point for all future learning. However, all seven areas are equally important, and although the curriculum may be weighted more to the prime areas for babies and toddlers, the specific areas should still be included. Likewise, for the children in pre-school or nursery and Reception Classes, the prime areas should not be neglected in favour of the specific areas. All are equally important and should be planned for and supported in a holistic way.

Thinking activity

How does each of the prime areas of learning and development support children's learning and development in the specific areas?

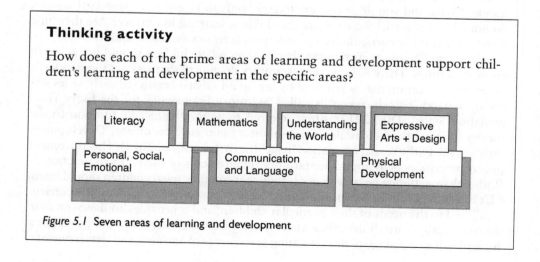

Figure 5.1 Seven areas of learning and development

There are four overarching principles that underpin the EYFS framework. These are:

- every child is a **unique child,** who is constantly learning and can be resilient, capable, confident and self-assured
- children learn to be strong and independent through **positive relationships**
- children learn and develop well in **enabling environments,** in which their experiences respond to their individual needs, and there is a strong partnership between practitioners and parents and/or carers
- **children develop and learn in different ways and at different rates.** The framework covers the education and care of all children in early years provision, including children with special educational needs and disabilities.

(DfE, 2017, p. 6)

These principles remind us that all children are **unique** and each child is born ready and able to learn with capacity to reach their potential. However, development and learning is not automatic. It relies on children feeling safe, emotionally secure and valued. It relies on adults developing strong and respectful **relationships** with children, interacting with them and building up their confidence and self-esteem. It also relies on having a safe and stimulating **environment** in which children are free and have time to experiment, explore, take risks and interact. The principles should underpin your practice as a student on placement. You should aim to treat all children equally, yet not necessarily the same. Treat each child as a unique individual and try to meet their particular needs through building positive relationships with them and their families. You should try to contribute to providing learning environments that will support the emotional and physical needs of each particular child. Your relationship with each child will be different, and so the learning journey that each child takes will be different. You may need to adapt the language you use, how you interact with them and the type of learning environment you provide to support individual children. Only then will **learning and development** take place in a way that results in positive outcomes for each individual child.

Unique child

The first of the principles, the Unique Child, is best understood when we consider what poses a risk to children's outcomes. Research evidence highlights poverty and poor attachments in the early years as being the highest risk factors to children not achieving their full potential and falling behind their peers in later life (DfE, 2011). The aim of the EYFS is to minimise these risk factors by providing an equal and strong foundation for all children so that they can grow into successful, healthy and independent adults.

The principle of the Unique Child reminds us that each child is unique and has the capacity to thrive, so it is our duty to ensure that no child gets left behind. Being committed to the belief that all children have potential to achieve, and that they "can be confident, capable and self-assured" (DfE, 2017, p. 6), will influence the decisions that you make about how you treat children during your time on placement. You will need to observe children closely, and spend time getting to know them well so that you can ensure that your interactions with them are supporting their learning and progress. This way you will come to know what interests or excites them, and also what irritates or frightens them. You will need to be respectful of the unique identity of each child, her or his family, culture, personality, capability, and any potentially limiting factors such as physical impairments or emotional traits. By spending time with them and getting to know them in all their uniqueness, you will be able to spot when extra or specific support might be needed, and you will be able to work with your mentor to provide that support or access it through the support of other professionals.

Positive relationships

The need to form positive relationships with children is informed by our understanding of Bowlby's attachment theory (Bowlby, 1953). Research into babies' brain development and the acquisition of cognitive skills suggests that babies who have developed a secure attachment to a significant adult will be more likely to succeed well at school and to form friendships and gain social fulfilment in late life (Gerhardt, 2004). These findings have led to the introduction of the key person (Elfer and Page, 2013) in early years settings, and this is now a statutory requirement in the EYFS (DfE, 2017, p. 21, 22). The key person is a practitioner who acts as the main carer for the child whilst in the setting. They get to know the child and the family well, and build a warm and positive relationship with them. The relationship with the key person is built on professional love and respect (Elfer and Page, 2013). It is a nurturing one that supports the child to develop a sense of self-worth, personal identity, pride and confidence to become more independent. The relationship with the key person is crucial in supporting the child to develop self-regulation. It is through this constant and unconditional attachment with the key person that the child will gain a sense of belonging and acceptance. This will support the child to develop self-confidence to explore, try things out and take risks within a safe and secure environment, with clear boundaries set by the key person.

Of all the four principles in the EYFS, this one may be the most challenging because it requires the practitioner to give something of themselves to the child and the family. It may challenge practitioners' assumptions and cause them to feel vulnerable at times. They therefore need to be deeply reflective and also supportive of each other, through the use of peer-to-peer support and formal appraisals.

As a student it will be important for you to try to develop positive relationships quickly with the children you are caring for, and with parents and professionals. It is not uncommon to feel slightly overwhelmed and nervous at the start of a new placement. It may seem daunting to have to get to know so many people in a short space of time. However, there is much to be gained from thinking about this prior to starting your placement, and planning how you intend to forge positive relationships with the children, staff and parents in your setting. Consider the following comments from early years students explaining how they developed positive relationships with children, staff and parents:

- I planned a conversation starter that I could use in the staff room – "Have you had a good weekend? Did you do anything?" or "Have you been busy this morning?"
- I just forced myself to smile and greet people when they came in the room, being friendly and cheerful all the time.

- I offered to help and always made sure I was busy doing something and not ever just standing around doing nothing.
- I waited till the parent had the child in their arms so I could say something to the child about what they had been doing. This was a good way of getting into a conversation with the parent and from then on it was easier.
- I found it hard to get the children to talk to me. They would always move away or go shy on me and then I felt really embarrassed in case anyone noticed. So now I always try to sit at a table or on the floor and just fiddle around with the resources as if I am playing and then the children stay and start to approach me instead of me approaching them.

Enabling environments

An enabling environment should 'enable' children to learn and develop well. It is an environment in which "all people are valued" and "learning is valued" (Early Education, 2012, p. 3). The two aspects to consider are the emotional environment and the physical environment.

The emotional environment can easily be overlooked in an early years setting, as the physical set up of the room and the resources are immediately visible, yet the influence of the emotional environment on children's learning and development is exceptionally powerful for such young children.

Children need to feel loved and secure in order to learn and develop well. They need to develop a sense of belonging and acceptance, so that they are not feeling anxious, upset or confused. For very young children, the only environment that is constant in their lives is their home environment. Sadly, for some children this may not be a secure and safe environment, but for most children it is the place where they know they belong and where they have an attachment to a constant adult in their life. Children will feel more secure and develop a sense of belonging more easily when the practitioners know about their home life and have a strong relationship with their parents or carers. The following story from my own practice as an EYFS teacher illustrates this well:

I know your grandma

Jake was just turned three when he started in nursery but he did not settle well. He was uncommunicative, withdrawn and often on the verge of tears. We had tried different ways to settle him but nothing seemed to work and his mother was also now becoming quite distressed at leaving him.

Then it happened that I was out shopping at the weekend and I bumped into an old friend of mine. She explained that she was a grandma now. She spoke with love and pride of her 3-year-old grandson, Jake, and how he was finding it hard to fit in to his new nursery class. I quickly realised that this was the same Jake and we enjoyed some time discussing his needs and also the needs of his mum who had experienced a bout of post-natal depression, which was unknown to us at the time.

The following Monday when I saw Jake I was able to welcome him and say, "Jake, I know your grandma, Jean – she's my friend and she told me all about how you help her look after her dog, Jess." Jake's face lit up and from that moment we had a breakthrough. We had made the connection between home and nursery that was the most valued by Jake and he then began to settle in quickly.

What was important to Jake was that we knew where he came from and who he was. Through making the connection with Jake's grandma, who was an important person in Jake's life, we had managed to affirm Jake and give him a sense of belonging. The emotional environment for Jake was now a welcoming and homely one, where he felt safe and accepted.

It can take detailed planning to ensure that the emotional environment meets each and every child's needs. Transitions into the setting will require careful planning with meticulous attention to the emotional needs of each child. More than anything though, there needs to be a cast-iron determination that each child will be supported to feel 'at home' in the setting, and an acceptance that this will require a flexible approach to settling in policies and daily practice. The practitioners you work with on placement will already know the children and their families well. It will be you, the student, who is making the transition into their setting. It is interesting to note that you may experience similar feelings to Jake, wanting to feel that you belong and knowing where you fit in. It is worth taking the time to reflect on your own emotional responses to transitions and then to consider how it feels for children too.

Thinking activity

- **Remember** – a time you were left at nursery or school. Try to relive the experience in your mind and remember the sights, sounds and smells that surrounded you. How were you feeling? Was it a positive or a negative experience for you?
- **Reflect** – what were the aspects of the environment that contributed to how you felt?
- **Take action** – find out how your placement setting supports children to feel comfortable, welcome and 'at home'. List three things you think they do well and one thing that you think might make it even better.

Of equal importance to the emotional environment is the physical environment that practitioners set up in their base rooms, classrooms and throughout the setting. The different play areas in an EYFS setting are referred to as 'areas of continuous (or permanent) provision' because they are permanently or continuously available for children to use. Some resources are left there permanently and different areas will be enhanced with specific resources from time to time in response to children's interests and development needs. The indoor and outdoor areas should be seen and valued as one continuous learning environment for babies and young children. Based on their knowledge of child development and learning theories, practitioners will ensure that the environment is first and foremost a safe and stimulating place to be.

Young children are typically physical, social and sensory learners and the learning environment should accommodate this. Routines to the day will need to be predictable and constant enough to provide security for children, yet flexible enough to accommodate the children's individual physical development needs with regard to eating, toileting and sleeping. Hungry, uncomfortable or tired children cannot learn. An enabling environment is one in which children can gain independence in regulating their physical needs with the individual level of support that they require. The physical layout of a room can accommodate this aspect of the children's development if it is carefully planned and adapted for individuals who are developing outside the expected parameters for their age group.

Here are some practical examples from early years settings that promote an enabling environment, both emotionally and physically. You may find similar examples in your placement setting:

- Culture – The environment shows evidence of different cultures and communities being welcome through welcome posters, displays and books showing different communities, artefacts from other cultures and displays of festivals, prayer and worship reflecting different faiths.
- Children feel at home and secure because they can find their way around – The environment inside and out is safe, there is a range of areas of permanent provision which are clearly signposted with visual symbols and labels.
- Key person – There is a display of key person groups and areas for groups to gather with pictures of the children who use that area. Routines include time for children to meet up with their key person and time is set aside for the key person to talk to parents/carers.
- Parents – Notice boards and information for parents is available in home language where required. Parents spend time in the setting with their children. Practitioners communicate with parents/carers in different ways to report on what the child does in the setting.
- Home languages – Visual symbols support parents and children who do not understand English and there are notices and labels to reflect the different languages spoken in the setting. Recording devices are used for children to hear messages from home in their home language and dual language books and displays will be seen.
- Routines – Routines are flexible and children have access to the outside area for most of the day throughout the year. They are able to follow their own interests by moving freely around the areas of continuous provision. They sometimes move resources from one area to another but know how to return them because the resources are clearly labelled and openly displayed.
- Time to become engaged in learning – Children have opportunities for uninterrupted play and become engrossed in deep level learning. Babies' routines follow their individual needs and the resources offered are stimulating to the senses, supporting them to become engaged in exploring and learning.

- Safe and accessible – The physical layout of the room allows for easy access and a clear pathway in and around the areas of continuous provision. A small child can easily find their way around the areas and into the outdoor environment and there is room for wheelchair users to safely get around. Large floor trays and low tables with open shelving are all used to provide easy access to babies and children, and the resources are displayed to meet their line of vision.
- Inviting and stimulating – Children are naturally curious and inquisitive. Interesting resources that reflect the real world are used to attract children's attention and engross them in learning. Natural materials such as bark, stones, plants, shells and sensory resources provide a rich stimulus for exploration and active learning.
- Well organised – Within each area of continuous provision the resources are clearly labelled and well organised. Small containers of different resources are photographed and labelled to support children to select resources and tidy away whilst developing mathematical and problem-solving skills at the same time.
- Carefully planned – Children learn in a holistic way, so the learning environment is planned to incorporate all seven areas of learning across all areas of provision. It may be that one area supports a particular area of learning predominantly but there is also scope for several aspects of learning to take place, depending on the stage of development and interests of babies and children.

You could use the following exercise to evaluate the emotional and physical aspects of the environment in your placement setting:

Thinking activity

Think of your placement setting . . .
   What do you see and what happens that shows that all people are valued?

- How are children's individual cultures represented and celebrated?
- How do children know where to find the resources they want to play with?
- How do children know who their key person is?
- How are parents/carers welcomed into the setting and how do they find out what their children have been doing?
- How does your setting communicate with parents who do not understand English?
- Are routines flexible so that children can choose to play where they want to, inside or outside, just like they would at home?
- How can you contribute to the emotional environment in your placement setting?

   What do you see and what happens to show that learning and all children are valued?

- Is there a clear pathway through the setting, between the indoor and outdoor, and around the areas of continuous provision? Is it accessible for wheelchair users?

- How does your setting create an inviting and stimulating environment?
- What sensory resources are on offer?
- Are there any natural materials for children to explore?
- How organised and inviting are the areas of continuous provision? Can the children quickly put resources away? Are the resources offered on open shelves in small containers that are clearly labelled?

How do you know what children are expected to learn through each area of continuous provision? Are the learning intentions documented and displayed?

Learning and development

The final principle, Learning and Development, is totally dependent on the first three principles being put into practice. Whilst on placement you will observe individual children to get to know their interests and development needs (Unique Child). You will provide professional love and nurture strong attachments. You will interact with the children, playing alongside and supporting their learning (Positive Relationships), and you will communicate with their parents and carers so that the children are secure, comfortable and confident enough to be able to explore and learn through a safe and stimulating environment (Enabling Environment). When you consistently apply the four principles to practice, you are providing children with the best opportunity to learn and develop in different ways and at different rates, depending on their unique identity and individual needs.

The principle of learning and development requires you to think about pedagogy. Pedagogy is concerned with the process of teaching. It involves thinking about how teaching and learning occur and deciding on the best way to teach in any particular situation. The EYFS statutory framework does not stipulate a preferred style of pedagogy as a statutory requirement. However, there are several references to play, and it is advised that practitioners should "teach children by ensuring challenging, playful opportunities across the prime and specific areas of learning and development" (Early Education, 2012, p. 3). Nevertheless, it is also a matter of ongoing professional judgement for practitioners to decide the balance between child-initiated and adult-directed teaching and learning (DfE, 2017). This may be a difficult decision for you as a student, especially in cases where the policies and educational culture of a setting may be predominantly outcomes driven. For example, you may believe that children need to be free to choose when to go outside and when to stay inside. Yet your placement setting may not provide for this type of free-flow play to take place, believing that children need more formal structure and adult-directed tasks in order to make progress towards the early years outcomes (the Early Learning Goals). In situations like this, you will start to appreciate that the principle of learning and development is, in fact, a *commitment* to supporting learning. There may be pedagogical disagreements about the balance of play and direct teaching, but what is vitally important in making decisions about this balance is the need to really understand how children learn and to make this your guiding criteria.

In the EYFS statutory framework there is concise guidance to support you to understand what effective learning looks like. Three characteristics of effective learning are described in detail, with clear guidance on how to support learning through positive relationships and how to provide for effective learning through an enabling environment. The detailed guidance on the 'Characteristics of Effective Learning' can be found on page 6 of the practitioners' supporting guidance document, 'Development Matters' (Early Education, 2012). You should take a pause now to read through it before continuing with the rest of this chapter.

The characteristics of effective learning

As a student on placement you will be required to plan activities for children to engage in. A common mistake that we often make is that we think first of the 'activity' and then decide on the learning. The guidance in the statutory framework, however, is very clear that we should start by considering how young children learn, and then plan the activities based on their needs and interests:

> in planning and guiding children's activities, practitioners must reflect on the different ways that children learn and reflect these in their practice.
>
> (DfE, 2017, p. 10)

The statutory guidance highlights the three characteristics of effective learning as:

1   playing and exploring
2   active learning
3   creating and thinking critically.

(DfE, 2017, p. 10)

Playing and exploring

Playing and exploring is about being fully engaged in learning. It involves:

- finding out and exploring
- playing with what you know
- being willing to have a go.

(Early Education, 2012, p. 5)

From the moment they are born, babies have a natural drive to find things out and explore. They respond to stimuli and seek out interactions with the environment and with the people who care for them. This supports the development of neural pathways in the brain, so that they are able to learn and develop (Gerhardt, 2004). It is fascinating to see how capable babies are of responding to and interacting with their parents through body movements, crying and feeding.

Children are enabled to explore and find out through social interactions when they feel loved and secure. In your placement setting you will see resources and activities that support children to find out and explore. For example, consider how a baby explores a treasure basket, and finds out about the properties of shape and the texture of materials through using their senses. Or consider the 3- and 5-year-olds in the outdoor play area, exploring nature through the physical experience of the outdoor environment, and finding out about skills and knowledge across all domains of learning, from the scientific and the mathematical to the creative and the imaginative. Through playing with what they know in the outdoors, using one object to represent something else, they are moving from exploratory play to imaginative play, which promotes their thinking and problem-solving skills. Their cognitive development is supported as well as their confidence and resilience, and it is this resilience and self-confidence that enables them to be willing to take a risk and have a go at stretching beyond their boundaries to reach their potential.

Learning through playing and exploring is dynamic and powerful. Yet, it can so easily be overlooked when we observe children and only record what they know or can do in an area of learning and development (for example, when we observe a child and record our observation as 'the child held the pencil in a tripod grip' – links to Physical Development, moving and handling 22–36 months). As a student you will have the greatest opportunity to spend more time observing how children learn. You will be able to take your time to tune in to children's learning, watching and listening to gain an insight into the hidden learning that goes on all around us and is often unnoticed. You should aim to use this opportune time wisely, taking the time to critically reflect on what you provide for children to support their learning.

Thinking activity

- **Think** back to your childhood – What did you love to play? Where? Who with? How?
- **Reflect** – Pick out the three aspects of Playing and Exploring in your account of your play experience. Identify how you were:

  o   finding out and exploring
  o   playing with what you know
  o   being willing to have a go.

  How did it feel? Why was this a good way to learn?

- **Take action** – Observe a child in your placement setting and record how you see her or him playing and exploring. Talk to your mentor about how you might support the child to strengthen this characteristic of learning, through your positive relationship or the enabling environment you provide.

Active learning

What do you think of when you see the words, 'active learning'? Most of us will automatically think of physical activity and presume that active learning is about learning through being physically active. However, active learning is about having the will to learn and being motivated to get involved. Active learning involves:

- being involved and concentrating
- keeping on trying
- enjoying achieving what they set out to do.

(Early Education, 2012, p. 5)

Children become involved and concentrate when they are interested or curious about something. It takes concentration and persistence to remain involved for some time, and when deeply involved and concentrating, a child will not easily be distracted. However, in order to become involved certain conditions for learning need to be in place, such as an environment that feels safe and comfortable for the child to learn in and a sense of well-being so that the child is free to be able to concentrate. As a student on placement, some of these conditions may be out of your control, but it is important for you to consider your role in supporting children to become involved and concentrate on their interests. You might do this by tuning in to the children's interests and getting to know them personally so that you can offer them new and appealing experiences or resources that will stimulate their curiosity, or by ensuring that you take into account their levels of health and well-being at all times so that you are aware of their needs and can know when and how to intervene to support or extend their learning.

When you are satisfied that a child is feeling well and comfortable, safe and secure, you can confidently allow the child to develop persistence – the ability to keep on trying. By allowing children to do things for themselves (even if it takes much more time) you are promoting their self-belief and their resilience. It can be difficult to stand by and watch the baby on her tummy attempting to reach out and grab the rattle that is just out of her reach. The baby wriggles and stretches and her fingertips brush against the rattle as she grunts and stretches. Given time and encouragement the baby will no doubt work out how to reach and grab the toy. The feeling of success, and the joy of watching you clap and celebrate that success, will be a far more powerful learning experience for that baby than the short term gratification of you handing her the toy at her first attempt.

Of course, some babies may not persevere to that extent and may become frustrated and give up early on. The motivation to learn needs to come from within us. This is called 'intrinsic motivation' as opposed to 'extrinsic motivation'. We are all born with intrinsic motivators that enable us to survive and to thrive. These key motivators can be described as:

1   Competence – to have the ability to be able to function in the world and look after ourselves.
2   Autonomy – the need to be in control and independent, to be able do what we want to do.
3   Relatedness – the need to belong, to be connected to others, to be loved and feel safe and secure.

(Deci and Ryan, 1985)

Being born with the intrinsic motivation to learn and develop is not, however, a guarantee for success. We need to nurture, support and encourage internal motivation, and more importantly, we need to be allowed to use these drives and to experience difficulties and success. As a student on placement you will be able to observe how your setting supports children to develop their intrinsic motivation. Try this short exercise to help you reflect on what you observe:

Thinking activity

Reflect on a day on placement:
    How did the adults support children to enjoy achieving what they set out to do? Did they . . .

- praise children's efforts and comment on the process of learning rather than the product (e.g. "Wow, I love the way you kept on building those blocks even when it was tricky and they were wobbling a bit", instead of "Wow, that is a great tower you built")
- allow children to do things for themselves
- support children's choices
- provide commentary of their efforts and feedback on their learning so that they are able to self-evaluate?

Choose one of the strategies described above and actively try it out next time you are in your placement setting. Write a short reflection on how it went – how did you support the children to develop their intrinsic motivation and enjoy what they set out to do?

Creating and thinking critically

Creating and thinking critically is about the process of thinking.
   It involves:

- having their own ideas
- making links
- choosing ways to do things.

(Early Education, 2012, p. 5)

If children are to have their own ideas, they will require a stimulating learning environment with open-ended resources, which support them to experiment, try things out and make links to what they already know or can do. They will need to be allowed to choose how to do things in their own way, rather than being expected to all produce the same product in the same way. This is why it is best to avoid over-directing children's activities or expecting them all to do the same thing. Being creative requires children to make decisions and choices about how to express their thinking. It involves imagination, social activity, cognitive ability and inner motivation. Therefore, as a student on placement, you will need to carefully observe and take note of their ideas to help you understand their thought processes. Take time to ask children about what they are doing and why. Ask them to explain the how and the why when they share their creative work with you and take every opportunity to share in their thinking through sustained concentration on a shared activity or sustained conversations about why things happen in the way they do.
   The following strategies are useful in supporting children's thinking skills. Be on the lookout for them in your placement setting. Do you see practitioners using these strategies? How do the children react?

- asking children to tell you how they tackled a task or to explain something to a friend
- providing an environment with lots of opportunities for open-ended play activities
- narrating to children what they are doing, paraphrasing, giving feedback

- acknowledging their ideas and not over-directing their play
- being an equal partner in conversations, trying not to dominate
- avoiding too many questions and asking open questions like "I wonder what might happen if . . . ?"
- supporting children to solve problems together.

Thinking activity

Ask your mentor to observe you supporting a child's play and to look for where you use some of these strategies.

Conclusion

In this chapter we have examined the four principles of the EYFS, the seven areas of learning and development and the three characteristics of effective learning. You should now be familiar with key terminology, and know where to locate information that you will need to be able to support children's learning and development whilst on placement. As a student on placement, you are in the ideal position to be able to start to apply the principles of the EYFS to your professional practice. Your role is to support children's learning and development through building positive relationships with them and their families, and through providing an environment that is safe, stimulating and homely. Through observing the children and tuning into their interests, you will be able to notice the extent to which they demonstrate the characteristics of effective learning. Where there are strengths, you can build on and extend these, and where there are gaps you can nurture and support the child to develop resilience, inner motivation and self-belief. As you become experienced and proficient in your professional practice, you will be able to critically reflect on the EYFS statutory framework. Over time you will develop your own pedagogical and professional values, but the principles of the EYFS should remain at the heart of your practice, and be the guiding principles that inform the daily decisions you will make to support each child to reach their potential.

Further reading

Palaiologou, I. (2013) *The Early Years Foundation Stage: Theory and Practice*, 2nd ed., Los Angeles: Sage.

Wood, E. (2013) *Play, Learning and the Early Childhood Curriculum*, 3rd ed., Los Angeles, London: Sage.

References

Bowlby, J. (1953) *Child Care and the Growth of Love*, London: Penguin Books.

Deci, E. L. and Ryan, R. M. (1985) *Intrinsic Motivation and Self-Determination in Human Behaviour*, New York: Plenum.

Department for Education (DfE) (2011) *The Early Years: Foundations for Life, Health and Learning – An Independent Report on the Early Years Foundation Stage to her Majesty's*

Government, Ref: DFE-00177–2011, Retrieved from www.gov.uk/government/publications, London: DfE.

Department for Education (DfE) (2017) *Statutory Framework for the Early Years Foundation Stage*, London: DfE.

Early Education (2012) *Development Matters in the Early Years Foundation Stage (EYFS)*, London: British Association for Early Childhood Education.

Elfer, P., Goldschmied, E. and Selleck, D. (2012) *Key Persons in the Early Years: Building Relationships for Quality Provision in Early Years Settings and Primary Schools*, 2nd edn., London: Routledge.

Elfer, P. and Page, J. (2013) The emotional complexity of attachment interactions in nursery, *European Early Childhood Education Research Journal*, 21(4): pp 553–567.

Gerhardt, S. (2004) *Why Love Matters: How Affection Shapes a Baby's Brain*, London: Routledge.

Chapter 6

How young children learn

Mary Dyer

Chapter aims

By the end of this chapter you will be able to:

- understand the relationship between the EYFS and theoretical perspectives of how young children learn and develop
- understand and evaluate different theoretical perspectives on how young children learn and identify key theorists and research within each perspective
- explore how theoretical perspectives are applied in practice when supporting children in the early years setting, and in promoting a positive approach to learning.

Introduction

As an early years practitioner you will use the EYFS on a daily basis to plan, observe and assess young children's learning. However, whilst this is a very thorough and broad-ranging curriculum framework, it is not in itself a theory of development or learning, but is, instead, developed out of a range of theoretical perspectives. This chapter explains a few of the more well known of these and their possible application to early years practice. It would therefore be helpful to you as you read this chapter to have a copy of Development Matters and the Statutory Framework on hand so you can see the curriculum framework within which you are trying to apply this knowledge.

The EYFS and young children's learning and development

In early years provision, young children's learning and development is measured in terms of their progress towards the Early Learning Goals (ELGs), which are reported on in their EYFS Profile as they come to the end of Reception Class. 'Development Matters in the Early Years Foundation Stage' (Early Education, 2012) identifies key stages or processes along the way that would indicate if children are making typical progress in their development, and their overall achievement of the ELGs is described in terms of them **exceeding** typical expectations of what they should be able to do as they reach the age of 5, **meeting** these expectations or if children's development is still **emerging** in these areas (Standards and Testing Agency, 2013). Whilst the ELGs and the statements identifying steps and stages in the progress children make are drawn from what we understand children can typically be expected to do at particular ages, they are not a theoretical framework themselves, but a guide to practitioners about what to expect and what subsequent development they might wish to support.

Alongside the ELGs sit the Characteristics of Effective Learning (CEL) which identify learning processes and dispositions children will benefit from developing if they are to be successful learners as they enter formal schooling. These focus on children developing a positive attitude to engaging with problem solving and social interaction; developing their own independence and confidence in learning so that they will take appropriate risks – physically, socially and emotionally; building up a resilience to be able to cope with small set-backs in the learning process; and also developing, expressing and pursuing their own interests as part of their early learning experience. However, again, you should remember that although the CEL have been drawn out of theory and research into the role of positive dispositions to learning, the framework presented in the EYFS is not in itself a theory.

Activity

Locate the Characteristics of Effective Learning in the EYFS, and ask your colleagues in your placement setting how these are promoted and used.

It is important to read and understand the different theories of how young children learn and develop, as this will support you in using the EYFS and Development Matters to guide your practice. Whilst the curriculum framework offers a great deal of information to practitioners, you need to understand the origins of this information, so that you can make an informed decision about the progress an individual child is making. The age bands within the EYFS framework, although they overlap with each other, are quite broad and do not always offer you the specialised information you require to understand an individual child's developmental needs. By being familiar with different theories of children's development and learning, you can be confident that as you plan the next steps for children's learning and development, the expectations you have are realistic and achievable for the children involved. You will also be able to make a more accurate judgement about whether a child's abilities in an aspect of learning or development really do meet or exceed expectations typical for their age, or if their abilities would be more realistically described as emerging. The next section of this chapter will consider some of the key theories concerning young children's social and cognitive development and how they might be applied to your practice. There will also be a brief discussion about the way the different theorists explain language acquisition and the role it plays in supporting children's understanding of their world. Further detail about language and particularly literacy development will be covered elsewhere in this book. Finally we will consider the role of learning dispositions and the importance of the CEL to young children's progress in their learning.

Theoretical perspectives on young children's learning and the role of the practitioner

Behaviourist perspective and social learning theory

The behaviourist perspective is based on the Thorndike's Law of Effect (Thorndike, 1913, cited in Schunk, 2004) that behaviour which has pleasurable outcomes or consequences for an individual is more likely to be repeated than behaviour that is not. This perspective does not only apply to the behaviour of young children and babies, but to anyone's behaviour regardless of their age. You might be able to apply this to your own behaviour, in the classroom, social situations, work situations and so on. If other people respond in ways that you like to your behaviour, then you will regard this as reinforcing what you have done and you will be more likely to do it again. Skinner (Doherty and Hughes, 2014) used Thorndike's Law of Effect to condition the behaviour of a range of different animals, and then to apply it to how we can shape the behaviour of humans. By offering reinforcement (often seen as a reward) for specific pieces of behaviour, he found he could increase the likelihood of that behaviour being repeated, and even the frequency with which it was repeated.

Underpinning this seemingly simple process, however, are some key issues to take account of. First of all, reinforcement needs to be offered consistently, and the frequency with which this is done will increase or decrease the likelihood of desired behaviour being repeated (Gray and MacBlain, 2015). Skinner found that if you reinforced appropriate behaviour every time, then as soon as you stopped reinforcing, the required behaviour disappeared very quickly. Unless you are prepared to offer reinforcement on an almost continuous basis, the behaviour you are trying to encourage and embed will not take hold. Skinner went on to discover that you could vary the frequency with which reinforcement was offered, in a fixed or a variable pattern, or you could vary the amount of time it took for the learner to receive reinforcement for their behaviour, again in a fixed or variable pattern. He referred to these patterns as schedules – fixed or variable ratio schedules, and fixed or variable interval schedules. The pattern most likely to lead to the learner continuing to behave in the required manner for the longest period of time was found to be the variable ratio schedule, as this means the learner cannot work out how many times they have to behave in a particular way in order to receive reinforcement. They must keep on behaving in that way, so that eventually they will be rewarded. This approach has been used effectively with children and adults to shape their behaviour, and may even have been part of your own upbringing.

Thinking activity

Can you remember being lavishly praised the first time you tidied your bedroom, or completed your homework on time, or some other everyday tasks from your childhood? How long did this praise and approval go on for before you were simply expected to continue with that behaviour as part of your usual routine?

For most children the amount of praise would start to vary, along with the frequency of it, as they completed this task day after day, week after week, so that before long they were carrying out their behaviour for very little reinforcement – it has simply become part of their behavioural repertoire. Reinforcing the desired behaviour from time to time, with unpredictable frequency, will then be enough to encourage them to continue to behave in this way.

However, as a way of teaching young children this perspective has significant limits. Whilst it can be used to increase the likelihood of certain behaviours being repeated, for that to happen, those behaviours must be presented in the first place, and the behaviourist perspective cannot control situations so that this will happen. Thus it can lead to practitioners having to wait for opportunities to react to children's behaviour, rather than being able to take a more proactive approach of discussing ideas of appropriate behaviour with children.

It also requires the 'teacher' (the parent, or the practitioner) to ignore any unwanted or inappropriate behaviour. Skinner's theory makes sense in the abstract, but in the real world of family life or the early years setting or school, we cannot ignore inappropriate behaviour, especially where it impacts on others and possibly puts someone at risk. Skinner would argue that then we are drawing attention to behaviour we do not want to be repeated, and that the attention we give to this can be regarded by some children as rewarding and therefore reinforcing. The behaviourist perspective by itself, then, is unlikely to offer the most effective way to support children as they learn how to behave in the social world.

The reinforcement being offered must also be of value to the child concerned, otherwise it will not be regarded as any kind of reward. Some children are very motivated by positive forms of attention – praise, approval, privileges and opportunities to do 'special' tasks within the setting or the home, the allocating of extra or increased responsibility. However, this does not apply to all children, and there may be others who actively avoid such notice, as they feel uncomfortable with it, so that the reinforcement on offer is now seen as a deterrent. Equally there are children for whom any attention, positive or negative, praise or criticism, is regarded as reinforcing, so that they may deliberately behave in ways that attract any kind of notice, rather than only in ways that would lead to praise and approval.

Finally, this perspective by itself only addresses behaviour, rather than the motivations and reasons behind it, not does it offer children an explanation for the responses to their actions. It may be effective in forming behavioural habits but not in developing an understanding of why those habits are appropriate or approved.

Where a behavioural perspective could be regarded as most effective in explaining and supporting young children's learning lies in the part it plays in Social Learning Theory (Gray and MacBlain, 2015). Bandura's research demonstrated that children will model or copy the behaviour of others, but most particularly when they have been able to see the consequences of that behaviour. Where it has been reinforced, and therefore has positive outcomes so far as the child can see, they are most likely to copy what they have seen. Social learning theory also explains how young children learn from each other. Children will focus on individuals they consider to be attractive, glamorous or powerful when choosing who to model and imitate – this will include parents, carers, teachers and practitioners as well as other adults, but equally it will include their siblings, both older and younger, and also their peers. Whilst it may be difficult to predict who a child will chose as a role model, in part this choice is determined by how others react to their model's behaviour. Where behaviour receives what the child considers to be a positive reaction or consequences (praise, approval, privilege or even simply attention) then this increases the power of that model, and the likelihood that their behaviour will be copied.

Your role as a practitioner

A behaviourist practitioner is a rule maker and a model. Both behaviourism and social learning theory place significant responsibility on you as a practitioner not only in terms of your own behaviour – how you talk to other people, how you cooperate and share with them, how well you work together with your colleagues – but also in how you respond to the behaviour of the other children within the setting. As a student you will need to present a positive and consistent role model in terms of your social interactions, demonstrating courtesy and respect to everyone at all times and taking a consistent approach to all children in your management of their behaviour. You will need to focus on behaviour you actively wish to encourage, and make difficult decisions about which inappropriate behaviour you must respond to, and which you can safely ignore, so that attention is not drawn to it. To ensure you do this appropriately, you can observe other practitioners and model their practice (and thus undertake your own social learning), speak to your supervisor and also refer to the setting's behaviour management policy to ensure you are consistent with the approach used in the setting. You will also need to have a good understanding of what motivates, and therefore can act as a reinforcement to, the children you work with, so that you can use this to shape their social learning effectively.

Activity

Imagine that you have to explain to a parent or colleague how you might use social learning theory and reinforcement to support an aspect of behaviour management (e.g. turn taking, or saying please and thank you) in the setting.

Constructivist approach

Constructivists argue that young children develop their own understanding of the world. They 'construct' their own ideas of how things work, and their own concepts of people, places, objects and events. As children get older, these concepts move from being concerned with concrete objects and experiences the child has personally participated in or encountered, to more abstract concepts such as fairness and morality, power and imagination, as well as concepts they may have no direct experience of, but which they can research or be told about, such as historical matters or life under the sea. An example of how children gradually move from the concrete to the abstract can be seen in how children come to understand the passage of time. It is difficult to explain this to a very young child when trying to explain when their birthday is – such a concept may have to be counted in concrete terms such as 'how many sleeps'. As the child gets older their understanding of a number of days or weeks passing can be demonstrated by the use of a calendar or diary without having to refer to their own direct experience.

The most prominent constructivist you are likely to encounter in young children's understanding of their world is Piaget (Garhart Mooney, 2000), whose research into cognitive development has significantly shaped early educational practice. Piaget identified four stages children pass through in the development of their reasoning and problem solving. His theory is not about the content of what children know, but about how they come to understand their world and make sense of it. Piaget argued that young children think and reason in different ways from adults and only gradually develop the mental structures necessary for adult reasoning. His four stages are:

- Sensori-motor period (0–18 months): learning through senses and reflexes, physical interaction with the environment
- Pre-operational (18 months–6 years): simple reasoning based on own perception and experiences, overgeneralisation
- Concrete operational (6–12 years): more sophisticated reasoning, beginning to decentre and consider perceptions and experiences of others
- Formal operations (12 years–adulthood): able to think in terms of abstract concepts and hypothetical situations, logical reasoning.

(Garhart Mooney, 2000)

He proposed that in order to understand our world we use two processes to build up what he called schema, stores of information, about how the world works:

- Assimilation – we take in new information as we encounter new experiences
- Accommodation – we adapt our existing knowledge structures, our concepts of how things work or what they mean, to fit this new knowledge in.

(Gray and MacBlain, 2015)

These processes continue to be used throughout our life to as we continue to learn from new experiences. For example: you have just purchased a new mobile phone handset, made by a different manufacturer. You already have a store of information about how mobile phones work, which buttons and menus to use for sending texts, accessing the Internet, making phone calls, storing contact information, taking photos and so on. You now have to learn how to manage these functions on your new handset. Thus you are assimilating new information (which buttons to press and so on) and accommodating your existing knowledge store to include this for future use. By the time you buy your third or fourth mobile phone, which again have different processes for the functions you want to use, you will have assimilated a lot of information about mobile phone use and accommodated your knowledge store by discarding information no longer useful to you, and drawing together information that is still of use to you. To a constructivist, then, experience plays a vital role for anyone developing an understanding of their world. The more you experience, the broader your knowledge base, giving you a wider and more detailed range of concepts about how your world operates.

Piaget argued that young children have to start with an understanding of the world based on their own experience alone, giving them an egocentric view of the world (Gray and MacBlain, 2015), literally a self-centred perception of how the world works. He proposed that children start with no concept of object permanence, i.e. they do not understand that objects, people and even events can continue to exist if they themselves cannot see them or interact with them. This explains why children may become distressed when people or objects move or are taken away from their immediate environment, e.g. a cup or toy falls off their high chair tray, or a person leaves the room. Their understanding that these things can continue to exist outside their own direct experience develops gradually during the sensori-motor stage.

This egocentrism would explain why most toddlers demonstrate quite self-centred behaviour and struggle with some social skills such as turn taking and sharing. As children get older, and their understanding of the world grows, they develop the capacity to understand that others have needs and wishes as well, and these may well be very different from our own.

Activity

Observe a group of children in your placement setting to see if they are able to take turns and share toys and resources. How old are they and how might this account for their behaviour? What do practitioners within the setting do to support children in developing these skills?

Children gradually understand that other people may not share their own knowledge and may quite literally see things from a different point of view. This is the process of developing a 'theory of mind' where a child learns that there are many different points of view to take into account in the social world, particularly when it comes to deciding who can play with particular resources, or who gets to speak at circle time. This decentring is an important part of their social development but relies on the child developing the mental structures to be able to process such information, which will only happen through time and experience.

Finally, Piaget also researched children's understanding of conservation, that size, volume or mass does not change even if shape or outward appearance changes. In his own studies he found that children did not appear to understand that if a ball of clay was rolled out into a long cylinder, for example, its mass did not actually alter. This is a basic principle that demonstrates how a child understands fundamental principles of quantity and mass, rather than focussing on the outward appearance of objects they see in front of them, which underpins their mathematical and scientific understanding. Piaget argued that children are unable, before the age of about 6 or 7, to understand and apply such abstract principles to their world. However, other researchers, for example, including Donaldson (Donaldson, 1987), argued that Piaget's findings were influenced by the way in which he carried out his research, and that it was not the concept that children did not understand, but the way in which the questions were posed.

Whilst there has been considerable debate about Piaget's claims over children's abilities to solve problems of conservation and the age at which they begin to develop more abstract reasoning (Gray and MacBlain, 2015), his findings about children's very early learning focussed on their senses and motor skills and their need to have hands-on experience in order to understand and learn about their world, have shaped early years practice for many years. The importance of active engagement in the learning process as one of the CEL, and the use of continuous provision areas where children can explore resources as they wish rather than always being presented with adult-led, structured activities, demonstrate the application of Piaget's theory to early education.

Your role as a practitioner

Piaget characterised the child as a 'lone scientist', exploring their own world and gradually making sense of it by forming hypotheses about how it worked and the people, objects and events within it, and testing these out. For the child to learn, they require experience which should be rich, stimulating, safe and engaging. This suggests a facilitating role for the practitioner, providing resources and experiences and offering opportunity for exploration, rather than one of rule making or boundary enforcing. Within an early years setting where there might be as many as 60 children at a time all conducting their own explorations and experiments in order to understand their own worlds, this can present you with some challenges, particularly in terms of managing social behaviour and cooperation. However, Piaget's response to this might well be to remind you that every experience, even those that might end in tears, presents a learning opportunity for a child and a chance to understand more fully how their social and emotional as well as their physical world works.

Activity

As part of your studies it is likely that you will have to plan activities to support children's learning. Using key points from Piaget's theories, plan an area of continuous provision to support children's understanding of two dimensional shapes.

Social constructivist approach

Social constructivists equally prize the role of experience and the importance of children being actively engaged with their environment to support their learning. However, this perspective also brings in a socio-cultural element to the learning process, by means of interaction with others, and the development of language and communication skills. Learning is no longer seen as a solitary process of making sense of your own experience but a shared one where individuals interact with each other to share knowledge and ideas, and they construct a shared or social understanding of their world. A good example of this theoretical perspective comes from Vygotsky (Garhart Mooney, 2000; Doherty and Hughes, 2014), who described the learning process any of us go through as an interaction between the novice and a More Knowledgeable Other (MKO), i.e. a relationship between a learner and a teacher. Vygotsky argued that learning is a process that builds upon what an individual can do now – their actual development, and what they may be able to do with assistance from the MKO – the proximal development. This process can be seen in in the following diagram:

Table 6.1 Zone of Proximal Development, adapted from Smith et al., 2011

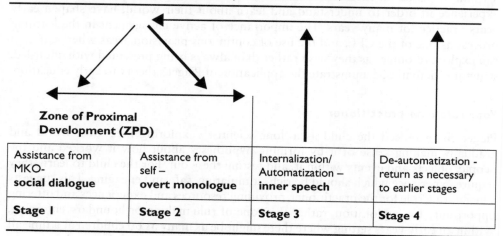

Assistance from MKO- **social dialogue**	Assistance from self – **overt monologue**	Internalization/ Automatization – **inner speech**	De-automatization - return as necessary to earlier stages
Stage 1	**Stage 2**	**Stage 3**	**Stage 4**

So for example, imagine you can swim front crawl (your actual development), but you wanted to learn how to swim breaststroke (your zone of proximal development, ZPD); what would a Vygotskyian approach to this look like?

First you would sign up with a teacher – perhaps a friend or relative who could already do this, or more likely, a swimming coach at your local pool – this is your MKO. They would explain to you what you needed to do (**social dialogue**) and probably even demonstrate the appropriate actions whilst talking you though them. You would then copy these moves whilst your teacher continues to talk you through them to ensure you follow the appropriate sequences.

Eventually, you should be able to practise the actions whilst talking yourself through them – first out loud (**overt monologue**), then in your head (**inner speech**). With practice, this sequence of actions will become a smooth process, and you will no longer be aware that you are deliberately talking yourself through what you need to do. In other words, learning has taken place and your ZPD – being able to swim breaststroke – has now become part of your actual development.

If, during practice, you find you are not improving your grasp of breaststroke, this indicates further teaching or instruction is required to analyse your mistakes and put them right, so you might have to return to earlier stages in the process (**de-automatization**) for this to happen, so that successful learning can take place. All this shows is that progress with learning is an individual process for all of us, which we do at different rates, requiring different levels of support and instruction.

Thinking activity

Now consider how this might be applied to supporting 3-year-olds in learning how to count from 1 to 10.

The key to learning for the social constructivists is the interaction that takes place between the teacher and the learner – whether this is an adult and a child, or two or more children with no adult intervention. Within this approach, those with greater experience or knowledge teach, while those with less experience or knowledge learn.

Whilst the social constructivist approach is based on a teaching relationship, it is still one that requires the active engagement of the learner if they are to develop their own understanding of their world. Language and effective communication skills underpin this approach to children developing an understanding of their world, as this is how such understanding can be expressed and shared. Bruner took this further and introduced the notion of scaffolding (Gray and MacBlain, 2015), a dialogue where the adult uses open-ended questions to support the child's growing understanding of a task or concept, encouraging them to predict or reason through stages in a problem or experience, to form hypotheses that they can test for themselves so that they are actively engaged in their learning rather than simply being the passive recipients of other people's knowledge. Whilst scaffolding is more usually undertaken by an adult practitioner supporting the learning of a child, do not overlook the value of peer learning in the early years setting – young children as quite capable of instructing each other and sharing their knowledge, even if they do not use such sophisticated skills as scaffolding to support this.

> **Activity**
>
> Observe the children on your placement and try to identify who are the knowledgeable or experienced leaders, and if this is always a matter of age, or if in fact it may be due to other factors such as greater experience or more confidence. Also identify in which areas of learning they offer instruction to their peers, and why this might be.

Your role as a practitioner

To support children's learning and development taking a social constructivist approach, you need to focus on their development of language and communication skills, and also on your role as the MKO. You should be planning activities and experiences that promote language development between children and practitioners, and between children and their peers, as only by sharing ideas can you implement a social constructivist approach to your practice. This does not mean that you should spend all your time deliberately teaching children by means of structured, adult-led activity, but it does mean you need to consider carefully what opportunities you might have for scaffolding children's learning and understanding, by use of open-ended, thought provoking questions, even when they are engaged in their own play and the use of continuous provision resources.

You should also consider how you could use a blend of structured activities, with yourself as the MKO to lead them, and set up continuous provision resources and free-flow play opportunities that encourage social interaction and therefore peer learning between the children. This then gives you opportunity for scaffolding learning as well as opportunity for children to develop their own interests and strategies for problem solving and reasoning. The social constructivist practitioner is engaged with the children in the early years setting, but manages to do this without taking over their learning and their interaction – their active engagement is promoted and protected at all times.

Activity

Plan a day's provision for 3- and 4-year-olds following one of the areas for learning and development from the EYFS, and taking a social constructivist approach to your practice.

The significance of language

Language development itself and its relation to emerging literacy will be discussed later in this book. However, it is worth briefly considering the relationship of language and communication development to cognitive and social development. Behaviourists regard language and communication as yet another element in the behavioural repertoire of the human individual, so that effective language and communication is simply an aspect of behaviour than can be shaped and reinforced. Thus the human infant begins to vocalise as their physical development progresses, and these vocalisations are shaped by responses from the caregivers (parents, practitioners, family members and so on). Vocalisations that are reinforced are most often repeated, and by varying the level and frequency of reinforcement, specific vocalisations are repeated and shaped, developing eventually into words and sentences. Whilst this may explain some adult responses to infant vocalisations and how some early utterances – mama, dada – eventually turn into recognisable words – mummy, daddy – this does not offer a satisfactory explanation for all language development, or for the mistakes children make when trying to produce more complex sentences. Nor does it suggest any link between language and understanding of the world.

Constructivists and social constructivists take a different view of the relationship between language and thinking. To a constructivist, experience and understanding emerge first at a concrete level, and are then conceptualised later by language as a symbolic tool, capable of representing a much wider range of abstract concepts. Once a child has a grasp of language she or he can begin to represent more complex concepts, such as past and future times, possibilities and imaginary or abstract ideas. However, language is driven by understanding and knowledge in this approach.

To a social constructivist, it is language itself that drives and supports understanding of the world, through dialogue and interaction with others. Language and communication play a vital role in the process of learning, as without these, ideas and experiences could not be shared, limiting access to any zone of proximal development, assisted by the knowledge of others. Language and communication then are vital tools that need to be developed if learning is to progress as smoothly and as efficiently as possible.

Promoting a positive and inclusive approach to learning

Regardless of which theoretical perspective you feel offers the strongest explanation for how young children learn, you also need to consider how your planning and practice can encourage all children to engage with the learning process. A child's overall disposition towards learning makes a significant contribution to the success of their learning, and all children need to be encouraged to develop positive dispositions. These have been identified by a number of different researchers and include: confidence, curiosity, intentionality, self-control, relatedness, communication, cooperation (Goleman, 1995, cited in Hall and Burke, 2004); resilience, resourcefulness, reflectiveness (Claxton, 1999, cited in Hall and Burke, 2004); and resilience, playfulness, reciprocity (Carr and Claxton, 2002, cited in Hall and Burke, 2004). Although this seems to be a long list of requirements for young children to be successful learners, on closer examination you can see that they centre on the child's curiosity, their independence and confidence, their communication and social skills and their willingness to reason and to experiment when encountering new learning experiences. Thus as you focus on activities and resources to support children's understanding of specific aspects of learning and development, it is essential that in your practice, you provide support for the development of these positive dispositions, so that children see that learning is an active and enjoyable process, within which the contribution they make is valued.

Within the EYFS, effective learning is characterised as:

- Playing and exploring
- Active learning
- Creating, and thinking critically.

(DfE, 2017, p. 10)

Children's progress will be measured not only in terms of their progress towards the ELGs, but also in terms of their development of these characteristics. It is your role as a practitioner to ensure that you support this development in your planning and your practice, no matter which theoretical perspective you choose to adopt for your practice. As you progress in practice you will come to realise that the different perspectives all have their part to play in explaining children's learning and underpinning your practice. It is your responsibility as a practitioner to consider how each of them can be applied to supporting the development of these characteristics, and how they might each influence your role and your practice.

Finally, practitioners have a duty under the EYFS and the revised SEND Code of Practice (DfE, 2017; DfE and DoH, 2015) to ensure that they consider the needs of all children – this is referred to as universal inclusive practice. This means you need to take into account the developmental levels (rather than simply the age), interests, learning needs and dispositions of all children, rather than making specialist adaptations to their activities for children with identified special needs. In your planning you need to show you are taking account of your children as individuals, in order to support their progress and help them develop positive dispositions to learning. A good understanding of theories of child development will inform your practice and your expectations in managing this to meet the individual needs of all children.

Activity

You are setting up an early years setting, to be called either Piaget's Play Group, or Vygotsky's Academy. Describe the role of the practitioner working with 3-year-olds in this setting. What would be the difference in practice in these two settings? How could either of them also borrow ideas for practice from each other, or incorporate social learning and reinforcement to support learning? How can universal inclusive practice be achieved?

Conclusion

This chapter has considered some of the main theories concerning how young children learn, which you can use to guide your practice and planning within the EYFS. However, what has been introduced here is only a beginning, and good practitioners need to read further and update their knowledge regularly, to ensure that their practice maintains a high standard of quality. Such research will also support you in your critical reflections and when you progress to a leadership role, guiding the practice of others. Further information sources have been identified below and in the reference list as an initial starting point.

Additional information sources

- Slater, A., Bremner, J. G. and British Psychological Society (2011) *An Introduction to Developmental Psychology*, 2nd ed., Chichester: BPS Blackwell.
- Gray, C. and MacBlain, S. (2015) *Learning Theories in Childhood*, 2nd ed., London: Sage.

References

Carr, M. and Claxton, G. (2002) Tracking the Development of Learning Dispositions. *Assessment in Education*, 9(1), 9–37.

Claxton, G. (1999) *Wise Up: The Challenge of Lifelong Learning*, London: Bloomsbury.

Department for Education (DfE) (2017) *Statutory Framework for the Early Years Foundation Stage: Setting the Standards for Learning, Development and Care for Children from Birth to Five, Ref: DFE – 00337–2014*, London: Crown Copyright 2014.

Department for Education (DfE) and Department of Health (DoH) (2015) *Special Educational Needs and Disability Code of Practice: 0–25: Statutory Guidance for Organisations Which Work with and Support Children and Young People Who Have Special Educational Needs and Disabilities, Ref: DFE – 00205–2013*, London: Crown Copyright 2015.

Doherty, J. and Hughes, M. (2014) *Child Development: Theory and Practice 0–11*, 2nd edn., Harlow: Pearson Education Ltd.

Donaldson, M. (1987) *Children's Minds*, London: Fontana Press.

Early Education (2012) *Development Matters in the Early Years Foundation Stage*, London: Crown Copyright 2012.

Garhart Mooney, C. (2000) *Theories of Childhood: An Introduction to Dewey, Montessori, Erikson, Piaget and Vygotsky*, Minnesota: Redleaf Press.

Goleman, D. (1995) *Emotional Intelligence*, New York: Bantam.

Gray, C. and MacBlain, S. (2015) *Learning Theories in Childhood*, 2nd edn., London: Sage.

Hall, K. and Burke, W. M. (2004) *Making Formative Assessment Work*, Buckingham: Open University Press.

Schunk, D. H. (2004) *Learning Theories: An Educational Perspective* 4th edn., New Jersey: Pearson Education Inc.

Slater, A., Bremner, J. G. and British Psychological Society (2011) *An Introduction to Developmental Psychology*, 2nd edn., Chichester: BPS Blackwell.

Smith, P. K., Cowie, H. and Blades, M. (2011) *Understanding Children's Development*, 5th edn., Oxford: Blackwell.

Standards and Testing Agency (2013) *2014 Early Years Foundation Stage Profile Handbook*, London: Crown Copyright 2013.

Thorndike E. L. (1913) *Educational Psychology Vol. 2: The Psychology of Learning*, New York: Teachers College Press.

Chapter 7

Key Stage I curriculum

Alison Ryan

Chapter aims

By the end of this chapter you will:

- have an understanding of the historical development of the Key Stage 1 curriculum
- be aware of how assessment of literacy and mathematics is carried out in Key Stage 1
- understand the key areas contained within the curriculum for literacy and mathematics
- have considered the barriers to learning within literacy
- have developed an understanding of how you can support children's development in literacy and mathematics.

Introduction

The Key Stage 1 curriculum follows on from the EYFS and is delivered to children in Years 1 and 2 of their primary schooling. The aim of the curriculum is to give children a sound grasp of the important skills and knowledge that they will need for a successful education, and so literacy and mathematics are key within this.

The primary curriculum – background and useful sources of information

In 1988, a National Curriculum was developed by the then Department for Education and Science as part of the Education Reform Act of that year. The National Curriculum was introduced into primary schools in 1989, and this was the first time that Key Stages (KS) were used to describe the different stages of education.

The National Curriculum has been revised in recent times to reflect changes in technology and now consists of 'core subjects' of English, mathematics and science, and the ' foundation subjects', which are

- art and design
- computing (ICT)

- design and technology
- geography
- history
- music
- physical education.

Schools are also required to teach religious education, and the syllabus for this is determined at a local level. They are also encouraged to teach Personal, Social and Health Education (PSHE) and citizenship. There are also two non-statutory skills frameworks, which mean that these skills should be taught, but are not separate assessed subjects. These are Key Skills, which include:

- communication
- application of number
- information technology
- working with others
- improving own learning and performance
- problem solving and thinking skills, covering information-processing, reasoning, enquiry, creative thinking and evaluation skills.

There are also five cross-curricular elements, which means that these should be considered in all taught subjects; these are:

- creativity
- ICT
- education for sustainable development
- literacy across the curriculum
- numeracy across the curriculum.

Guidance on what is to be taught now is contained in the Primary National Strategy, and the Primary Curriculum can be obtained from www.gov.uk/government/publications/national-curriculum-in-england-primary-curriculum.

There was an additional focus on the role of Primary literacy and mathematics through the introduction of the National Literacy and Numeracy Strategies in 1997 and 1998. These were in response to concerns that children were not reaching the expected level at the Key Stage 1 (KS1) Standard Attainment Tests (SATs). These strategies gave schools a very clear structure for what should be taught at each level of learning, and emphasised the importance of subject knowledge for teaching staff, and parental involvement in the child's literacy and mathematics development. These have been developed further and are now included in the Primary curriculum guidance.

In 1990 SATs were introduced for 7-year-olds at the end of KS1, followed by SATs for 11-year-olds at the end of KS2 in 1994, and for 14-year-olds at the end of KS3 in 1997. These tests focussed on literacy, mathematics and science. This gave schools a progress measure to work with, and although there have been reforms of these SATs, including the removal of tests for 14-year-olds, they still provide very important feedback for schools, parents and the government about how children are achieving in literacy and mathematics. The revision of KS1 tests in 2016 mean that children currently take tests at the age of 7 in reading, writing (including grammar, punctuation and spelling) and mathematics. These tests are marked by the teacher, and examples can be found here: www.gov.uk/government/collections/national-curriculum-assessments-practice-materials.

There is also a phonics screening check at the end of Year 1 which assesses children's understanding of letter sounds (for further details see www.gov.uk/government/publications/phonics-screening-check-2016-materials).

Literacy

The rest of the chapter should be read with reference to the curriculum for Literacy and Mathematics for Key Stage 1 – please see the further reading section at the end of this chapter for details.

The curriculum for Key Stage 1 emphasises the importance of English in children's development. It does not give details of how children should be taught, or any underpinning theory. However, there are many reviews that have been done of teaching methods and guidance documents that the government have produced that have had an impact on the way that children will be taught. Some of these are contained in the further reading section for this chapter, such as Riley (2006). Each school will have its own methods and resources; however, there are things that all schools will use that are the same.

Speaking and listening

Spoken language is particularly important as this underpins not only a child's ability to progress in formal English study, but also their ability to understand instructions and to communicate socially with others in the school. The guidance for all National Curriculum subjects, which contains details of what should be taught at each stage, is known as the Programme of Study. The Programme of Study for Speaking and Listening is the same for Years 1 to 6 in the curriculum, and this reflects that fact that children will develop language at different rates, especially if they are learning it as a second language. This is discussed later on in this chapter. The Programme of Study includes areas such as asking and answering questions, and the importance of learning Standard English rather than dialect or regional words and phrases or slang words. Examples of this might be phrases such as, 'going to the loo', rather than using the more formal, 'toilet'. It also mentions children having to learn to use appropriate registers when speaking, which refers to the choice of formal or informal language depending on who you are talking to.

Reading

There are two main areas of skills that children need to develop when learning to read. These are recognising the words that they are reading and being able to pronounce them correctly, and being able to understand the meaning of the words in the context of the text. The skills of comprehension involve both speaking and listening, and the role of the adult is to help children make sense of what they are reading through supportive explanations and questioning, to make sure that they understand the meaning of what they are reading. This can be complex as the English language has lots of words that sound the same but have different spellings (homophones), for example, *hair/hare*, or *bare/bear*; words that look the same but have different sounds (homographs) such as 'wound' as in, '*I have a wound on my leg*', and wound as in, '*she wound the ball of wool*'; and those that look the same but have different meanings, depending on which context they are being used in (homonyms), such as, '*I am a cook and I love to cook*', where the word is being used as both a noun and a verb. Children need to develop their knowledge of the meaning of each word, along with their knowledge of the function of each word, and that will help them distinguish between them.

When learning to read children are taught to use decoding skills, looking at the word and its context within a sentence. Children in Key Stage 1 will usually have been taught to read using a phonics scheme which teaches the 42 sounds, or phonemes, of the English language in a structured way, and by Year 1 will be using this knowledge to work out the sounds of unfamiliar words. The schemes use the key concept of grapheme/phoneme correspondence, to help children to start learning words where the sound the letters make can be easily worked out from the word. A grapheme is the way that we write a sound and a phoneme is the way that we say it. Children will initially be taught words where the graphemes and phonemes correspond. For example a simple word like '*sat*' is made up of three sounds, 's-a-t'. The children will later develop the skills to be able to decode words where the graphemes do not correspond to the phoneme sounds such as *cough*, which is sounded out as '*coff*'.

There is very useful guidance within the curriculum documents to the phonemes and for spellings for children in Years 1 and 2, and the vocabulary, grammar and punctuation requirements for both years as well as an explanation of terms used in grammar.

It is important to remember that children develop these skills at very different rates so you will often be supporting children who are still developing their phonic knowledge. You need to be familiar with the phonemes and how the children have been taught before they come into Key Stage 1. For more information on phonics teaching you should refer to the further reading section at the end of this chapter.

When on your placement you will have a key role in helping children to develop their reading skills. Children really appreciate having time spent in small groups or one to one to share books. When reading with children you should consider the following sequence of activities to help them get the most out of the book:

Table 7.1 Reading a book with children

Sequence	What the practitioner can do
The context of a book	Before you start to read, look at the cover and the illustrations. Ask the children questions such as: what is the title, what do you think it will be about, who is the author?
Discussion of the characters	When you are looking at the pictures, make sure the children know the names of the characters; ask them questions about the characters to involve them in the story; for example, a story about a cat could involve discussion of who has a cat and what are the cats' names, or who has other types of pets.
Developing predicting when reading	Before turning the page, ask the children what is going to happen next.
The importance of repetition in reading	Children love reading the same book over and over again, and even though you may get bored they won't! You can use this to ask 'do you remember questions' in rereading sessions, where they can tell you what happens next; or questions to help children think about the story such as asking about alternative endings.

Activity

Choose any book used in your placement, and think about the context of the book – what is it about, what are the main themes within it?

How would you support a child with understanding those themes when reading that book together? Make a list of the sort of questions you would ask and what additional information you could offer.

Many books have additional themes, aside from just the story, such as the very popular Elmer book, which is about fitting in to a group. This can be used to discuss issues of diversity with the children, and can also be used for creative activities which help the children not only get the most from reading the book, but also inspire them in art and design areas. For example, The Gruffalo could be used to get the children thinking about creating their own imaginary monster.

A wide range of books should be used for reading, including traditional tales from European and other cultures, and non-fiction texts to stimulate interest in reading for everyone. These can link in with other topics such as Science, History and Geography. Many children's books use rhyme as well as there are many great examples of poetry for children. Rhyme is very important when learning to read, as most of the way that we learn early letter sounds is in thinking about words that rhyme with words we already know. If a child has learned '*sat*' then they can more easily learn '*pat, mat, cat*' and so on.

Children love it when adults also use expressive voices when reading, especially if you can vary your voice when you read. Developing confidence in reading with children is one of the key things to do early on in your placement, and like most things it gets better with practice!

Activity

Choose a book from your placement and record yourself reading it as you normally would. Listen to the recording and see if you can add to your reading by varying the tone and pace with which you speak. Can you use different voices for different characters? Try speaking in a higher or lower pitch of voice to distinguish between characters.

There are also links between literacy and mathematics when reading, so when you are looking at a book, think about where the maths themes are in the books you are sharing with the children. For example, Elmer has lots of opportunity to talk about different patterns, and non-fiction books often have lots of maths facts in them such as weight, height, age and so on.

Writing

Being able to write consists of two key skill areas, which link to the reading and speaking and listening skills already discussed. The first skill area, transcription, is about being able to spell the words that you want to use, and links very strongly to reading. Children also need to read widely to develop their knowledge of vocabulary and to learn that there are alternatives to words that can make their writing in Key Stage 2 more interesting. So it is important that children see the links between what they are reading and their ability to write similar types of text. Often an activity will be set that takes a book that has been used for reading, and asks the children to do writing tasks of different types. This also links into other curriculum areas such as recording investigations in Science or learning about the world in Geography and History.

The second skill area in writing is composition. This is about articulating ideas, and links to language skills and wider knowledge of the world. When you are support- ing children with this skill area, you can use visuals and role play to stimulate ideas for writing. It is important to encourage children to talk about their ideas, and to be able to structure those ideas verbally before they start to write things down. It is also important to develop the idea of writing as a process, and the different stages that you might go through to produce a final piece of work, such as initial thoughts, pictures to illustrate, first draft of writing and finished piece.

Handwriting

Developing handwriting that can be easily read is a challenge for many children, and emphasis is placed on developing both the formation of letters and also the ability to join them up so that they can still be understood. Most schools will have a hand- writing policy which will be shared with parents, and children will be encouraged to write as much as they can for different purposes. Handwriting progress depends on the children having developed fine motor skills in order that they can hold a pencil or pen, and lots of activities will have been done in the Early Years to support children with this development.

Activity

Look at the range of different writing implements that your setting has. What are the different sorts of tools that younger children need such as differently shaped pens and pencils or pencil grips?

Barriers to learning and supporting children with additional needs

Learning to read, write and spell is a complex process, and all children develop these skills at different rates. Some children will need additional support due to a visual or hearing impairment, or conditions that affect their ability to control fine motor control such as cerebral palsy. Left handed children often find learning to write more of a challenge, due to the fact that they tend to cover what they have written in the process of writing, or use a hooked grip which is more tiring for their hands than right handed children, meaning that work can take longer and be less neat. You can find sources for more information on working with children with additional needs in the further reading section.

English as an additional language (EAL)

Since the introduction of the National Curriculum in 1988, we have seen changes in the UK as a society, particularly in terms of changing patterns of migration. We now live in a far more multicultural society than previously, with more people coming to settle in the UK from the newer European Union countries such as Poland and Lithuania, and others arriving as refugees and asylum seekers from conflict zones such as Syria, Sierra Leone and Afghanistan. This has meant additional support is needed for language development, as there are now many more children who have English as an additional language in primary schools, and more languages to be supported for communication with parents. Statistics from 2013 show that 1 in 6 primary pupils do not have English as their first language, and it is estimated that over 300 languages are now spoken in UK schools (Telegraph, 2013; Naldic, 2016).

Thinking activity

How many children in your setting have English as an additional language? What percentage is that of the total number of children in the setting? How many different languages do the children in your setting speak? Are they using the same alphabet as we are in English, are they reading from right to left as we do?

It is important to be aware of this, not only as these children may need additional support, particularly if they have only recently started school in the UK, but also to be aware of what languages they already know and the type of language they are using at home. Languages do not all use the same alphabets, and so they may need help with learning the English alphabet, as well as things like the fact that we read and write from left to right. It is also important to find out what languages their parents are using so that you can support communication about their children's development.

Mathematics

Communication and maths

In this chapter we have previously mentioned maths themes in reading books, and the link between literacy and maths is very important, as much of early learning in maths is about language. By the end of Key Stage 1 children need to know and understand large amounts of subject specific language, some of which is used in other contexts.

Thinking activity

The words 'square' and 'count' are used in maths but also have non-mathematical meanings. Think about all of the other meanings of these words aside from their mathematical definition – use a dictionary to help you if needed. What is the difference between the mathematical meaning and other everyday uses of these words? How would you explain to a child what the maths terms mean and what the other terms mean? How could you use visuals to help you with this?

The Key Stage 1 maths curriculum

Maths in Key Stage 1 is split into two areas, Numbers; and Measures, Shape and Space, which also includes basic statistics. This follows on from the EYFS, where the emphasis is on children being able to understand the names for 2D and 3D shapes, and use positional language including 'behind' or 'in front of', and being able to sort and order things. The Numbers part of the curriculum includes counting, addition, subtraction, multiplication, division and fractions. Measures, Shape and Space includes knowing about length, height, weight/mass, and time, the names and properties of 2D and 3D shapes, and positional language such as 'half turn' and 'quarter turn'. Statistics is taught in Year 2, and children need to be able to count objects and represent them as pictograms, tally charts, block diagrams and tables.

Learning number symbols and names

We make numbers using the digits 0–9. Young children need to learn to recognise both the shape of these digits when written and to be able to write them, bearing in mind that digits are sometimes different in written and printed formats. Often, digits like 1, 3, 4, 5 and 7 will be written in different ways by different people, and that may be confusing for children.

They also need to learn that each digit has a name, sometimes more than one, as in *nought*, *nothing* and *zero*. These digits are then combined to make numbers of any size. Sometimes the numbers will have the same name as the digit name, for example, 2 is called *two* and represents the number 2; but for larger numbers, the digit combination gives a number with another name, so that 12 is not *one two* but *twelve*. This is quite a complex concept for a young child, and they will need lots of support with this.

The concept of place value

Although we only have ten digits, we can make any size of number using the concept of place value. This is a very important concept in Key Stage 1, and underpins the more complex maths in KS2 and beyond. You cannot do things like long multiplication and borrowing without a sound understanding of place value, and the fact that when you borrow a 1 from the next column along in a sum, what you are really doing is borrowing 10. Children need lots of support in being able to make larger numbers from the digits 0–9 and lots of practical activities where they can combine different digits to make numbers. As a practitioner you will need to be familiar with place value and concepts of divisibility and the times tables in order to support children's learning.

Activity

What is the largest number that you can make from this set of digits below?

| 0 | 4 | 3 | 2 |

Figure 7.1 Numberline

What type of number is it? What can it be divided by? How do you know that?

Resources to support maths learning

Your setting will use many different types of resources to support maths learning, the emphasis being on giving children access to all of the resources they need to really understand a maths concept, and to enable them to represent it in different ways. The Concrete, Pictorial and Abstract approach (CPA) is used to enable children to start with objects that they can see and touch, then move on to pictures representing those objects, before later being able to understand the operation as a more abstract calculation.

This approach is based on Bruner's theory (1957, in Beckett and Taylor, 2016) that children learn through enactive, iconic and symbolic representations, and Piaget's theory of development (Slater and Bremner, 2010), which describes children going through different stages of development at different ages. Young children between the ages of 2 and 7 are said by Piaget to be in the Pre-Operational Stage, which means that children still find it more difficult to do things mentally without a physical representation. They can, however, understand and represent things with pictures or symbols. Piaget argues that it is not until between 7 and 11 years old that children can start to use logic to work out problems, and therefore then they do not need as much input with actual objects. It is important to remember that all children develop at different rates and that many children such as those children with learning difficulties and disabilities will need to use these concrete resources for longer.

Number work

The emphasis in Year 1 is on counting. This is a visual, kinaesthetic and oral skill, and needs to be practised repeatedly. It is important that children are given the opportunity to count forwards and backwards, and are supported in their learning by the use of objects to actually count, and by visuals that reinforce counting, such as number lines. Children also need to know that there is a practical reason for counting, so there are lots of opportunities within a normal school day for doing that, such as counting the number of children in the class or any given area, the number of pens needed for an activity, number of books in the reading corner, and so on. They also need to use language such as *less, more, fewer, most* and *least*. Again, you can help this by asking questions such as '*do we have fewer pens than we need*', '*do we have more girls than boys in our group?*'

Thinking activity

Within your placement have a look at where the opportunities are for children to learn how to count. What resources are there to help them do this? What areas of the provision could be used for counting aside from during maths sessions?

For example, are there role-play areas within the classroom? Are there displays where they can use counting skills? Is there opportunity for counting in the playground, for example hopscotch? What other subjects could children practise counting in?

You could keep a diary of a day at placement and see how many opportunities there are for counting practice during that time.

It is also important to give children lots of opportunities to count and compare. Many schools use resources for both counting and comparing, such as comparing bears, frogs, dinosaurs and so on. These can be used initially for counting, and later in the Measures, Shape and Space element of the curriculum, for looking at different sizes. They also encourage the learning of colour names, and positional language such as describing which is *in front of*, *behind*, *next to*.

Adding and subtracting

In Year 1, the emphasis is on number bonds to 20. Children need to be able to add and subtract confidently all of the combinations that make up twenty such as $10 + 10$, $20 + 0$, and $15 + 5$. By Year 2, they will need to be confident in using those number bonds to help them with number facts up to 100. Children need to practise these skills both with actual objects, and with representations such as visuals and symbols, and to understand that whatever the format used, you should still get the same answer. Children need also to understand that it does not matter which way round you write an addition sum, you will still get the same answer, but it does matter which way round you write a subtraction sum.

$$3 + 6 = 9 \qquad 6 + 3 = 9 \qquad 3 - 6 = -3 \qquad 6 - 3 = 3$$

This is known as the commutative nature of addition and subtraction. Again, this is best explained with objects to start with, so that the children can see what happens if you try and take away a greater number from a smaller one.

Multiplying and dividing

Multiplying and dividing can be difficult concepts for children to understand, and need to be taught by practical methods, such as thinking about sharing objects into groups and counting how many are in each of those groups. This can be supported by them having access to lots of resources where they have to share counters, pasta shapes, beads, buttons and so on between receptacles. Children also need to understand that the commutative principle also applies to multiplication and that 3×6 will give you the same answer as 6×3 but that 3 divided by 6 is a very different sum to 6 divided by 3.

When you start work on dividing, it is also important for children to know about odd and even numbers, as this will underpin their work on more complex multiplication in KS2. At this stage they are not expected to understand the concept of prime numbers, (those that can only be divided by themselves and 1 such as 2, 7, 13), but activities such as counting in 2s will help reinforce ideas of even numbers, as will sharing activities using things such as counters.

Words for the different symbols used in maths

As well as number words, children will need to understand the different ways of using words for the symbols for addition, subtraction, multiplication and division. Instead of using the + sign we could say *and*, *total*, *plus*, *more*, *altogether*. As well as saying multiply for the X sign we can use *times, groups of, lots of.* You will need to model this language when you are working with children as it is important for their understanding of word based problems that they will encounter in the Key Stage 1 tests such as the examples below:

Sam has three marbles; his friend Ansar gives him four more marbles. How many marbles has he got altogether?

Figure 7.2 Addition

Children in Year 1 need to know how to find, recognise and name a half and a quarter from a variety of different objects and shapes. This could involve sorting activities like those described above for multiplication and division, where a set is halved or quartered, or a visual activity such as finding half a circle or a square. This can be a good opportunity to let children practise their fine motor skills with using pens, pencils or scissors, and getting them to colour in or cut out shapes to show half or a quarter. It is important that children understand that half and a quarter are not fixed numbers like 2 or 10 but that the amount will vary depending on what is being halved or quartered. Games such as Bingo and matching cards can be used to help children develop their skills at recognising fractions in visual forms.

Children will also need to be able to work with fractions in word type problems such as this example:

Chloe has 8 sweets. If she gives half to her friend Zak, how many will she have left?

Figure 7.3 Measurement shape and space

In Year 2 children will extend their skills to being able to write factions in the standard format of ½, ¼, and will also be dealing with equivalent fractions such as ²⁄₄ and larger fractions such as ¾.

Measurement shape and space

As well as learning to measure height, length and mass/weight, children need to learn dates, times and money; they need to be aware of the names of days and months; they need to understand and use language such as *this afternoon, tomorrow, last week*. This gives lots of opportunity for you to talk to the children about the routine of the classroom and reinforce their use of time on a daily basis. Children will not be expected to be able to write the time accurately to five minutes, e.g. *twenty-five past three, ten to seven*, until the end of Year 2, but they can be helped to understand the sequence of the day by talking about regular routines, or by saying how long an activity is going to take, and repeating that information at the end of the activity. Parental involvement in learning is vital here, as so much of this can be done when out and about, talking about sizes of products in shops, the time it takes to cook meals, and by practical cooking activities such as baking cakes.

In the geometry section of the curriculum children will be learning the names of 2D and 3D shapes such as *circle, square, cuboid, pyramid*, and so will need support with saying and spelling these as well as recognising them. By the end of Year 2, children will be able to sort and categorise shapes using their properties such as numbers and shapes of sides, faces, edges and vertices.

There are also lots of opportunities for environmental maths in this topic, looking for shapes around the classroom and the playground or when out on trips and setting up activities in the playground that reinforce the language of shape and position. This area also links in with subjects such as PE and Art and Design and Technology.

Thinking activity

Observe children at playtime or in a PE session. What maths language and activities can you see? Is positional language used such as *forwards, backwards, turn*? How are children using maths language at playtime, maybe playing counting games or hopscotch or using differently shaped play equipment such as hoops and balls?

Think about how you could develop those activities with use of specific questions or equipment, such as scoring when children are throwing balls.

Data handling

In Year 2, children will be taught the use of tally charts and pictograms to record data. At your placement, you can help by developing displays around the setting that illustrate different ways of recording data, such as a weather chart with symbols that can be used to record each day's and week's weather, a height chart that children can use to measure themselves, or a pictogram showing when (in which month) the birthdays are for all the children in the class. There are also many cross-curricular links to other subjects such as Science here. For example, in Year 1, pupils have to study living things and record how they grow, which gives opportunities to measure plants, or use tables and charts to record when plants flower or leaves change colour.

Conclusion

Helping children to learn the vital skills of reading, writing and understanding maths is one of the most rewarding areas of early education. The joy on a child's face when they can understand text and can start to read their own choice of books is wonderful, and as a student on placement you can have a significant impact on that development.

Further information and resource sites

Teaching phonics

>   www.gov.uk/government/collections/phonics – a collection of material about phonics teaching.
>   http://jollylearning.co.uk/overview-about-jolly-phonics/ – the website of one of the main companies providing phonics schemes to schools.

Primary resources website

>   www.primaryresources.co.uk – this is a resource site created by teachers with lots of useful free material.

Twinkl

>   www.twinkl.co.uk – a great source of resources for KS1 subjects, some free but you can also pay to access more material.

Working with deaf and hearing impaired children

>   www.ndcs.org.uk – Especially these video clips with information about working with deaf children: www.ndcs.org.uk/professional_support/our_resources/here_to_learn/index

Working with visually impaired children – includes advice on strategies and resources

>   www.rnib.org.uk/services-we-offer-advice-professionals/education-professionals

Working with left handed children resource website

>   www.anythingleft-handed.co.uk/kids_help.html

References

Beckett, C. and Taylor, H. (2016) *Human Growth and Development*, 3rd edn., Los Angeles: Sage.
Department for Children Schools and Families (DCSF) (2008) *Sir Peter Williams' Independent Review of Mathematics Teaching in Early Years Settings and Primary Schools*, London: DCSF.
Department for Education (DfE) (2016) *National Curriculum*, Retrieved from www.gov.uk/government/publications/national-curriculum-in-england-framework-for-key-stages-1-to-4, The above document contains the Appendix for English mentioned in the chapter.
Naldic (2016) www.naldic.org.uk/research-and-information/eal-statistics/eal-pupils/
Riley, J. (2006) *Language and Literacy 3–7: Creative Approaches to Teaching*, London: Sage.
Slater, A., Bremner, J. G. and British Psychological Society (2011) *An Introduction to Developmental Psychology*, 2nd edn., Chichester: BPS Blackwell.
Telegraph (2013) www.telegraph.co.uk/education/educationnews/11761250/More-than-300-different-languages-spoken-in-British-schools-report-says.html

Chapter 8

Practising safely

Amanda Crow and Tina Froggett

Chapter aims

By the end of this chapter you will:

- have an understanding of the importance of safeguarding and promoting the welfare of children and young people
- be clear about your responsibility as a student practitioner when working in Early Childhood Education and Care (ECEC)
- have an insight into legislation and policy that governs the work of practitioners.

Introduction

This chapter will support the development of your academic and practical knowledge and skills in relation to safeguarding. Having confidence in your abilities and knowing who to talk to when you are worried and supporting the child are crucial aspects of working safely in ECEC. Therefore, understanding your role as a student practitioner and being clear about your responsibilities will contribute to you becoming a confident and capable early years practitioner. This chapter will challenge you to reflect on legislation and previous serious case reviews that have influenced current practice. Early years practitioners are in the privileged and influential position of working with children and their families in their earliest and most informative years of life. The first few years of life, and particularly from birth to 2, are critical for the developing brain and a time when children grow and develop (Marmot, 2010), so safeguarding and promoting their well-being is the most important role you will undertake as the following definition explains:

> Safeguarding and promoting the welfare of children is defined for the purposes of this guidance as protecting children from maltreatment; preventing impairment of children's health or development; ensuring that children grow up in circumstances consistent with the provision of safe and effective care; and taking action to enable all children to have the best outcomes.
>
> (HM Government, 2015a, p. 5)

The Department for Education (DfE) is responsible for child protection in England, and legislates through local authority arrangements a range of policies and guidance for professionals who work with children and young people. Northern Ireland, Scotland and Wales each have their own separate laws that cover education, health and social care, including the protection of children (NSPCC, 2016). This chapter will focus on the child protection system in England; however, it is significant and important to recognise that each nation in the United Kingdom is understood to follow a set of shared principles when keeping children and young people safe from harm (NSPCC, 2016).

Thinking activity

- What do you understand 'safeguarding' to mean in practice?
- Are you aware of your responsibilities as a student practitioner?
- Why is it important you know who the safeguarding lead is in your setting and what you must do if you are worried about a child?

When working with children and young people, practitioners have a duty of care; safeguarding is everyone's responsibility (HM Government, 2015a, p. 9); therefore, it is essential as a student that you are prepared for your future professional responsibilities and role. Understanding and developing a sound knowledge of safe practice is therefore important. Effective safeguarding means keeping children at the centre of everything you do, and is a crucial aspect of your developing professional learning. Your early years placement setting will have a duty, under section 40 of the Childcare Act 2006, to comply with the welfare requirements of the Early Years Foundation Stage (EYFS) framework (DfE, 2017). It is essential to note that the term 'safeguarding' encompasses all aspects including protecting children at risk of harm, ensuring their safety and intervening when they are vulnerable (Palaiologou, 2016).

What does the EYFS say about safeguarding?

Safeguarding children is a statutory requirement of the EYFS framework (DfE, 2017) and underpins all aspects of early years practice; Section 2 of the EYFS outlines the safeguarding and welfare requirement (DfE, 2017, p. 16) Here we will consider the requirements for safeguarding children and the suitability of adults as the most relevant sections to students.

Safeguarding children

It is a statutory requirement for all early years settings to have a lead practitioner for safeguarding (DfE, 2017, p. 16). All members of staff and students must report any concerns they have about a child, and these will be taken up by the safeguarding lead. Whilst the safeguarding lead takes overall responsibility, it is essential that all adults are aware of safeguarding policies and procedures.

The setting's safeguarding policy must clearly outline what action will be taken if someone is concerned about a child, as well as the rules regarding the use of phones and cameras on the premises, and how to address situations when an allegation is made against a member of staff (DfE, 2017, p. 17).

Activity

Take some time to look at Section 2 of the EYFS (DfE, 2017) and read about the safeguarding duties placed on the setting. Read your placement setting's policies around safeguarding to see how these duties are incorporated into safeguarding practices. There might be a collection of policies to look up; for example, safeguarding, employment and the use of mobile phones.

All practitioners must receive training in how to safeguard children from unsuitable adults, and this includes staff who behave inappropriately. Settings are also required to report safeguarding issues to Ofsted and to follow current government guidance (DfE, 2015a).

Suitable people

Settings have a duty to protect children from coming into contact with unsuitable people (DfE, 2017, pp. 17–18). The "effective systems" referred to in the EYFS consist of a number of procedures, for example, references and security checks (DfE, 2017, p. 17). As a student, you will be asked to undergo a Disclosure and Barring Service (DBS) check before being allowed to work with children on placement, which forms part of the "effective system". The placement setting may also ask for proof of your identity and a reference.

Suitability extends to include physical fitness to work with children (DfE, 2017, p. 20). Employers have the right to ask any student or member of staff to leave the premises if they are under the influence of alcohol or other substances. Medical conditions and their treatment should be discussed with the manager of the setting, to ensure that medication does not impair the adult's ability to carry out their role effectively.

Point for reflection

As a student, you will not be expected to take on safeguarding responsibilities but you will be expected to follow policy and procedures. Reflect on how the requirements of the EYFS (DfE, 2017) will affect you whilst you are working on placement.

Keeping yourself safe

As a student new to the setting you should receive an induction before you start. The induction process provides you with the opportunity to raise issues around suitability, and to ask any questions you might have about safeguarding. Make sure that the setting is aware of any medication that you are taking, especially emergency medicines such as inhalers, and who to contact in an emergency. You will be asked to provide your DBS certificate and reminded of your ongoing responsibility to declare any convictions (DfE, 2017, p. 20).

It is essential that you read the setting's safeguarding policy, and understand your safeguarding responsibilities. Some settings have a separate policy regarding the use of mobile phones and cameras following the conviction of Vanessa George in 2009.

The case of Vanessa George, 2009

Vanessa George was jailed in 2009 after admitting to abusing toddlers at a nursery in Plymouth. She admitted to seven sexual assaults and six counts of making and distributing indecent pictures of children. She used her mobile phone to take images of herself abusing children at the nursery and passed them on to a man she met on Facebook. He then forwarded them on to two other women. The report into the case stated that there was no evidence that Vanessa George had sexual interest in children until she became involved with this man.

The serious case review carried out by the local council found that good practice was compromised by personal relationships and this provided an ideal environment for abuse. Sexually explicit conversations about adults were normal, but staff didn't feel that they could challenge this inappropriate behaviour. There was a lack of staff supervision opportunities for staff to raise sensitive issues and this was thought to have contributed to the abuse taking place.

Adapted from 'Little Ted's was "ideal" place for Vanessa George abuse' (BBC, 2010)

The EYFS sets out the required ratios of adults to children (DfE, 2017, p. 21). As a student, you would not normally be counted within these ratios unless you have been on placement for a long period and are deemed suitable. It is important, therefore, to establish whether or not you will be working unsupervised, for example, changing nappies, taking children to the toilet or working alone with a small group. It is good practice to have an experienced practitioner working with you at all times.

Whilst working with young children, they may want to tell you all about themselves, their family and what they like to do at home. If you have any concerns about the content of these conversations you must raise them with a member of staff. As the case of Vanessa George illustrates, inappropriate conversations or behaviour by staff must also be reported (DfE, 2017, p. 20).

The EYFS requires that staff have regular supervision meetings, where sensitive issues can be discussed. It is good practice for this to be offered to students. It is essential that, as a student, you take these opportunities to raise any concerns. A good manager will welcome comments from students as they provide fresh insight into practice.

Thinking activity

- Think about ways in which you need to keep yourself safe.
- What information do you need to provide to the setting?
- What behaviours do you need to adopt to keep yourself safe?

It is difficult when arriving at a new setting to have the confidence to speak out. However, it is everyone's responsibility to keep children safe and a responsibility that must be taken seriously. The government's guide 'What to do if you're worried a child is being abused' (HM Government, 2015b) provides clear advice to practitioners and is a useful introduction to safeguarding for students.

Legislation

It is vital that you are familiar with legislation that governs the work of profession-als, as during your time in training and throughout your practice, you will be bound by statutory duties in relation to protecting children from harm (HM Government,

Table 8.1 Key legislation and policy guidance

Children Act 1899	Provides the legislative framework for child protection in England; places a duty on Local Authorities to promote and safeguard the welfare of children.
United Nations Convention on the Rights of the Child (UNCRC) 1989	Details the importance of protecting the rights of children and is a legally binding international agreement.
Children Act 2004	Introduced legislation that requires cooperation between agencies-partner organisations who work with children and their families. Including health, education, social care, police and housing associations, the Act also introduced Local Safeguarding Boards to coordinate services.
Childcare Act 2006	Requires early years providers to comply with the welfare requirements of the Early Years Foundation Stage.
Equality Act 2010	Brings together a number of discrimination laws and protects children and young people from discrimination, harassment and victimisation.
Protection of Freedoms Act 2012	Merged government departments responsible for safeguarding vulnerable groups and amended the Vulnerable Groups Act 2006, resulting in the development of the Disclosure and Barring Service (DBS).
Children and Families Act 2014	Introduced reforms to support the welfare of children with special education needs by introducing a single assessment process. The Act has a clear focus on fostering, adoption and care arrangements for children.
Working Together to Safeguard Children (WTSC) 2015	Statutory guidance issued by law for anyone working with children and young people in England. It explains the practice element of the aforementioned Acts, detailing how organisations should work together and how practitioners should conduct the assessment children.
What to Do If You Are Worried a Child Is Being Abused 2015	Advice for practitioners and intended as a complementary gu' WTSC.
Keeping Children Safe in Education 2016	Issued by the Department for Education, statutory guidan' schools and colleges including nursery schools.

2015a). The 1989 and 2004 Children Acts place clear responsibilities on settings, both private and voluntary including schools, to promote the welfare of all children and young people. In addition, both national and international law legislate for children's wishes to be respected (HM Government, 2015a).

Keeping up to date with changes in legislation and policy is necessary, in order to ensure you have relevant and current knowledge. The DfE provides guidance and key documents that will help you to keep informed. There are also a number of other organisations, for example, the National Society for the Prevention of Cruelty for Children (NSPCC), Barnardo's and the Children's Society. These are all major charities who provide regular updates for practitioners, especially in relation to the most vulnerable children who may need care and protection. Details of their websites can be found at the end of the chapter.

The following table highlights the key legislative documents that guide practitioners working in the early years field. Although this is not an exhaustive list, it details policy developments and changes in law that you will find informative when working in your placement settings.

Collaborative working

Professionals who work with children and young people are required by law to work in a collaborative way, and by doing so are in an opportune position to protect and promote children's welfare. Early years settings will be required to work within the legislative policies set by their local authority, and this will include following policies and procedures set by the Local Safeguarding Children Board (LSCB). Established in response to legislation set out in the Children Act 2004, these local boards have responsibility to develop inter-agency policies and procedures, alongside providing training; they also undertake reviews into cases where children have been seriously harmed or killed, and scrutinise organisations to ensure they are carrying out their statutory duties.

Activity

Access your Local Safeguarding Children Board (LSCB) website.
What information do they have for professionals about the following:

- training
- information for parents and carers
- information for children and young people

How can you use this information to inform your understanding of safeguarding legislation and practice?
LSCBs offer training for practitioners. Take the opportunity to access training if possible.

Assessing need

Helping children and families early is much more effective than waiting for a crisis to happen or for more invasive action to be necessary at a later date. Practitioners who intervene when problems first become apparent are in a better position to promote the welfare of children and offer support to their families (HM Government, 2015a). Assessment, therefore, is an integral part of early years practice, and professionals are continually assessing the needs of children, whether that be in relation to attending to a baby when they are hungry, or ensuring a play environment is suitable and stimulating. The Early Years Foundation Stage describes assessment as a means to recognise children's progress alongside attending to and understanding their needs and recommends this is done in partnership with parents and or carers and other relevant professionals (DfE, 2017).

Working Together to Safeguard Children describes 'Early Help' as the assessment necessary when individual children are identified as needing coordinated support from more than one agency (HM Government, 2015a, p. 12). As an example, in practice you might see children and their families benefiting from the help of a health visitor, housing agency and speech and language therapist and they will be working to one coordinated plan, often called a 'team around the child'. The Early Help assessment, therefore, facilitates the joining together of all the important information that each professional holds, and enables information to be shared as part of a continuum of help and support. Where need is believed to be manageable through the coordination of services, the professionals involved will work together with the family until such a time that intervention is no longer needed.

There will be some children who have more complex needs and the provision of coordinated services through an Early Help assessment may not be enough. In such circumstances help may need to be provided under Section 17 (children in need) or Section 47 (child protection) of the Children Act 1989 (HM Government, 2015a, p. 15). This will involve the local authority social care services, as they have the duty under the Children Act 1989 to provide services for identified children in need and protect them from harm. This duty involves working with services and parents to identify any issues that will impact on the child. Agencies will use the assessment framework to guide their work, as it provides a conceptual model for the assessment of need and delivery of services. Underpinned by research, the framework, represented as a triangle (see Figure 8.1), takes account of the interrelating factors that impact on a child's life (HM Government, 2015a, p. 22). What can clearly be seen in the following diagram is the importance of the child at the centre, and the relationship between a child's development, their family and environment, and the capacity of the parent to offer care and protection.

Information sharing

Working collaboratively includes taking seriously the importance of communicati? professionals must be clear about their responsibilities and share information timely and sensitive way (HM Government, 2015a). The gathering of inform? on the child, siblings and wider family enable risk factors to be analysed, and e the child's needs are assessed in a coordinated and holistic way. The early sha? information is central to providing effective early help, especially important f young children who are reliant on adults for their basic needs.

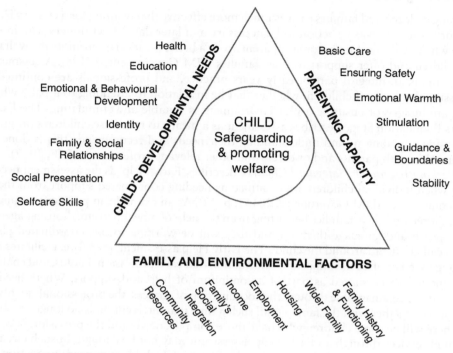

Figure 8.1 Assessment framework

Source: Assessment Framework (HM Government, 2015a)

The case of Child G, 2013 – information sharing

In May 2013, 3-month-old Child G was taken to hospital with serious head injuries inflicted whilst in the care of the child's mother and her new partner. Both parties received custodial sentences for the injuries they inflicted on this little baby.

Child G's mother has learning difficulties and already had a 3-year-old child. Her new partner has a significant history of crime, resulting in periods spent in prison. His child from a previous relationship had been placed on the child protection register as a result of physical abuse to the child and its mother, for which he also received a custodial sentence.

There were a number of occasions when incidents or changes in family circumstances were not recorded by health professionals, particularly around the mother's new relationship with a man known to be a risk to women and children. Therefore, information was not shared effectively which resulted in decisions being made without knowing the full picture. This was found to be particularly important in cases where a family is known to be vulnerable.

Source: Assessment Framework. Information taken from serious case review published on the NSPCC website (Wonnacott, 2015)

When professionals work together, they have a duty to share information that is appropriate and in a timely manner. Alongside *Working Together to Safeguard Children* (HM Government, 2015a), the government has published information sharing guidance that includes seven rules for practitioners to follow, and describes information sharing as an intrinsic part of any frontline worker's role (DfE, 2015a). As such, it is important to understand how much information to share and who with. As a student, it is essential that you understand the importance of sharing information. You must also be clear what constitutes appropriate information. Your responsibility is to the child first and foremost, and when you are on placement, there will be procedures that you will have to follow.

Thinking activity

Look up the seven rules of information sharing and consider how they might impact on your practice:

- Identify which rule requires you to be open and honest unless it is unsafe to do so.
- Can you think of a situation where it might be considered unsafe or inappropriate to directly discuss a concern with the family of a child?

Practitioners must be aware of the legal framework for confidentiality, which can be found in the Children Act 1989, the Human Rights Act 1998 and the Data Protection Act 1998. All relate to the use of personal information and equality (DfE, 2015a, p. 14). Permission or consent to share information, as a general principle, should be requested from the child if they are of an age to understand, and from the adult with parental responsibility. It is always better to be honest, as this will usually help when planning and coordinating services. There are exceptions, however, and you should not promise complete confidentiality if the interests of the child are compromised by doing so. The law permits the disclosure of confidential information necessary to safeguard a child or children (DfE, 2015a, p. 14).

Children's rights and the importance of the child's 'voice'

The United Nations Convention on the Rights of the Child (UNCRC) (UNICEF, 1989) is an international agreement that outlines the rights offered to children by member states. The United Kingdom signed the Convention in 1990, and it became law in 1992. Children are viewed by the Convention as citizens in their own right, with the family as the natural environment for children to grow up "in an atmosphere of happiness, love and understanding" (UNICEF, 1989, p. 3).

The Convention also states that children have the right to have their 'voice' hea and that all decisions should be made in their best interests. This is echoed in the rent government guidance on safeguarding:

> the child's needs are paramount, and the needs and wishes of each child, b
> a baby or infant, or an older child, should be put first, so that every child ʻ
> the support they need before a problem escalates.
>
> (HM Government, 20ʻ

Whilst some children may not be able to verbalise their thoughts, feelings and wishes, their 'voice' needs to be heard through observations of who they like to spend time with, the activities they enjoy and the routines that make them feel comfortable, in order to uphold the right to grow up in the "atmosphere of happiness, love and understanding" outlined in the UN Convention (UNICEF, 1989, p. 3).

Thinking activity

- Look up the list of things that children have said they need (HM Government, 2015a, p. 11)
- How can you as a student practitioner ensure that children's 'voices' are heard?
- Think about ways in which you could ensure that children have what they have said they need.

Inclusive practice

The UN Convention on the Rights of the Child (UNICEF, 1989) clearly outlines in Article 2 that children must not be discriminated against.

1   States Parties shall respect and ensure the rights set forth in the present Convention to each child within their jurisdiction without discrimination of any kind, irrespective of the child's or his or her parent's or legal guardian's race, colour, sex, language, religion, political or other opinion, national, ethnic or social origin, property, disability, birth or other status.
2   States Parties shall take all appropriate measures to ensure that the child is protected against all forms of discrimination or punishment on the basis of the status, activities, expressed opinions, or beliefs of the child's parents, legal guardians, or family members.

(UNICEF, 1989, p. 4)

In 2014, the Children and Families Act set out a new way of working with children with special educational needs and disabilities (SEND). The new act clearly places the child's needs at the centre of SEND provision, and provides parents with greater influence over how funding is used to meet those needs. This spirit of inclusion features prominently in the EYFS (DfE, 2017) and is reinforced by the Equality Act 2010, which settings are also required to comply with. Government guidance on safeguarding states that equality of opportunity for all children must be maintained (HM Government, 2015a, b). The setting's commitment to inclusive practice may be found in each of their policies, or they will have a separate inclusion policy that applies to all aspects of what they do. As a student, you need to be aware of the setting's approach to inclusion and how this is upheld in practice.

> **Activity**
>
> Read through your placement setting's inclusion policy.
>
>   Take some time to look around the setting and observe practice to see how the setting's policy is incorporated into everyday practice.

Contemporary issues

Consequential abuse concerns the impact that adult actions and behaviours can have on the development of their children (Ventress, 2014). It specifically refers to the capability of parents and family members, and how their capacity to parent can be affected by a number of environmental factors. Whilst some are un-intentional, for example parents who have an impairment or disability, there are a number of actions that can result in harm to children. The term 'Toxic Trio' (Ventress, 2014) describes the effects for children when parents suffer mental illness, misuse substances and/or live in abusive relationships. To explain further, a report commissioned by the Department for Education from 2009–2011 to investigate serious case reviews found a correlation between all three elements of the 'Toxic Trio' in many neglect cases (Brandon et al., 2012, p. 30).

The case of Hamzah Khan, 2009 – Toxic Trio

Hamzah Khan died aged 4 in December 2009 as a result of chronic neglect by his mother who was convicted in October 2013 of manslaughter and child cruelty. This case was particularly shocking as Hamzah's body was not discovered until nearly two years after his death.

Hamzah's parents met when his mother was just 16 and she went on to have 7 children. Relationship problems culminated in Hamzah's father becoming abusive and he was later convicted of assaulting Hamzah's mother on several occasions. The breakdown of their relationship coincided with the death of Hamzah's maternal grandmother who had previously provided much needed emotional support for her daughter. Hamzah's mother was alone, depressed and became dependent on alcohol and cannabis.

Despite reporting incidents of abuse, Hamzah's mother refused help. She was also disengaged from other services, for example, the GP and pregnancy support, and soon became socially isolated. The younger children, including Hamzah, were not registered with local pre-schools or schools and virtually disappeared as far as universal services were concerned. Very little was known to professionals about the family or their whereabouts.

Police visited the house following reports of anti-social behaviour and poor living conditions but they were denied access. The persistence of a Police Community Support Officer later resulted in the police gaining entry, and a search revealed Hamzah's dead body.

The serious case review makes reference to the fact that the trio of alcohol abuse, depression and domestic violence increase the chances of child neglect (Maddocks, 2013), but on this occasion, domestic violence had not been linked to the possibility of child neglect.

Information taken from serious case review published on the NSPCC website (Maddocks, 2013).

Although it should not be perceived as fact that all children who live in family circumstances where parental mental illness, substance misuse and domestic violence are present will suffer harm, the presence of one or more factors are significant (see the case of Hamzah Khan above). Research confirms that their presence can have both short and long term consequences for children (Ventress, 2014). Practitioners need, therefore, to be mindful and observant, and aware of the vulnerabilities that can arise when families are affected.

Early years settings have a number of legal responsibilities, and many have been discussed throughout this chapter. Keeping children safe and healthy in the setting and wider community has always been important, but legislation has now been produced as part of the counterterrorism strategy, with the aim of reducing the threat of terrorism in the UK (DfE, 2015b). The Counter-Terrorism and Security Act 2015 legislated that all public organisations must "have due regard to the need to prevent people from being drawn into terrorism" (the Prevent duty). Early years settings are required to follow the statutory requirements detailed in Section 26 of the Act, and see protecting children from the risk of radicalisation as an integral aspect of their wider safeguarding duties. In particular managers of early years settings are required to have in place procedures to assess any risks for children and carry out reasonable checks on staff and visitors for links with extremism (Ofsted, 2016).

Conclusion

This chapter has covered many aspects of safeguarding practice, and will help to prepare you for your student placement. It is not, however, meant to replace the need to be familiar with government legislation and guidance, nor is it a substitute for local policy and procedures. Safe and secure provision for all children is core business for early years providers, and requires vigilant but caring practitioners who keep the needs of the child at the centre of their practice.

Useful websites

Barnardo's work to transform the lives of vulnerable children and young people: www.barnardos.org.uk/.

National Society for the Prevention of Cruelty to Children (NSPCC): www.nspcc.org.uk

The Children's Society – A national charity that runs local projects, helping children and young people when they are at their most vulnerable, and have nowhere left to turn: www.childrenssociety.org.uk.

National College for Teaching and Leadership – Teacher's Standards (Early Years).
This chapter provides underpinning knowledge for Standards 1.1, 2.7, 5.1, 5.5, 7.1, 7.2, 7.3, 8.1, 8.2, 8.3, 8.7.

References

BBC (2010) Little Ted's Was 'Ideal' Place for Vanessa George Abuse, Retrieved from www.bbc.co.uk/news/uk-england-devon-11682161

Brandon, M., Sidebottom, P., Baily, S., Belderson, P., Hawley, C., Ellis, C. and Megson, M. (2012) *New Learning from Serious Case Reviews: A Two Year Report for* 2009–2011 *DfE- RR226*, Retrieved from www.gov.uk/government/uploads/system/uploads/attachment_data/file/184053/DFE-RR226_Report.pdf (Accessed 14 October 2016).

Department for Education (DfE) (2017) *Statutory Framework for the Early Years Foundation Stage: Setting the Standards for Learning, Development and Care for Children from Birth to Five*, London: DfE.

Department for Education (DfE) (2015a) *Information Sharing Advice for Safeguarding Practitioners*, London: Crown Copyright, Retrieved from www.gov.uk/government/publications/safeguarding-practitioners-information-sharing-advicd

Department for Education (DfE) (2015b) *The Prevent Duty Departmental Advice for Schools and Childcare Providers*, Crown Copyright, Retrieved from www.gov.uk/government/uploads/system/uploads/attachment_data/file/439598/prevent-duty-departmental-advice-v6.pdf

HM Government (2015a) *Working Together to Safeguard Children: A Guide to Inter-Agency Working to Safeguard and Promote the Welfare of Children*, London: Crown Copyright, Retrieved from www.gov.uk/government/uploads/system/uploads/attachment_data/file/419595/Working_Together_to_Safeguard_Children.pdf

HM Government (2015b) *What To Do If You're Worried a Child Is being Abused: Advice for Practitioners*, London: Crown Copyright, Retrieved from www.gov.uk/government/uploads/system/uploads/attachment_data/file/419604/What_to_do_if_you_re_worried_a_child_is_being_abused.pdf

Maddocks, P. (2013) *A Serious Case Review: Hamzah Khan: The Overview Report*. Bradford: Bradford Safeguarding Children Board.

Marmot, M. (2010) *Fair Society, Healthy Lives: A Strategic Review of Health Inequalities in England Post-2010*, London: UCL Institute of Health Inequality.

National Society for the Prevention of Cruelty to Children (NSPCC) (2016) Retrieved from www.nspcc.org.uk

Office for Standards in Education (Ofsted) (2016) *Inspecting Safeguarding in Early Years, Education and Skills Settings*, Manchester: Crown Copyright.

Palaiologou, I. (ed.) (2016) *The Early Years Foundation Stage: Theory and Practice*, London, UK: Sage.

UNICEF (1989) *The United Nations Convention on the Rights of the Child*, London: UNICEF, Retrieved from www.unicef.org.uk/Documents/Publication-pdfs/UNCRC_PRESS-200910web.pdf

Ventress, N. (2014) Socialisation and Consequential Abuse, in J. Reid and S. Burton (eds) *Safeguarding and Protecting Children in the Early Years*, Oxon: Routledge, pp 73–81.

Wonnacott, J. (2015) *Serious Case Review: Child G*. Essex: Essex Safeguarding Children Boⁱ

Chapter 9

Observation and assessment

Samantha McMahon

> ## Chapter aims
>
> By the end of this chapter you will:
>
> - understand the purpose of observation
> - be familiar with a range of observation methods
> - understand some of the ethical dilemmas to be considered when observing young children
> - be aware of how to interpret observational data to assess and support a child's learning and development.

Introduction

This chapter outlines the purposes of observation, focussing primarily on observing young children. However, the chapter also acknowledges that you, the student, have much to learn from observing other practitioners and from being observed. The chapter provides a brief overview of some of the different methods available for observing young children, and offers guidance on how to carry out accurate observations. You will be encouraged to consider some of the ethical dilemmas faced by the observer, and bias in observations will be explored. The chapter then provides an overview of how observational data can be interpreted and analysed to assess and support children's learning and development.

The purposes of observation

Observing the environment

Starting university can be daunting and many students can find themselves overwhelmed when they begin their first placement. Students are expected to undertake observations whilst on placement, and these often form part of an assessed professional practice portfolio. In these first few daunting weeks you may struggle to decide who, what, how and when you should observe. During this settling-in period at placement, you should spend time observing the environment. Ask permission to photograph the room layout (not including children) and the outside area so that you can identify key areas of provision. Make a note of the daily routine, including how children are dropped off and picked up. Identify the notice board for parents and observe how children's work is displayed. Collecting and then reflecting on these early observations should help you begin to understand how the environment supports the children's learning and development, and it should help you settle into placement.

Observing children

In everyday practice, observations of children are central to the formative assessment process articulated in EYFS (DfE, 2017) which states:

> Ongoing assessment (also known as formative assessment) is an integral part of the learning and development process. It involves practitioners observing children to understand their levels of achievement, interests and learning styles, and to then shape learning experiences for each child reflecting those observations.
>
> (p. 13)

Observation lies at the heart of the observation, assessment and planning cycle as illustrated below:

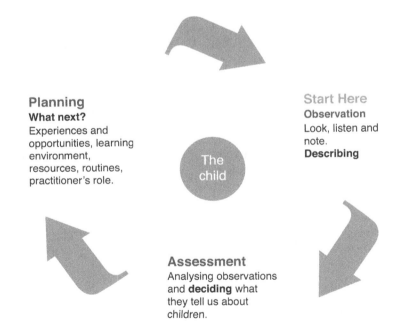

Figure 9.1 Assessment framework sample observation

Source: Development Matters (Early Education, 2012, p. 3)

The purpose of observation in the formative assessment process is for practitioners and students to get to know the children really well, and over time, to build a clearer picture of their needs, interests and learning styles, and decide how to respond (Carter and Nutbrown, 2014). Students can also use observations for a variety of purposes:

- to develop their knowledge and understanding of how children learn and develop
- to get to know a child
- to acquire and practice skills
- to collect data for a research project or professional practice portfolio
- to develop their knowledge and understanding of inclusive practice.

The following case study, drawn from a real student's experience, illustrates how observations can promote and support inclusive practice.

Case study

Lewis is a first year undergraduate student on an early years course. He is on placement in a Reception Class which has two female teachers, two female teaching assistants and fifty-nine children, forty girls and nineteen boys. He has completed eight days of placement over a period of four weeks. He has arranged to speak to his tutor at university, as he feels uncomfortable in placement. Lewis explains that he has noticed that when he is in the class the boys gravitate towards him and can become rather boisterous; he feels that the setting is too feminised, and is not meeting the boys' needs. Lewis does not feel confident enough to discuss his feelings with his mentor in placement. During the discussion with his tutor, Lewis explains that a large area of provision in the class is assigned to the home corner and role-play area, which he thinks the boys do not access. The tutor suggests that Lewis should observe the home corner/role-play area, to investigate if his thoughts and feelings are supported by the observational data.

Lewis explains to his placement mentor that he would like to focus some observations on the home corner/role-play area, as he is interested in how boys and girls access it. His mentor is delighted and is keen to discuss his observations. Lewis observes the area for thirty minutes, four times on separate occasions, and counts how many girls and boys access the area for five minutes or more. Lewis observes that eighteen girls played in the area for more than five minutes but only four boys. A number of other boys approached the role-play area to find props: two boys wanted lasers and one a captain's hat.

Points to consider

As a student how might Lewis use this information?
  What changes could be made to the home corner/role-play area?
  What might be the consequences for the boys and girls' learning and development if no changes are made to this area of provision?

As a result of Lewis sharing his observations with his placement mentor, changes were made to the home corner and role-play area. New props, including old remote controls and mobile phones, were added which could be used as lasers. Lewis was asked to work with a mixed group of children for new ideas for the area, and one boy suggested it should be a ship because his brother was in the navy. Lewis worked with the children to change it into a ship. His mentor, one of the class teachers, allocated more adult time to the area to promote more inclusive access and to scaffold the children's learning.

Ethical considerations

Before moving onto how to observe young children, it is important to take time to think about ethical practice when observing. The ethic of care underpins all practice in early years, and concerns promoting, developing and maintaining caring and respectful relationships with children, parents and carers, staff and other professionals (Siraj and Hallet, 2014). This ethic of care should extend into the practice of observing young children, so that observations are respectful and sensitive to the feelings and needs of the child.

Thinking activity

Imagine that you are sitting, engrossed on your mobile phone, and a relative stranger sits down beside you with a note pad and begins to watch you and take note of everything you are doing.

What would you think and feel?

You might wonder what the person was looking for and what they were writing and you might alter your behaviour. Keeping the thoughts and feelings in mind that this activity has provoked, how might you adopt a sensitive and respectful approach to child observation?

Students should be mindful that they do not have a 'right' to observe a child, and that the act of observation can disturb a child's feelings and change their behaviour (Harvell and McMahon, 2016). In order not to disturb the feelings of the child and risk altering their behaviour, it might be tempting to observe them secretly. However, respectful and ethical practice means that the child should give informed consent to be observed. This can be challenging. For example, how can informed consent be collected from a 2-year-old? In practice, informed, written consent from parents is usually considered to be adequate. Nevertheless, it is important that you, the student, remain alert to verbal and non-verbal cues that indicate that a child does not want to be observed. In doing so, you are demonstrating sensitive, respectful and ethical practice. It is essential that parents, staff and children are reassured that any data you collect will be anonymised to ensure that there is no possibility that a child, their family or member of staff can be identified from the observation.

Confidentiality is integral to ethical practice.

Ethical practice in observing young children also means that you are careful to be objective and unbiased. This is difficult, because observation is affected by **perception**, that is, our individual interpretation of what we see, hear, taste, smell and touch (Hobart and Frankel, 2004). In addition, people's perceptions are influenced by their experiences, fears and anxieties. First impressions of a child can often linger, particularly dominant characteristics such as how chatty or friendly they are, or how well they behave. Observers can unwittingly distort their data so that it fits these first impressions. Such first impressions can lead to **bias** in observations, as can prior knowledge about a child and their family. Bias can be avoided by accurately recording the child's actions using neutral, **objective** language. Consider the following example of an observation.

Lulu

Lulu is *very contented* as she sits on the floor. She is playing with a treasure basket, which she **often plays with**; she reaches out with her left hand and grasps a sponge. She shakes the sponge, drops it and reaches for a short brush. *She is curious* about how the brush feels and strokes her face with it. She then puts the brush in her mouth. She *does not like the taste* of the brush and drops it.

The words and phrases written in italics indicate that the observer is being **subjective** rather than objective. By describing Lulu as very contented, they have made a judgement about her state of mind rather than recording what they have seen or heard. Similarly when the observer comments that Lulu is curious and does not like the taste of the brush, the observer is making a judgement about the child, rather than recording what they have seen and heard.

The phrase written in bold suggests that the observer is including prior knowledge about the child in this observation, and therefore, it is not an accurate record. The observer may well have seen the child playing with the treasure basket on a previous occasion, but if an observation is to be trusted as an accurate record of the child's actions, it must only contain what the observer actually saw.

A more accurate and objective observation would be:

Lulu smiles and babbles as she sits on the floor with a treasure basket in front of her. She reaches out with her left hand and grasps a sponge. She shakes the sponge, drops it and reaches for a short brush. Lulu strokes her face with the brush, and then puts it in her mouth. She grimaces and drops the brush.

Cultural bias

Hobart and Frankel (2004) remind us that many of the children you observe may have been brought up in a different culture, which may have different expectations of children's behaviour. Some children, for example, are discouraged from getting messy at home, and so are reluctant to take part in messy play. Some children from another culture will not look an adult in the eye as this is viewed as disrespectful. As an observer you are likely to make value judgements based on your own upbringing and cultural values. Try to develop your knowledge and understanding of other cultures to lessen the likelihood of cultural bias in your observations.

Student concerns

Before this chapter moves on to focus on the process of observation, it seems timely to consider some of the concerns students have before they observe. It is natural to feel anxious about starting a new placement and about sitting observing children. Students often feel awkward and as if they are intruding, or that their supervisor might think they are not busy. However, observing children is a well-established practice in ECEC and you can reassure yourself, and your supervisor, that the observations will be put to good use. You will be integrating theory with your observations to develop your understanding of how children learn, and to promote the development of the children.

Students occasionally witness bad practice, and rightly question whether they should record it. As the observation would normally be focussed on a child or children then it should capture their reaction to the practice, rather than the bad practice. For example, you might record that children you are observing aged between 24 and 36 months were expected to sit on the carpet for story time that lasted 25 minutes. This story time was led by one practitioner and included children aged between 24 and 60 months, and in total there were 17 children seated on the carpet. What is important here is to focus on how the younger children reacted to sitting in this large group for this amount of time. If the younger children were restless and seemed to distract the older children from the story, then this should be shared with your supervisor. As a student you might feel apprehensive about drawing attention to this practice, and you could discuss it with your tutor first, but your supervisor is a professional and will be keen to reflect on practice.

Very occasionally, a student may observe practice which is unsafe, or through their observations become concerned that a child is being abused in some way. The student must share this information with their supervisor or the manager of the setting immediately who will take the appropriate action. The student should also discuss this with their tutor who can provide support, and follow up on any action that may need to be taken.

You can find more information about what to do if you are concerned about safeguarding at: www.gov.uk/government/uploads/system/uploads/attachment_data/file/419628/Information_sharing_advice_safeguarding_practitioners.pdf.

How to observe young children

Often in settings, practitioners use a range of digital devices to photograph and record children as part of the observation process. Photographs and videos can be powerful tools in observing children and a great way of sharing the child's learning and development with the child and their parents. It is also possible in many settings to upload photographs into a software package which links the digital observations with the EYFS framework to create a digital portfolio of the child's learning and development. However, in order to ensure that children are kept safe, it is not normally appropriate for a student to photograph and video record them. Bruce et al. (2015) also warn that there are disadvantages to digital record keeping, as they can constrain what a practitioner would like to record. Therefore, students are encouraged to try a range of different methods of observation.

Methods of observation

The starting point for most observations is to look, listen and note, and it is very important for the student to practise these skills by planning regular and frequent opportunities to observe. As a student, you should keep a notebook on hand and try observing a child for five minutes, just writing what you see and hear. Always make a note of the child's age in months, gender and any other details which might be important; for example how many other children they are playing with, and if any other

Table 9.1 Different observation methods

Observation methods	Advantages	Disadvantages
Snapshot A brief, spontaneous record of what the child is doing often written on a post-it note.	Quick. Useful to record developmental milestones.	Contains a very limited amount of information. An inexperienced observer might struggle to capture important details.
Time Sample Observe a child for a brief amount of time, e.g. for one minute at regular intervals or for ten minutes during a session.	Useful to capture data about a child you are concerned about or to discover which equipment or areas of provision are being accessed.	Time consuming. Observer might lose concentration and miss a recording.
Event Sample (sometimes referred to as ABC) A log is completed over as long a period of time as possible to capture particular types of behaviour.	Can reveal underlying causes or patterns of behaviour, specifically: what came before the behaviour, Antecedent; what occurred, Behaviour; and what happened as a result of the behaviour, Consequences.	Allocating time. The expected behaviour may not occur during the time allocated to observe. Making it obvious to the child that they are being observed.
Checklist/Tick list A pre-prepared list of developmental milestones, or children's skills to be ticked off when observed.	Quick. User-friendly and easily repeated. Results are obvious and readily understandable.	Checklists may not give a true picture, e.g. if the child is unwell or feels they are being tested. Challenging to maintain objectivity if you believe a child has previously achieved a milestone.
Longitudinal Study Takes place over a period of time and may consist of a number of different types of observation. Students may be required to complete this type of study to closely record a child's progress over time. Sometimes known as a child's learning journey.	Provides detailed insight into the individual and unique child. Can reveal how effectively the environment is supporting the child's learning and development. Can be shared and enjoyed by parents, children and staff.	The child might leave the setting, or become ill. Your observations might upset parents particularly if the child shows atypical development or behaviour.
Target child A pre-coded observation usually to study concentration and interaction.	Allows the observer to focus clearly on one specific aspect of development. Shows how the setting promotes language development.	Time consuming. Codes need to be learned and practised before use.

adults are present. These short **narrative** observations are a way to gain confidence and skills in observing, and an excellent way to build knowledge of child development.

When you first start observing children, you will probably focus on **narrative** observations. Narrative is a frequently used technique because it requires little preparation and generally involves you watching a child, or an activity, and writing down as accurately and objectively as possible everything that you see and hear. However, there are a range of methods of observation available, and as a student you have a great opportunity to try different methods and to reflect on the alternative perspectives they give you on the developing child. The table on the previous page presents an overview of some of the different methods of observation along with their advantages and disadvantages.

How to use observations

As a student, you will be expected to analyse and interpret your observational data to assess the child's learning and development, and to suggest how you might plan to meet their learning and developmental needs. As a student, you may have to submit a number of completed observations which have been interpreted with reference to theory, and assessed according to Development Matters statements and Early Learning Goals in the EYFS. At the university we provide the student with a template, which supports and guides the interpretation and analysis of their observations. The student is expected to transfer relevant excerpts from their records to the template and to make time to regularly share their observations with their supervisor on placement. As a student, making time to discuss your observational data is essential, as it is an opportunity to reflect on your analysis and to check your objectivity. Your supervisor will be experienced in carrying out observations, and can offer advice on which aspects of learning and development you should focus. Students sometimes attempt to assess every aspect of a child's learning and development from one observation. Remember, one observation will never give you the total picture of a child, and definitive claims about a child's learning and development should not be made from such a limited sample of data.

Here is an example of a completed observation drawn from a student's portfolio.

Name of Child: G	**Age** (in months): 54	**Observer:** **Type of observation: Narrative**
Number of children: 14 **Number of adults: 3**	**Date: 3/3** **Time** (from – to): **10.35–10.45**	**Reference points** (link to appropriate framework): PSED

Type of Setting: Reception Class. The observation took place outside and the children were free to choose their play.
Aim: To observe if G is able to play cooperatively with other children.
Objective: Previous observations of G suggest that he can struggle to share resources when playing inside. I want to see if he is able to share and play cooperatively in the outdoor area.

Observation (write everything you see, hear . . .)

G has a pink ball. He's kicking it about and glancing around at the other children who get close to him and frowning at them. Several children individually approach and ask to join in or seek to join in by tackling the ball away from him. G responds to each that he would rather play on his own. He keeps the ball close to him and constantly looks around at the other children nearby, rushing to regain the ball if it strays near to other children. G sees M playing with a teacher using a white football. G approaches M and holds out the pink ball to her; M smiles and accepts the ball. G then takes the white football away from M and walks away. M and the teacher look surprised. All the other children go in and J comes out and finds his own ball. G and J kick their respective balls around, both commenting to each other and laughing and drawing attention to high kicks or near misses over the wall. Each retains complete ownership over their own ball. More children come out and W approaches G and asks to join in (there are no other free balls). W complains to me that G will not let him join in the game. I approach G; he holds the ball tightly against his chest as I approach. I explain that G has had a long turn, there are no other free balls and W would like to play so G has two choices: he can either give the ball to W to play on his own OR give the ball to W and join in with his game. There is a long pause. . . . "I don't know which to choose yet . . ." says G. I say "Ok, I'll give the ball to W so he can start his turn and if you decide you'd like play with him then you can." I take the ball and give it W who runs away to play with it. G says nothing and I walk away. G then starts crying very loudly with his head held back. He then approaches me, still crying, "I want to play with W!" I ask him if he has asked W if he still wants to play. G replies "No!" and resumes louder crying. "I can see you really enjoy playing with the ball and are really upset now. . . ." W approaches and says, "I'd like G to join in with my game." G gasps and raises his eyebrows . . . and then grasps W tightly in a spontaneous hug. They both run away and play with the ball together.

Evaluation including relevant theory

Dowling (2014) points out that social learning forms a major part of EYFS and that is why there are some concerns if a child struggles to play cooperatively with other children. She also points out that children under 5 are inexperienced with interpersonal skills and so disputes occasionally flare up. It seems from the observation that G is inexperienced with his interpersonal skills as he struggles initially to share the ball, and then to communicate with W to say that he would like to play. Dowling (2014) argues that for children who start school very shortly after their fourth birthday, as is the case for child G, they can find the transition into reception very daunting. Neaum (2010) also reminds us that children aged 4 can take turns but not consistently, and if a child is upset they will turn to an adult for comfort as G did in this observation. In this observation the adult had to support G to take control of his emotions, and she acknowledged his feelings and helped him find a solution. Here the adult is a more knowledgeable other and is scaffolding (Bruner, 1975) G's social and emotional development and learning. The EYFS (DfE, 2017) emphasises the importance of the practitioner responding to each child's emerging needs and guiding their development.

It is interesting that G swapped his pink ball for M's white ball, without asking M. Perhaps, G did this because he thought M, a girl, would prefer the pink ball. This might be an example of gender socialisation and perhaps G was trying to understand how M might be feeling about playing with the 'wrong' coloured ball. In order to build friendships children do need to develop social intelligence and see things from another child's point of view (Dowling, 2014).

It seems from this observation that G is demonstrating some expected patterns of behaviour linked to his social and emotional development. He is able to play cooperatively when supported by an adult and is developing knowledge of social rules. He may need further support and practice to understand what is involved in being a friend.

EYFS Links (include specific statements from Development Matters and age ranges with examples of where they link to in the observation)

> PSED: Making relationships 30–50 months. Can play in a group, extending and elaborating play ideas. G struggled with this aspect of development although with some support from the adult he did go and successfully play with W, as evidenced at the end of the observation.
>
> PSED: Managing feelings and behaviour 30–50 months. Begins to accept the needs of others and can take turns and share resources, sometimes with support from others. G did need support in order to be able to share his ball with W; however, when he swapped his ball with M, perhaps, he thought she would prefer the pink ball.

Next steps

Development Matters (Early Education, 2012) suggests that the adult should model how they manage their own feelings and explain that while all feelings are understandable, not all behaviours are. The adult can use persona dolls and puppets to help children consider feelings and behaviour, and provide photographs and pictures of emotions for the children to look at and talk about.

The adult can also support children in building positive relationships by challenging negative comments and behaviour. They should encourage children to play with a variety of friends.

An activity that could be provided and why it would support learning and development

G appeared to enjoy playing outdoors with a ball therefore it might be possible to build on this, and support him with collaborative and cooperative play. The adult could organise ball games which include a small mixed group of children and different coloured balls. The children have to work together to score goals or get points by kicking the ball into a hoop on the floor. G could also be encouraged to collaborate in other games; for example, parachute games, board games and building projects. The adult could also read stories which focus on friendships and playing together.

Supervisor's name:	Supervisor's signature:	Student's name:	Student's signature:

Thinking activity

Take a few minutes to read and reflect on the observation presented above. Consider how confidentiality is maintained and check if the observer maintains objectivity.

Can you identify other theoretical perspectives that could be included or additional links that could be made to Development Matters or the Characteristics of Effective Learning?

What other activities would you plan?

Assessment in EYFS

Formative assessment is understood as ongoing assessment, and it involves practitioners observing children to understand their level of achievement, interests and learning styles, and to then shape learning experiences for each child (DfE, 2017, p. 13).

Summative assessment collects all the information from formative assessment at a particular point in time. The EYFS includes a requirement that summative assessments must be provided when a child is aged between 2 and 3, and also in the final term of the year in which the child reaches age 5.

Progress check at age 2

The 2-year-old progress check was introduced to provide a summative assessment of children aged between 24 and 36 months, and there is an emphasis on the need for early identification of children who are at risk of failure, or where there are concerns regarding specific aspects of their development (Dubiel and Early Excellence Centre for Inspirational Learning, 2014). The progress check is built around the prime areas of development – Physical Development; Personal, Social and Emotional Development; and Communication and Language. A key component of the assessment is for the practitioner to detail how they have responded to any concerns which have emerged, and where necessary, identify if additional support is needed from other professionals. The National Children's Bureau has provided guidelines for practitioners, and crucially parents should be partners in the process. Initially, it was envisaged that the progress check would contribute to developmental checks undertaken by the Health Visitor.

The EYFS profile

Typically, the EYFS profile is to be completed by the Reception teacher at the end of the summer term. The profile must reflect ongoing observation, and all relevant records held by the setting, including discussions with parents, carers and any other adults the practitioner and the parents consider to offer a useful contribution. The profile should provide a well-rounded picture of a child's knowledge and understanding against the expected levels. Practitioners must indicate whether children are meeting, exceeding or not yet reaching (emerging) expected levels of development. More information on expected levels of development can be found in Chapter 5. Year 1 teachers receive a copy of the profile, and schools must share results of the profile with parents. In addition, EYFS profile results must be provided to the Local Authority, and this data will be returned to the DfE.

At the time of writing this chapter there is some uncertainty about the timing and format of summative assessment in reception. The DfE has been keen to introduce a standardised baseline assessment, which would provide a starting point from which to measure children's progress. However, at this time the DfE has scrapped its plans for a mandatory baseline assessment as the Reception Baseline Comparability Study (Standards and Testing Agency, 2015) found that there was insufficient comparability between the different models of baseline assessment for them to be used in an accountability system. This decision has been welcomed by teachers, academics and parents who were united against the government's model of baseline assessment, which they say would put unnecessary pressure on children, labelling them as failures at the start of their academic careers. Many schools do carry out their own baseline assessments, but these are different as they are focussed on the child's learning and development rather than an accountability measure for the school. Although plans for a mandatory baseline assessment are on hold, Early Years Teachers are expected to "observe and assess children's development and learning, using this to plan next steps" (NCTL, 2013, p. 3); therefore, observation remains central to effective practice.

Thinking activity

Spend some time reading and researching the contrasting perspectives on baseline assessment in EYFS. What do you think?

Conclusion

This chapter has provided an overview of the purposes of observation and some of the methods you might use. It has also considered ethical issues and how and why it is important that the observer should be objective. The chapter included an example of a completed observation, which illustrated how observational data might be interpreted using theory. Finally, the chapter presented an overview of the mandatory summative assessments, which are included in EYFS.

Further reading and research

www.foundationyears.org.uk. This website provides essential resources to support effective observation including EYFS, Development Matters and guidance on how to complete summative assessments.

Forman, G. and Hall, E. (2009) Wondering with children: The importance of observation in early education, *Early Childhood Research and Practice*, 7(2), [online] Retrieved from http://ecrp.uiuc.edu/v7n2/forman.html. This article includes short video clips to develop understanding of the role of observation and how it can be used to support children's learning and development.

References

Bruce, T., Louis, S. and McCall, G. (2015) *Observing Young Children*, London: Sage.

Bruner, J. (1975) The ontogenesis of speech acts, *Journal of Child Language*, 2: pp 1–9.

Carter, C. and Nutbrown, C. (2014) The Tools of Assessment: Watching and Learning, in G. Pugh and B. Duffy (eds) *Contemporary Issues in the Early Years*, London: Sage, pp 127–144.

Department for Education (DfE) (2017) *Statutory Framework for the Early Years Foundation Stage*, London: Crown Copyright.

Dowling, M. (2014) Young Children's Personal, Social and Emotional Development, 4th edn., London: Sage.

Dubiel, J. and Early Excellence Centre for Inspirational Learning (2014) *Effective Assessment in the Early Years Foundations Stage*, London: Sage.

Early Education (2012) *Development Matters in the Early Years Foundation Stage (EYFS)*, London: Early Education.

Harvell, J. and McMahon, S. (2016) Observation, in L. Trodd (ed.) *The Early Years Handbook for Students and Practitioners: An Essential Guide for the Foundation Degree and Levels 4 and 5*, Routledge: London, pp 402–415.

Hobart, C. and Frankel, J. (2004) *A Practical Guide to Child Observation and Assessment*, 3rd edn., Cheltenham: Nelson Thornes.

National College for Teaching and Leadership (NCTL) (2013) *Teachers Standards (Early Years)*, Crown Copyright.

Neaum, S. (2010) *Child Development for Early Childhood Studies*, 1st edn., Exeter: Learning Matters.

Siraj, I. and Hallet, E. (2014) *Effective and Caring Leadership in the Early Years*, London: Sage.

Standards and Testing Agency (2015) *Baseline Assessment Comparability Study*, London: Crown Copyright.

Chapter 10

Leadership in ECEC

Samantha McMahon

Chapter aims

By the end of the chapter you will have:

- an understanding of why leadership in ECEC is important
- considered a number of different leadership models
- considered the key skills required to be an effective leader in ECEC
- explored how to develop your own skill in leading practice.

Introduction

It may seem strange to include a chapter focussing on leadership in a book which is primarily designed to support undergraduate students at the start of their academic career. However, as you will be the future leaders in ECEC, this chapter will introduce you to the skills and attributes which make an effective leader. The chapter will explain why leadership is important and provide an overview of some key leadership models relevant to ECEC. This chapter also presents you with an opportunity to reflect on leadership in your placement setting, and encourages you to take a reflective approach to developing your skills as a future leader.

Why is leadership in ECEC important?

Effective leadership has been identified as essential to the delivery of high quality provision, and research into Effective Leadership in the Early Years Sector (ELEYS) suggests that strong leadership leads to better outcomes for children (Siraj-Blatchford and Manni, 2007). However, the concept of leadership in ECEC can be problematic. It developed from educational models of leadership found in schools, where leadership is associated with a single person with authority to lead. Leadership and management roles in ECEC often merge, and Hallet (2014) points out that the administrative duties associated with management often take time away from pedagogy and practice. A manager normally takes a planning and organisational role and is responsible for the daily running of the setting. The leader, according to Whalley (2011), provides direction, offers a vision shared by others and inspires and demonstrates effective practice. It can be difficult in a small setting, with a traditional, hierarchical organisational structure, to strike a balance between leading and managing.

The development of professionalism in ECEC, through the introduction of Early Years Professional Status (EYPS), and more recently the graduate level Early Years Educator (EYE) and the Early Years Teacher (EYT), is bringing about a new way of thinking about leadership in ECEC settings. Leadership in ECEC is being reconceptualised as a shared responsibility whereby people within the setting work together to influence and inspire each other. Siraj and Hallet (2014) describe an emerging understanding of leadership in ECEC that is a "relational and communal concept where all can be a leader and engage in leadership, benefit from leadership and exercise power and individual agency" (p. 10). This emerging understanding of leadership has a place within it for the undergraduate contributing to the team and exercising agency. Nutbrown (2012) suggests that all practitioners, regardless of qualification level, should be capable of demonstrating pedagogical leadership. The following section provides an overview of some key models of leadership beginning with pedagogical leadership in ECEC.

Key models of leadership

Pedagogical leadership

Siraj and Hallet (2014) state that "pedagogy relates to a holistic approach to supporting children's overall development" (p. 110), arguing that it is where education and care meet. Pedagogy is often defined as the approach to teaching and learning, and is informed by the personal values, beliefs and principles of practice of the individual. Therefore, pedagogical leadership is concerned with creating conditions in which members of the organisation can give their best in teaching and learning to support the holistic development of the child. Hallet (2014) states that the pedagogical leader must:

- have a sound knowledge and understanding of how young children learn and develop
- have a sound knowledge and understanding of ECEC principles and practice
- be able to develop a clear vision based on a sound understanding of children's learning and development
- articulate their vision with passion.

Leadership is often associated with vision (Bolman and Deal, 2013), whereby the leader creates a sense of direction which drives the organisation. In ECEC, the vision of the leader is informed by the primary purpose of any setting, which is to improve the educational, social and health outcomes for children (Siraj-Blatchford and Manni, 2007).

Thinking activity

Consider your placement experience to identify and describe an example of pedagogical leadership. How did it influence your practice?

Refer to the description of pedagogical leadership above, and with reference to your placement, try to identify the conditions which allow members of the organisation to give their best in teaching and learning, to support the holistic development of the child.

Distributed leadership

Although it can be difficult to move away from the traditional idea of an authoritarian leader who holds all the power, there is a move towards a vision of leadership which is more collaborative and inclusive. Distributed leadership describes a model of shared responsibility, and is defined in terms of influence rather than power (Rodd, 2006, p. 17). Lockwood (2016) highlights a number of advantages associated with this model of leadership including:

- it makes leadership more accessible to the individual practitioner
- it can help the individual practitioner overcome their reluctance to take on a leadership role
- it promotes collaboration and develops professionalism
- it is democratic and participatory.

However, a manager must be wary of delegating too much responsibility where practitioners are inexperienced and under-qualified. Distributed leadership requires the ongoing commitment of all staff to increasing their expertise through continued professional development. Lockwood (2016) points out that the EYE occupational standards emphasise the importance of continued professional development, and the EYT qualification highlights the need to "take responsibility for leading practice through appropriate professional development for self and colleagues" (NCTL, 2013, p. 5).

Thinking activity

In your placement setting, a distributed model of leadership may mean that leadership tasks and responsibilities are delegated to specialist roles, for example, safeguarding, family support, special needs and behaviour management.

What do you think are the benefits of this system of leadership?

What do you think some of the challenges of this system might be, and how are these addressed in your setting?

Leadership for change and catalytic leadership

The drive for continuous improvement to ensure high quality provision is at the heart of government policy (Ofsted, 2015), and the role of the graduate leader, whether an EYP, EYE or EYT, is to be a change agent to shape and improve practice. McDowall Clark (2012) envisioned a new model of leadership, which sees the leader as a catalyst for change. The catalytic leader recognises the possibility for change, and through a supportive, non-confrontational, reflective process, exerts influence to bring about small incremental changes. Change is not imposed from above, but emerges through continual reflection and is democratic; it is a way of working together with a common purpose. Catalytic leadership, in common with the models for distributed and pedagogical leadership, is a participative model, which focusses on change to improve practice.

Figure 10.1 Leading from within as a catalytic agent
Source: McDowall Clark, 2012, p. 398

Thinking activity

Reflect on the model of catalytic leadership illustrated above. How might this model influence your practice?

Gender and leadership

The composition of the workforce in ECEC is overwhelmingly female, and it was hoped that professionalisation would attract more men into the sector to provide positive male role models for children. However, there are complex social and cultural reasons for this imbalance. Siraj and Hallet (2014) point out that sensitivity about child abuse may mean that men meet with prejudice and mistrust. Furthermore, the long and widely held view that working in ECEC is women's work and has low status and low levels of pay (Nutbrown, 2012) may affect the recruitment of men into the workforce. However, when men do enter the workforce there is a tendency for them to gain promotion (Lumby and Coleman, 2007). There are gender stereotypes which cast men as leaders, and women as supporters and nurturers. Hallet (2014) suggests that through higher education, women are moving to the forefront of leading provision in ECEC, through a shared, distributed model of leadership rooted in an ethic of care.

The models featured here are a small selection of leadership models pertinent to ECEC, and cannot fully represent practice in every setting. The most effective model of leadership depends on the context of the setting, and successful leaders will adapt and be responsive to the needs of the stakeholders in the organisation. Leadership in ECEC is being reconceptualised away from the view that leadership resides with a nominated individual with authority and power, towards a participative and shared model. The participative approach is a sustainable, inclusive model, which builds leadership capacity and potential in the workforce and moves away from the dependency culture created when leadership is seen as residing with one individual. Being a leader in ECEC requires particular skills and attributes which are discussed in the following section.

Skills and attributes for leading in ECEC

Communication

During her time on placement working towards EYPS, one of my students, Laura, described her leadership role: "you have to be a leader but don't want to come across as taking over, you have to explain, talk things through and that includes with the manager." Another student, Karen, explained how she included the other practitioners: "I say to them, tell me what's niggling you about practice in your room, even little niggles, what could we do improve things?"

These quotes illustrate beautifully that leadership in ECEC "is a matter of communication more than anything else" (Rodd, 2013, p. 63). It is through the capacity to communicate clearly that the leader can foster collaboration and participation, and as Siraj and Hallet (2014) point out, the leader who communicates effectively is likely to command a greater capacity to influence others. Leadership is explicit in how leaders use their everyday talk to interact with others. Karen, for example, provides practitioners with an open, non-threatening way to discuss practice, and she is keen to hear their ideas. Siraj and Hallet (2014) state that effective communication is multi-faceted involving talking, encouraging, questioning, listening, reflecting, translating, interpreting, consulting, debating, summarising, understanding, acknowledging, negotiating, decision making, verifying and reporting.

Active listening

Effective communication also requires active listening. Active listening is described by Siraj and Hallet (2014, p. 51) as:

> Engaging with the words spoken, gaining meaning and understanding behind the words articulated, and using all the information given, including underlying feelings, to understand the meaning of the message as it was intended.

In active listening the listener receives non-verbal and verbal messages from the speaker, and must reflect on both to clarify meaning. Similarly, the listener uses verbal and non-verbal cues to respond to the speaker.

Thinking activity

Consider your time on placement, and give an example of when you communicated effectively. How did active listening enable this interaction? Could there be an improvement? If so how?

Managing effective communication

In a busy setting, it can seem almost impossible to find time to communicate properly, and communication often takes place in an inappropriate environment, for example in a corridor or hallway where others pass and may overhear (Hallet, 2014). Background noise can be a distraction, as can interruptions from children, parents and other members of staff. However, these barriers can be overcome by arranging a specific time when an uninterrupted meeting might be held. Students often find it difficult to meet with their placement mentor, who may be a busy classroom teacher or room leader. This can be overcome by the student offering to come in early or stay late. Time for effective communication may require advanced planning and organisation.

Reflection

As a student, you are encouraged to engage regularly in the process of reflection. The process of reflection looks back at what has occurred, reconstructs it, and reforms it to improve practice. As a student you should keep a journal which provides a safe space for your individual reflections. However, it is equally important to engage in reflective dialogue to make learning explicit. In daily practice, the process of reflection is no less important for the leader. Effective leaders continue to reflect on their own practice and encourage reflection in their staff (Siraj and Hallet, 2014). Leaders should facilitate reflective conversations, and it is possible to use records of children's learning and development as a springboard for reflective dialogue. It is possible in these reflective discussions to make the learning processes and strategies used by each child and practitioner visible. Siraj and Hallet (2014) suggest that leaders' reflective conversations provide a vehicle for developing collective knowledge, and a focus on professional issues allows for roles and practices to expand and develop.

The process of reflection must be underpinned with specialist knowledge and understanding. As students in higher education, you have a unique opportunity to access and discuss theory, research and policy which determine pedagogy in the EYFS. Hallet and Roberts-Holmes (2010) in their research study, *Leadership of Learning in Early Years Practice* (LLEaP), found that specialised knowledge gained in higher education gave leaders professional confidence to articulate their knowledge, to lead pedagogy and to develop a vision shared by staff and parents. The LLEaP study demonstrated that reflective dialogue, drawing on specialist knowledge and understanding, encouraged reflective practice and the development of a professional leadership identity. Therefore, as students you are acquiring specialist knowledge and understanding of the field, which can be married with your experiences from placement to inform your reflections, and contribute to the development of your professional leadership identity.

Thinking activity

Referring to examples in your journal, review the quality of your reflections. Identify where you have used specialist knowledge and understanding. Could they be improved? If so how?

Passion

Hallet and Roberts-Holmes (2010) identified passion as a driver of leadership in ECEC. Passion is not a skill, but it might be understood as an attribute or characteristic of the effective leader in ECEC. Passion is described as a deep emotional enthusiasm for children, families and the community in which the leader works and is a defining feature and motivating factor of leaders in ECEC (Hallet and Roberts-Holmes, 2010). It is likely that a passion for working with young children has led you to study early years or childhood studies at university, and passion is deeply embedded in the culture of practice in ECEC. Passion is a valuable strength, for the student and the leader. It fuels enthusiasm and commitment, and underpins nurturing and inclusive practice. Passion is often a feature of a collaborative and empowering style of leadership. However, such an emotional commitment to working with young children can leave practitioners open to financial and emotional exploitation (Taggart, 2011), and as a potential future leader it is important to support and protect the workforce, rather than reinforce exploitative practices.

Emotional intelligence

Emotional intelligence (Goleman, 1996) is an essential characteristic of an effective leader. It is closely linked to reflective practice because it requires the leader to be self-aware, and also underpins effective communication. Emotional intelligence is the ability to manage one's own feelings and respond sensitively to others feelings in a professional manner (Goleman, 1996). Goleman (1996) suggests that emotional intelligence is the aptitude that affects all other leadership abilities, and includes the ability to tune into people so that you can interact with them effectively.

Rodd (2013) suggests that emotionally intelligent leaders:

- are good listeners and responders
- ask appropriate questions and engage in meaningful dialogue
- nurture and value emotional intelligence of staff, children and parents.

As a student you need to develop emotional competence by being aware of your own feelings and managing your emotions. Emotional competence also requires you to have empathy and to be able imagine what it would be like to be in that person's situation. To reflect upon your emotional intelligence and to see how emotionally literate you are, complete the quiz at www.mindtools.com/pages/article/ei-quiz.htm.

Challenges of leadership in ECEC

Lockwood (2016) suggests that one of the most significant dilemmas facing early years is encouraging more individuals to embrace leadership. She argues that it is difficult to encourage individuals to take on additional responsibilities in a sector characterised by low pay, low status and limited expectations in terms of qualifications and training. Rodd (2006) argues that the perceived reluctance of practitioners to engage in leadership is due to the contradiction between caring and traditional notions of leadership with authority and power. Therefore, to encourage more individuals to embrace leadership it is time to adopt more collaborative and participatory models of leadership, which better suit the needs of the sector. McDowall Clark (2012, p. 292) states that "Leadership can be grounded in the common professional motivation to make a difference and work for the well-being and education of young children and their families." In this way leadership becomes everyone's right and responsibility to be engaged in it. However, as Lockwood (2016) highlights, current leaders and managers may be reluctant to 'let go' of their responsibilities, not least, because of greater government emphasis on accountability and meeting performance management targets.

Thinking activity

Before continuing with reading this chapter take some time to consider what you have learned so far about leadership in ECEC. What were new insights for you?

Leading children's learning

As a student, your focus whilst on placement will be on leading children's learning. Research evidence from Researching Effective Pedagogy in the Early Years (REPEY) (Siraj-Blatchford et al., 2002) demonstrates the valuable role that the adult can take in leading children's learning. You will be expected to observe and assess children's learning and developmental progress, and also to plan appropriate activities to meet their learning and development needs. It is also important that you reflect on the effectiveness of the environment. Is it an enabling environment (DfE, 2014) which responds to their individual needs?

The following case study presents an example of a student leading a change in practice which improved the learning environment.

Case study

Nadia was on placement in the pre-school room in a private day nursery, and during a routine visit from her university tutor she was asked to think about the purpose of the displays of children's work, and how often the children viewed their displayed work. Nadia started to think about the displays in the room, and spent time observing the children to see how often they looked at their work on display. Her observations suggested that the children very rarely looked at their work on display. Nadia decided to read about the purpose of display in an early year's environment, and also how to develop it. From her reading, she found that it was important to get children involved in displaying their own work, and that this would be a way to support child-centred learning.

Nadia approached her placement mentor and explained that she had been reading about display, and would like to work with a group of children on planning and setting up a display of their work. The supervisor agreed and worked with Nadia to find a display space that was at child level so that it would be accessible to the children. Nadia worked with the children as they framed and annotated their work. Nadia also asked them if they thought it would be a good idea to put their photograph alongside their work. The children agreed, and set about taking photographs of each other which were mounted alongside the children's work.

The children took great pride in their display and wanted to show their parents, staff and the other children. The inclusion of the photographs and the display being accessible to the children meant that they regularly revisited their work. As a result, the setting, whenever possible, includes the children in displaying their work. They invested in child height display boards and include photographs of the children alongside their work.

The case study demonstrates that it is possible for a student to use leadership skills to improve practice and provision to support children's learning and development.

Thinking activity

Can you identify which leadership skills Nadia used?

How could you develop your practice in light of this case study?

Which areas of children's learning and development did Nadia's work enhance?

What do you think all those concerned felt about the change? Consider Nadia's feelings, the children's and their parents' feelings, and also the feelings of other members of staff.

One of the aims of the LLEaP research project was to identify 'best leadership practice', and a focus on best leadership of learning practices identified eight areas of expertise including:

- leading pedagogy in settings
- leading pedagogy for transitions
- leading children's learning in the outdoor environment
- leading a learning culture and community of practice
- leading continuing professional development
- leading, creating and sharing knowledge with parents
- leading change for transformation
- leading, creating and sharing reflections.

(Siraj and Hallet, 2014, p. 30)

As a student you are not expected to be an expert in each of these areas; however, you are expected to be developing your knowledge and understanding of pedagogy, transitions and supporting children's learning and development in the outdoor area. You are also expected to participate and contribute to the learning culture in the setting, and be active in your own professional development. Where appropriate, you should negotiate opportunities to engage with parents, and continue to reflect on your practice and on practice and provision in the setting. Again, where appropriate, you might share these reflections with team members and with your peers at university.

Teamwork

Sometimes on placement, students can face hostility and resistance from other members of the staff team, and it is very important for students to understand team dynamics and why some staff may not welcome input from a student. One student described spending her first few weeks on placement as trying to work out 'the pecking order', referring to the informal positions of leadership, power and authority assumed by members of the team. It can be challenging for a student to find a place in the pecking order. The chapter on communication and teamwork outlines the different stages that that teams go through in their development, for example, forming, storming, norming and performing (Tuckman and Jensen, 1977), and you should read this chapter for more information on the different stages. When a student joins, the team may revert to one of the earlier stages such as forming or storming where some can feel threatened or challenged. Thus the student may face resistance and hostility. The team needs to learn how to deal with differences, and resistance is often short lived if the student is prepared to listen, takes time to get to know the others and pulls together with the team. Collaboration in the team relies on high-level communication skills. By spending time working out the 'pecking order', the student can identify which stage of development the team is at.

It can also help the student and the leader to be aware that Belbin (1981) argued that a successful team is well balanced, fulfilling a range of roles, including:

- *action-oriented roles* such as the shaper who keeps the team on task, the implementer who puts ideas into action and the completer/finisher who ensures deadlines are met
- *people-oriented roles* such as the coordinator who acts as a chairperson, the team worker who supports others and encourages cooperation and the resource investigator who develops contacts and negotiates on behalf of the team
- *cerebral roles* such as the planter who is creative and comes up with new ideas, the monitor evaluator who is best at evaluating ideas and the specialist who is an expert in a field.

Belbin (1981) suggests that by understanding your role within a team, you can identify and develop your strengths and manage your weaknesses. Knowing the team roles can help both the student and the leader understand how the team is performing. Of course, these roles are only a guide and are not prescriptive; team structures and roles are dependent on the situation.

> **Thinking activity**
>
> In placement, speak to your mentor about the possibility of observing the other individual members of the team. Explain that this is so that you can try and understand your role within the team. Seek permission from each individual. It is likely that they will want reassurance that the data you collect will be kept confidential and will not be used to assess their performance. Explain that you would like to analyse the data with reference to Belbin's (1981) work in order to identify how you might contribute to the team.

As a student you will be part of an immediate team based in a room or class, but that team will be part of a wider team in the setting or school and possibly across settings into the community. As a leader, you will be required to work in a multi-agency team with other professionals in order to improve outcomes for children. In multi-agency teams there can be difficulties in finding time to establish links with other professionals, barriers in communication due to different ways of working and problems in understanding specialist knowledge. Team formation can take time and relies on staff being flexible and inclusive, and the leader must support the development of a team culture of trust and respect.

Developing students as leaders

The recognition of the importance of the early years in determining a child's future success is now firmly established (Pugh, 2014), and a critical feature of high quality provision is effective leadership. It is essential that future leaders are well prepared through gaining appropriate qualifications. In addition, you as the student should consider working with a more experienced member of staff, or mentor, in the placement to develop your leadership skills. For this mentoring relationship to be successful requires commitment from both the mentor and the mentee (McMahon et al., 2016). It is essential that both parties are in agreement from the outset about roles, expectations and boundaries, and that achievable goals are set. The student (mentee) should identify their strengths and areas of development, and be proactive in arranging time to meet with their mentor. It is important for the mentee to keep records and consider how meeting their goals can benefit the setting as well as their professional development.

Conclusion

This chapter has provided an overview of leadership in ECEC and how it is being reconceptualised. It has presented key models and outlined the skills and attributes that you as a future leader need to develop. The chapter included case studies and thinking activities to encourage you to reflect and develop your understanding of leadership in ECEC.

Further reading and research

The National College for Teaching and Leadership (NCTL) offer a range of advice and publications focussing on improving early years teaching and learning, drawing on Ofsted examples of good practice. www.gov.uk/government/organisations/national-college-for-teaching-and-leadership

The Ministry of Education in New Zealand has published excellent downloadable resources to stimulate conversations about leadership in ECEC. England has looked to New Zealand for ideas about curriculum design and pedagogy in ECEC, and their resources on leadership are equally relevant. www.education.govt.nz/early-childhood

References

Belbin, R. M. (1981) *Management Teams: Why They Succeed or Fail*, London: Butterworth-Heinemann.

Bolman, L. and Deal, T. (2013) *Reframing Organisations: Artistry, Choice and Leadership*, 5th edn., San Francisco: Jossey-Bass.

Goleman, D. (1996) *Emotional Intelligence: Why It Can Matter More Than IQ*, London: Bloomsbury Paperbacks.

Hallet, E. (2014) *Leadership of Learning in Early Years Practice: A Professional Learning Resource*, London: Institute of Education, University of London.

Hallet, E. and Roberts-Holmes, G. (2010) *Research into the Construction of the Early Years Professional Status Role to Quality Improvement Strategies in Gloucestershire: Final Report*, London: Institute of Education, University of London.

Lockwood, S. (2016) Leadership, in L. Trodd (ed.) *The Early Years Handbook for Students and Practitioners: An Essential Guide for the Foundation Degree and Levels 4 and 5*, Abingdon: Routledge, pp 416–432.

Lumby, J. and Coleman, M. (2007) *Leadership and Diversity: Challenging Theory and Practice in Education*, London: Sage.

McDowall Clark, R. (2012) 'I've never thought of myself as a leader but . . .': The early years professional and catalytic leadership, *European Early Childhood Education Research Journal*, 20(3): pp 391–401.

McMahon, S., Dyer, M. and Barker, H. (2016) Mentoring, Coaching and Supervision, in L. Trodd (ed.) *The Early Years Handbook for Students and Practitioners: An Essential Guide for the Foundation Degree and Levels 4 and 5*, Abingdon: Routledge, pp 433–447.

National College for Teaching and Leadership (NCTL) (2013) *Teachers Standards (Early Years)*, London: Crown Copyright.

Nutbrown, C. (2012) *Foundations for Quality: The Independent Review of Early Education and Childcare Qualifications: Final Report*, London: DfE.

Office for Standards in Education (Ofsted) (2015) *The Report of Her Majesty's Chief Inspector of Education, Children's Services and Skills 2015: Early Years*, Manchester: Ofsted.

Pugh, G. (2014) The Policy Agenda for Early Childhood Services, in G. Pugh and B. Duffy (eds) *Contemporary Issues in the Early Years*, 6th edn., London: Sage, pp 3–20.

Rodd, J. (2006) *Leadership in Early Childhood*, Maidenhead: Open University Press.

Rodd, J. (2013) *Leadership in Early Childhood*, 3rd edn., Maidenhead: Open University Press.

Siraj, I. and Hallet, E. (2014) *Effective and Caring Leadership in the Early Years*, London: Sage.

Siraj-Blatchford, I. and Manni, L. (2007) *Effective Leadership in the Early Years Sector (The ELEYS Study)*, London: Institute of Education, University of London.

Taggart, G. (2011) Don't we care? The ethics and emotional labour of early years professionalism, *Early Years: An International Journal of Research and Development*, 31(1): pp 85–95.

Tuckman, B. and Jensen, M. (1977) Stages of small group development revisited, *Group and Organisational Studies*, 2: pp 419–427.

Whalley, M. (2011) *Leading Practice in Early Years Settings*, 2nd edn., Exeter: Learning Matters.

Chapter 11

Developing academic reading, writing and research

Andrew Youde and Lindsey Watson

Chapter aims

By the end of the chapter you will have:

- an understanding of critical reading to support finding and reviewing academic literature sources
- developed skills in self-analysis including identifying your strengths and weaknesses as a student
- considered how to use academic literature to support Early Years degree assignments and practice.

Introduction

Many different factors influence students' ability to carry out their degree studies successfully. This chapter is concerned with the development of early years student's key skills, including the ability to undertake critical reading to facilitate analysis and evaluation of literature sources and their own professional practice, whilst exploring how students can effectively transfer these skills to their academic assignments.

Critical reading

This section discusses how to find academic literature, and then how to review the quality of the literature, the first step to critical reading. The development of criticality skills in your reading and writing not only supports your continued professional development (CPD) through assisting you academically, it also supports your ability to think critically about your own and others' professional practice (Lindon and Trodd, 2016).

As an undergraduate student, you will be expected to carry out research in terms of searches for specific academic material, and reading appropriate literature sources to support your thinking and written work. The term 'literature' is used to refer to all published material, for example, books, journal articles, government documents and websites (see section on 'How do you review academic literature?' for a further discussion of these types of literature). You may also come across the term 'academic literature', which is particularly difficult to define; however, there are safeguards that students can apply to determine a source's suitability for use within an academic assignment at this level of study. It is important to use appropriate academic literature because:

- you will become up-to-date with the latest and/or key research, theories, policies and practice
- it will support you in becoming a more informed practitioner and professional
- through engaging with appropriate academic literature, you will strengthen your ability to effectively reflect on practice
- an appropriate and effective literature search potentially increases your grades.

In order to identify appropriate academic literature, a number of steps need to be taken. Figure 11.1 outlines an example of the process with play as the broad area of the search.

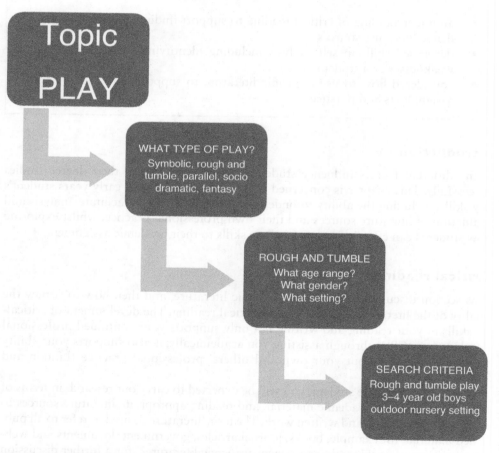

Figure 11.1 An example to illustrate the process of defining a topic and developing appropriate search criteria

When searching for academic literature, consider the following steps:

- **Define the topic** – what is the broad topic of the search? In our example, 'play' is the broad topic area.
- **Use keywords/specific search criteria** to help narrow down the focus of your topic. You need to feed these keywords into online academic search engines (such as Google Scholar) or library catalogues (such as a university library search tool), to help you find relevant literature sources (Dochartaigh, 2007). By noting down any possible synonyms for the topic, such as physical/active play for the above example, you are potentially creating opportunities for conducting a more thorough review of the literature available to you.
- **Begin the search and consider**: books, journal articles, government documents, statistics, reputable websites, reputable newspapers.
- **Refine the search** – at this point, you need to review what you have, and ask yourself, does the literature review enable you to complete a good assignment or inform aspects of early years practice? It may be necessary to further narrow down the search criteria to match the specifics of the topic, such as the example in Fig. 11.1, where the term play is further refined to symbolic, rough and tumble, parallel, socio-dramatic, fantasy.
- **Continue searching** – continue to sort literature into categories, for example, different themes or issues emerging from your literature searches, assessing whether the sources support or contradict each other or your own opinions.
- **Consider the date of sources** – it is important to consider the date of sources. This is especially important within the ever-changing early years sector, as updated government policies and initiatives and a thriving research community constantly add to the academic literature available. However, some academic literature remains current for many years, for instance, examples of the work of prominent psychologist Piaget (1964) and sociologist Vygotsky (1978), which are often found within contemporary literatures.
- **Finishing the search** – literature searches are ongoing, as different themes and issues can present themselves throughout the whole research/writing process. An abundance of literature can be overwhelming at times, so a good time to finish your search is when new sources are not adding any new information to the research, or if you already have enough information to sufficiently support your work.

It is important when searching for academic literature that you record details about the sources used. You need to find your own preferred method to record information, such as notes on individual sources, or themed mind maps of multiple sources. Source information should include themes, important points and quotes, and the relevance these have with your own work. It is also necessary that you record specific information that will allow you to correctly reference your sources, according to your own institutional rules. The information needed for accurate references potentially includes author/s, date, publication title and type of source (e.g. book, journal or website), volume and issue number (for academic journals), web address and page numbers. It can be extremely frustrating and time consuming for students to finish their work and then attempt to compile an accurate reference list.

Searching for academic literature is time consuming, so it is particularly important to develop techniques, such as skim reading, to quickly locate relevant information. When reading books, you need to use the information available to you, such as contents pages and the index, to determine if the book is relevant for your current studies. Reading introductions and conclusions within chapters is helpful in signposting any relevant content, as are headings and subheadings. Finally, reading the first line of each paragraph, which usually contains a topic sentence (detailing the content of the paragraph), should indicate what will be covered.

The above principles will help in reviewing all literature sources. However, there are some tips that will help with specific academic sources. Academic journals generally have an abstract at the start, between 200–500 words in length, providing a comprehensive summary of the research (Gray, 2009). The abstract helps determine whether the content has interest or relevance. Carefully reading the abstract, followed by the introduction and the conclusion, allows you to consider how relevant the article is before moving on and committing to reading the main body of the article.

Electronic sources often have a 'find' option which immediately locates keywords within a document. When using web sources, pressing 'control and f' on a device brings up a find box where keywords can be entered and searched. Some e-books have the added advantage of tools that allow the reader to search for key terms within the book. Institutional library databases often have a search option, as do other e-book readers, such as Google Books. These 'find' tools can often save you a great deal of time.

Activity

Complete a web search for a current early years related document, such as 'Statutory Framework for the Early Years Foundation Stage' (DfE, 2017). Once you have located and opened the document, use the 'control and f' function suggested above to find keywords you think may appear in the document. Suggested words or phrases for 'Statutory Framework for the Early Years Foundation Stage' (DfE, 2017) could include:

- early learning goals
- welfare
- assessment.

How do you review academic literature?

This chapter separates discussions regarding searching for academic literature and reviewing the quality of sources for ease of explanation and presentation; however, in reality, these activities commonly occur simultaneously. Determining the value and quality of a piece of literature – and, in essence, getting to the heart of critical reading – considers the merits and weaknesses of a piece of literature for a particular purpose, namely your assignments or placement practice.

In some respects, reviewing literature is relatively easy, as it is a skill you have been using and developing all your life. For example, if a student has just been to the cinema, his or her friends will ask what he or she thought of the film. The said student will give an answer and provide some supporting evidence – "I enjoyed the film, the special effects were great and I didn't see the twist at the end coming." When reviewing academic literature, students follow a similar process. Ask questions such as:

- what did I think of the work?
- did I learn anything?
- what evidence was provided to help justify the arguments being made?

Knowing more about the type of literature sources can be a useful first step in determining the potential value of a source. A brief overview of the main types of literature is now provided.

Academic journal articles

These are periodic journals, such as *Early Years* and the *Journal of Early Childhood Research*, which contain articles relating to a particular academic discipline. They refer to scholarship in that area, including presentation and scrutiny of new research, policy or early years practice, and also critique existing work in the disciplinary area. Each journal contains articles around 4,000 to 7,000 words in length – much shorter and focussed than books. Articles are peer reviewed (checked for accuracy and content by other academics knowledgeable of the area) and, as a result, are considered valid and reliable sources of academic literature. Those new to reading academic journals can find it daunting to begin with, due to the inclusion of academic language. You should persist with reading academic sources, as reading these types of literature will expose you to the academic language and criticality that will be required in your own written assignments.

Academic books

These tend to be written to cover early years theory, policy or practice. They are usually written by someone knowledgeable about the area, and provide a broad overview of particular topics. They are not 'peer reviewed', so can contain some bias if the author is particularly passionate about a position.

Early years practitioner periodicals

These periodicals, such as *Nursery World* and *Early Years Educator*, are aimed at informing early years practitioners. These types of sources are not peer reviewed; however, they are good at relating theory to practice. Early years practitioner periodicals are sometimes a good place to start to try to understand a new topic, before moving on to potentially more sophisticated thinking within academic journals. When using these types of sources to back up your own arguments, you should also consider doing so alongside more academic sources.

Government publications

These publications commonly outline legislation or guidance on particular areas of early years practice, safeguarding for example. These sources tend to be more directive, and contain less discussion of differing views on a particular area. The agenda of the government at the time of publication may sometimes raise the question of bias, and you must also consider the date of publication. Unless you are placing the publication within an historical context, you should aim to use the most relevant up-to-date literature.

Web sources

These can include early years websites, blogs, discussion forums and videos. These types of sources can be tempting as they can have a simple layout and be easy to follow and understand. However, sources may not be outlining what is typically considered to be effective early years practice. You need to consider the credentials of the author or organisation associated with the website to determine their suitability as an academic source. For example, the Joseph Rowntree Foundation (2016) is an independent organisation working to inspire social change through well-respected research, policy and practice, with a well-established website offering access to many academic sources and is considered a suitable academic source.

To further review literature, consider the following questions:

What is the purpose of the literature?

Sources of literature can be for a variety of purposes:

- to discuss and develop theory
- to consider or evaluate government policy
- to report research findings
- to examine early years practice
- or a combination of these points.

For you to understand the contemporary environment of current early years research and practice, it is important that you have read and considered what has gone before (Gray, 2009). You are advised to review your topic and think about which of the above purposes are most relevant. Also, you should consider the intended audience of the source – is it for academics, early years practitioners, students, parents or the general public? Again, you need to look at your topic and consider which sources, and their intended audience, would be of most relevance and value. Generally, sources which require a certain level of expertise to understand, such as those aimed at academics and senior practitioners, are likely to be the most useful for this higher level of study.

What is the authority or expertise of the author/s?

There is commonly a brief biography of the author or authors within a source and, if not, a quick Internet search can often provide an overview of their experience and expertise. Some issues to consider include:

- are they an academic who has researched and taught the area?
- are they an experienced practitioner?

- have they developed government policy in the area?
- is it written by a government department or a reputable early years body?

Is the source objective?

Objectivity within a research context is connected with personal feelings and opinions. A lack of bias, judgement or prejudice allows a piece of work, an individual or group to be considered as being objective (Opie, 2004). Ideally, there should be at least two sides of an argument presented. You can potentially recognise arguments from the use of different sources when discussing a point, or possibly from the use of connective language such as *however, in contrast, arguably*. For example, the author may be a strong advocate of outdoor play; however, when considering children's access to outdoor play in a typical early years setting, the source may not consider the relevance of universal inclusive practice and fail to recognise some of the challenges to ensure the learning experience is both valuable and safe for all children. Therefore, this particular author has displayed a potential lack of objectivity.

Is the source accurate?

Determining the accuracy of a source can be challenging for undergraduate students; however, the more you critically examine sources, the better you will become at judging whether a source is reliable and free from error. When reading a source, you should consider whether the points being raised support the conclusions. Also, what evidence (research or experience of practice) is presented to support the work? Another method for checking source accuracy is considering what sources have been cited within. Good research provides a trail; you should be able to use a source's own reference list to help clarify some of the arguments presented. However, probably the best way of judging the accuracy of a source is to read a variety of sources about a topic, and compare the arguments being made across a particular theme.

Does the source contribute to your research?

Drifting away from the focus of a topic is a potential danger when faced with the mass of literature available within institutional library catalogues and online search facilities, which can be distracting. There is nothing wrong with enjoying reading broadly around early years literature as this makes for a better student. However, at some point, an assignment has to be completed or placement work has to be prepared. Keep the focus of the literature search and review written down and close by.

Activity

Identify three specific academic literature sources related to a topic within early years degree studies.

Critical reading to inform placement practice

During an early years degree, you will more than likely complete a placement or be employed in a relevant setting. These settings will provide you with the practical experiences to undertake observations on practice, which will underpin the work for one or more of your degree modules. Reflection on practice will commonly start with relatively small issues, for example, planning and putting up a display within the setting. Reading should inform this practice and could be focussed on the following areas:

- why are displays important?
- who and what are displays for?
- what is an enabling environment?

Initially you would focus on the first two questions here at the start of the literature search. As you become more informed about this area, your reading would take you to a discussion of what is an enabling environment, and why are they important within early years settings? This, therefore, strengthens your reflections and helps you become a more informed student.

Also, during your first year, your reflections on practice will include critical incidents (as discussed in Chapter 4) you have observed or experienced. To illustrate, a quite extreme but not uncommon incident is now considered followed by a discussion of appropriate reading:

A student is in a setting with a child, who is having a snack. The child suddenly starts to choke. Quickly, another practitioner comes along and takes action that removes the food from obstructing the child's throat.

As the student reflects on this incident they should initially consider the EYFS and its requirements to safeguard and promote the health, safety and welfare of children (DfE, 2017). The student read and reflected on how this incident was conveyed to the child's parents, as the practitioners in the setting did not want it mentioned. This is an example of bad practice, as such incidents should always be communicated to parents. The student should then read about effective communication with parents, and the importance of parent partnerships. This would include the impact of not communicating such incidents to the parents, should somebody else, or the child, tell the parents. In this case, parents would lose trust in both the practitioners and setting. When reading and reflecting on such an incident on placement, theory could be considered here to help analyse this situation. In this instance, reading about communication theory and effective parental partnerships would be the most relevant. Recognition of the important themes of the incident, as above, should inform initial literature searches. It is this reading that then assists with the analysis and evaluation of the incident leading to critical reflection from linking the theory (reading) to practice (the incident).

Student self-analysis

Early years degree students should undertake self-analysis to help improve both their academic studies and placement practice. This encourages critical reflection on strengths and weaknesses and consideration on how to improve. This section outlines a useful framework (Figure 11.2) to support self-analysis before discussing some common points raised by undergraduate students when they are reflecting on strategies to improve.

SWOT analysis

This framework can provide a structure and depth to your reflective practice by considering your own strengths and weaknesses, and also opportunities you could take to improve, such as undertaking extra placement hours in a different socio-economic area, or mitigating the threats of being asked to do additional hours in a setting when university assignments are due. As you progress through the early years degree and update your SWOT, weaknesses should develop into strengths, you will identify greater opportunities to improve practice, and you will develop knowledge, understanding, skills and qualities that will stand you in good stead should any threats arise.

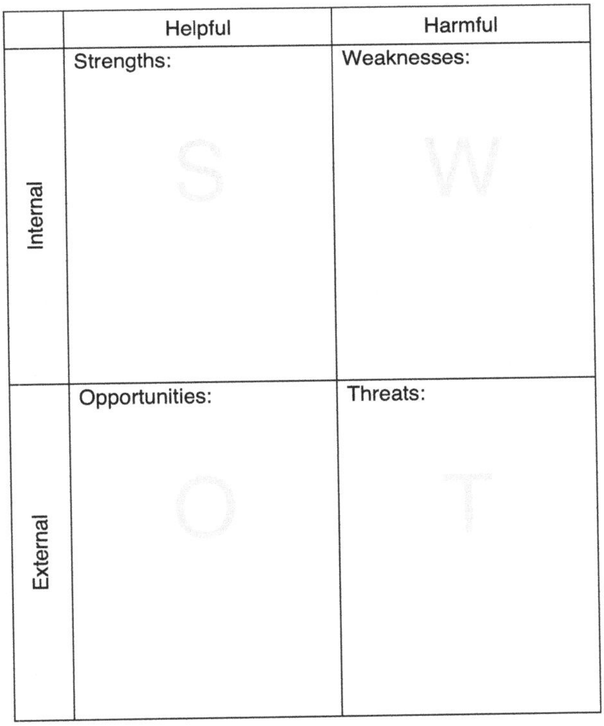

	Helpful	Harmful
Internal	Strengths:	Weaknesses:
External	Opportunities:	Threats:

Figure 11.2 A SWOT analysis framework depicted as a quadrant

> **Thinking activity**
>
> Undertake a SWOT analysis of your own practice. Include your internal strengths and weaknesses. Then, consider factors that are largely beyond your control that could impact on your practice. If they could enhance your practice, note them as opportunities. If they could impair your practice, note them as threats.

A common mistake made by first year early years degree students when carrying out their first SWOT analysis is to identify a lack of reading as their biggest threat. This should be noted as a threat at first, until you have learned how to critically read academic sources (see discussion within the critical reading section). Once you possess this skill, it is then within your control regarding how much reading is actually undertaken. A lack of reading would therefore be a weakness, whereas extensive reading would then be included as a strength. For those that say their biggest threat is not reading, this has important implications for both their understanding of theory, and the quality of their research for both assignments and practice. Reading is the key to research and can provide the biggest opportunity or strength!

Critical analysis to inform critical writing

This section develops the earlier discussion of critical reading, to outline how this can inform and improve both your writing and practice. Differences between descriptive writing and critical analysis are considered, with supporting examples, as well as a key approach to research that you will undertake during the course.

To move your work to encompass critical writing, you must first critically analyse a topic, issue or incident. The advice provided in the 'Critical Reading' section earlier in this chapter provides the start to the critical analysis process. But whereas this advice was just for a particular source of literature, you will use a range of sources to help you critically analyse an aspect of assignment or practice work.

Critical analysis means to break down the topic, issue or incident and consider constituent parts, such as arguments for and against a particular approach, and use a combination of sources to help. Within the context of early years, sources can include:

- theory
- academic literature
- secondary research
- primary research (such as your observations)
- government policy and guidance.

The purpose of critical analysis is not to inform, which would be classed as descriptive writing (see section on 'Descriptive and Critical Writing'), but it is there to evaluate the value, validity or truth of a particular area within early years. Critical analysis can then inform critical writing, whether that is for university assignments or reflection on practice. Aspects of critical writing include:

- being open-minded and fair when considering strengths and weaknesses of other's work and ideas
- comparing and contrasting one approach against another
- judgement that is critical, but not dismissive, based on evidence and not assertions without support, through making assumptions
- demonstrating the links between different sources of information
- making a case underpinned with supporting evidence
- justifying why an approach is the most appropriate
- clearly arguing the significance
- justifying the timing of events.

All of these points have the notion of 'supporting evidence' in common, again stressing the importance of reading around the topic area. You can express your opinions; in fact, it is encouraged, but these should always be presented as arguments, and backed up with evidence. Following such analysis, you can then evaluate the area, that is, give your opinion or recommendations, also known as your academic voice, based on the evidence you have reviewed. An academic voice is a careful evaluation of published work, providing a critical judgement of other people's work, without being dismissive. Backing up your arguments needs to be balanced, and avoiding overstating the impact of your work is helped by the use of cautious language, such as hedging words, for example, *possibly . . . probably . . . potentially . . . it could be argued that. . . .* This is considered an important aspect of academic writing, and crucial in avoiding overstating, whilst still encouraging critical analysis and evaluation. Therefore, by extensive reading around a broad range of sources and research, you will become a more informed student who is able to clearly justify arguments made in assignment work and approaches adopted in practice.

Descriptive and critical writing

The main characteristic of descriptive writing is that it describes something (as you would probably expect), but does not move the discussion or argument beyond this. Within your degree work, there are times when descriptive writing is needed, for example:

- to describe a setting
- to describe a child's background and prior learning
- to outline the timing of a piece of research
- to provide a summary of events leading up to an incident
- to give a brief general description of an academic source, although the discussion should quickly move on to analysis.

Point for reflection

Limiting description within your work to a minimum allows for a greater focus on analysis and evaluation. Focussing on analysis and evaluation is a more effective way for you to produce higher quality academic writing.

Examples of critical analysis and critical writing

The following extracts of student's work are good examples of critical analysis. They are presented first, with a discussion of their strengths provided underneath.

Example 1 – Child A and her language development

This could suggest that Child A's language development has also impacted her learning and development in 'literacy' and 'mathematics'. It is thought that speech delays and incomprehensibility in children can cause later problems with print recognition and processing (Whitehead, 2010), indicating how Child A's delay in her language development could impact her in 'literacy'. In addition, much of what is involved in mathematical understanding can be linked to connections between language, symbols, concrete materials and pictures (Haylock and Cockburn, 2013). This could suggest that if Child A's language is underdeveloped, she may struggle with understanding mathematics as she will be unable to effectively link high levels of language with the other components needed to fully understand mathematics.

This is a good example of how the student is not simply describing what theorists have said, but is actually using that to explain what she has seen in the child's development. Note the mix of sources underpinning this passage and the cautious tone adopted through the use of hedging words ("this could suggest") to introduce the student's justified opinion at the end.

Example 2 – Behaviour and the development of Child L

Observations (see Appendix 8 and 9) demonstrate that Child L can use her imagination to play out the role of a princess. Harris (cited in Hallet, 2016) argues, children who participate in pretend play can act out the roles of someone else along with pretend actions such as L showing a curtsey. Rogers and Evans (2008, cited in Hallet, 2016) would argue that through pretend play, L will enhance her social competence and a sense of well-being, which suggests L's improving her interactions with peers and adults around her. This also relates to the EYFS under 'Communication and Language', as at 40–60 months, she demonstrates she can recreate the roles of cartoon characters (Early Education, 2012).

Again, this student can link what she has read in terms of theory to the curriculum framework for current practice, and also use it to explain, rather than simply describe, the child's development – all key skills within the national occupational Early Educator and Early Years Teacher standards (National College for Teaching and Leadership, 2013a, b). A range of evidence underpins the extract, including the student's own primary research (through observations), academic literature, government policy and guidance (reference to the EYFS) and non-governmental charitable organisations, such as Early Education. Also, good links are made between sources, for example, between the Roger and Evans source and observations of practice in the penultimate sentence, and then the link to the EYFS in the final sentence.

Example 3 – Student discussing key person working when she evaluates the behaviour and development of Child A. She refers to the practitioner as F.

As F is Child A's key person, it is her responsibility to form a respectful, reciprocal relationship with her parents (DfE, 2014, p. 21). When F visited Child A at home, this was the beginning of the relationship (Beckley, 2013, p. 175). Knowing that F is Child A's key person enabled her parents to build a relationship with a specific person. It also gave them somebody to communicate with and somebody to reassure them during Child A's transition (Elfer et al., 2012, p. 18). As F and Child A's parents communicated throughout Child A's transition, it will have helped Child A to feel more comfortable in the setting (Woods, 2015, p. 25; Pugh and Duffy, 2007, p. 152).

This is a very strong example of a student using a range of different reference sources to explain and evaluate how theory and legislation is put into practice. Students are required to use theory along with current policy and legislation to explain and evaluate practice. Here the student draws on attachment theory and the key person approach.

Students as researchers

During an early years degree, students will be increasingly asked to undertake research around practice within settings. This section outlines Action Research as an approach to evaluating their own practice within settings. This is commonly achieved by obtaining their own data to research their own specific questions or issues. This is known as primary research, whereas secondary research involves using the research of others, say in books, journal articles or government statistics, to explore specific questions or issues. Example 2 above (see section 'Examples of critical analysis and critical writing') included student observations in the analysis of a child's behaviour and development, and this is a common example of the integration of primary research into early years degree work. Whilst Action Research commonly draws on primary research to evaluate practice, this is supported with reference to a range of secondary sources including theory and academic literature.

Kemmis and McTaggart (1992, p. 10) describe Action Research as "to plan, act, observe, and reflect more carefully, and more rigorously than one usually does in everyday life". Figure 11.3 outlines Kemmis and McTaggart's Action Research Spiral based on their description:

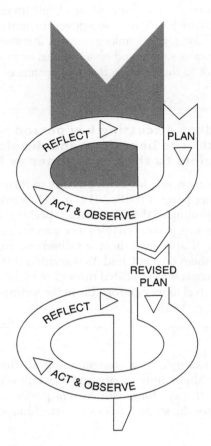

Figure 11.3 The Action Research Spiral
Source: Kemmis and McTaggart, 1992, p. 11

In an early years context, this refers to the more systemic and rigorous reflection and research underpinning decisions made by a setting or individual practitioners. For example, a setting may want to introduce free-flow play as part of their daily activities. They would plan carefully how to introduce this by reading extensively around the area of play, including relevant theories and good practice. A practitioner may go and observe free-flow play in another setting that had successfully implemented this approach. The setting 'acts' by implementing this new aspect of practice, and then 'observes' the impact by collecting evidence or data – maybe through observations. Following a period of time, maybe a month, the practitioners within the setting will 'reflect' on the new approach, drawing on the collected data, and then decide whether to continue and consider improvements going forward into the next Action Research cycle.

There are two key features that separate Action Research from other research approaches – it is practitioner-led, and cyclical in nature. Action Research concerns practitioners improving their own practice and, as a result, they have a dual role in the process – practitioner and researcher. Practitioners drive the research forward. There is 'action' involved, i.e. 'doing' or intervening in practice within the setting, before researching and reflecting on its impact. Following this reflection, changes can be made to the next cycle of the practice, and a continuous process of action, research, reflection and (hopefully) improvement occurs. This, therefore, suggests a cyclical nature to the research as practitioners continue to improve their practice.

Data or evidence to support decisions made when conducting Action Research, or any educational research, is commonly categorised as quantitative or qualitative:

- quantitative data has a numerical basis, for example, measures of improvement against EYFS criteria, and is adopted in larger scale research projects, for example, a survey of the impact of a new phonics reading scheme across a number of settings
- qualitative data is more commonly used in small-scale early years research and explores meanings, experiences and opinions. Interviews and observations are key methods of collecting this data as they afford a deeper understanding of particular areas of practice.

As with any educational research, Action Research should be conducted with due attention to ethical practices. Guidelines should be referred to, such as the British Educational Research Association's (BERA) Ethical Research Guidelines (2011), throughout all stages of planning and conducting research. This is particularly important within early years context, as children are commonly involved and are unlikely to understand the nature and impact of their participation in the research process. Key ethical practices (BERA, 2011) that must be considered include:

- voluntary informed consent
- openness and disclosure
- right to withdraw
- incentives
- detriments arising from participation in research
- privacy.

When conducting research, steps should be taken to minimise the impact of the researcher's values and beliefs on all stages of the process. This is particularly important when undertaking Action Research, given the dual role of practitioner and researcher, and the potential for bias in the research outcomes. At the heart of this section is the notion of subjectivity – how your background (such as age, life experiences, gender, education) influences and conditions your judgements. For example, if two degree students were conducting observations of outdoor play, they may draw differing conclusions from two boys wrestling on the grass. One, who had been bullied at school, may view that situation as potentially dangerous and could get out of hand quite quickly. The other, who has two twin brothers at home and regularly sees this type of play, may view it as normal for boys of their age.

Conclusion

This chapter has provided an overview of critical reading to inform critical writing. It has highlighted key skills that will help you develop criticality within your studies. The chapter included examples of students' academic writing and thinking activities to encourage you to reflect and develop your understanding of what it means to be critical.

Further reading and research

Roberts-Holmes, G. (2014) *Doing your Early Years Research Project: A Step by Step Guide*, 3rd ed., London: Sage.

Ratcliffe, J. (2016) Becoming an Undergraduate: The Transition from Level 3 to Level Four and Five, in L. Trodd (ed.) *The Early Years Handbook for Students and Practitioners: An Essential Guide for the Foundation Degree and Levels 4 and 5*, Oxon: Routledge, pp 15–27.

References

Beckley, P. (2013) *The New Early Years Foundation Stage: Changes, Challenges and Reflections.* Maidenhead: Open University Press.

British Educational Research Association (BERA) (2011) *Ethical Guidelines for Educational Research*, Nottingham: British Educational Research Association.

Department for Education (DfE) (2014) *Statutory Framework for the Early Years Foundation Stage: Setting the Standards for Learning, Development and Care for Children from Birth to Five*, London: Department for Education.

Department for Education (DfE) (2017) *Statutory Framework for the Early Years Foundation Stage: Setting the Standards for Learning, Development and Care for Children from Birth to Five*, London: Department for Education.

Dochartaigh, N. (2007) *Internet Research Skills: How to do Your Literature Search and Find Research Information Online*, London: Sage.

Early Education (2012) *Development Matters in the Early Years Foundation Stage (EYFS)*, London: Crown Copyright 2012.

Elfer, P., Goldschmeid, E. and Selleck, D. (2012) *Key Persons in the Early Years: Building Relationships For Quality Provision in Early Years Settings and Primary Schools*, Oxon: Routledge.

Gray, D. (2009) *Doing Research in the Real World*, 2nd edn., London: Sage.

Hallet, E. (2016) *Early Years Practice: For Educators and Teachers*, London: Sage Publications.

Haylock, D. and Cockburn, A. (2013) *Understanding Mathematics for Young Children*, 4th edn., London: Sage Publications.

Joseph Rowntree Foundation (2016) *Joseph Rowntree Foundation: Inspiring Social Change*, Retrieved from www.jrf.org.uk (Accessed 26 September 2016).

Kemmis, S. and McTaggart, R. (1992) *The Action Research Planner*, 3rd edn., Geelong, Victoria: Deakin University Press.

Lindon, J. and Trodd, L. (2016) *Reflective Practice and Early Years Professionalism: Linking Theory to Practice*, 3rd edn., London: Hodder Education.

National College for Teaching and Leadership (NCTL) (2013a) *Early Years Educator (Level 3): Qualifications Criteria*, Manchester: National College for Teaching and Leadership.

National College for Teaching and Leadership (NCTL) (2013b) *Teachers' Standards (Early Years)*, Manchester: National College for Teaching and Leadership.

Opie, C. (2004) What Is Educational Research? in C. Opie (ed.) *Doing Educational Research*, London: Sage, pp 1–14.

Piaget, J. (1964) Cognitive development in children: Piaget development and learning, *Journal of Research in Science Teaching*, 2(3): pp 176–186.

Pugh, G. and Duffy, B. (2007) *Contemporary Issues in the Early Years*. 4th Edition. London: Sage.

Vygotsky, L. (1978) *Mind in Society: The Development of Higher Psychological Processes*, (M. Cole, V. Steiner, S. Scriber and E. Souberman, Eds, Trans.), Cambridge: Harvard University Press.

Whitehead, M. (2010) *Language and Literacy in the Early Years 0 – 7*. 4th Edition. London: Sage.

Woods, A. (2015) *The Characteristics of Effective Learning: Creating and Capturing the Possibilities in the Early Years*. Oxon: Routledge.

Chapter 12

Working with parents

Amanda Crow and Tina Froggett

Chapter aims

By the end of the chapter you will have:

- an understanding of the policy requirements for working with parents
- explored parent and practitioner partnerships
- reflected on the judgements and stereotypes made on parents and families
- considered the barriers to parental involvement
- developed an understanding of current thinking and practice on working with parents.

Introduction

As practitioners of the future, students undertaking an undergraduate course of study related to childhood and early years need to be prepared for working collaboratively with parents. By 'parents' we mean 'any adult who has parental rights and caring responsibility for children'. It is unlikely that as a student on placement in a setting you will be involved in working directly with parents; however, it is important to be aware of the underpinning principles of this essential aspect of practice. In this chapter we will discuss a set of approaches and ideas that inform the way practitioners work with parents, carers and families to support children attending early years settings. We will also introduce a conceptual framework, or system of assumptions, beliefs and theories, that informs early years practice in this area.

Thinking activity

Ask yourself the following questions and consider your answers as you read through the chapter.

1   What do you understand by the term 'parenting'?
2   What influences parenting?

3   How has early years legislation influenced our understanding of parenting?

4   Is there an ideal parenting style that works for all?

Think about how you were parented. How might this experience affect your practice?

What does the Early Years Foundation Stage (EYFS) framework say about working with parents?

Working with parents is a continuous theme that runs through the EYFS, particularly with regard to learning and development (DfE, 2017). There are two assessments, the Two Year Check and the Early Years Foundation Stage Profile, that require the practitioner and the parent to work together (DfE, 2017). However, this relationship should be ongoing, developing over time. Parents must be provided with full details of the setting's policies and procedures, including information about how the EYFS is being delivered, curriculum content, how children with additional needs are supported, and how parents and carers can share home learning experiences, in order that they can engage with their child's early years education (DfE, 2017). "Good parenting and high quality early learning together provide the foundation children need to make the most of their abilities and talents as they grow up" (DfE, 2017, p. 5). "Children learn and develop well in enabling environments, in which their experiences respond to their individual needs and there is a strong partnership between practitioners and parents and/or carers" (DfE, 2017, p. 6).

The EYFS acknowledges the findings of the Effective Provision of Pre-school Education (EPPE) Project (Sylva et al., 2004), that involving parents in children's education has a positive effect on their learning outcomes. The nature of partnership working will vary across settings, so it is important for students on placement to be aware of the strategies used to engage parents.

Working with parents is achieved principally through the key person system. The allocation of a key person to each child is a statutory requirement of the EYFS (DfE, 2017), stressing the importance of establishing good relationships with children and their families. The key person system is the bringing together of practitioner, parent and child to nurture and support positive relationships, and this requires adult involvement (Elfer et al., 2003). The key person approach builds secure attachments that encourage children to feel safe and secure in the setting (Elfer et al., 2003). This relationship is of particular importance when working with children under 3 (Goldschmied and Jackson, 2004). The key person plays a crucial role when working with children with special educational needs, liaising with the Special Educational Needs Co-ordinator (SENCO) to seek the specialist help and support the child's needs, but at the same time ensuring that the needs of the parents are met too. However, the intention of the key person relationship is not to be a substitute parent, but to act as a secure base from which the child is able to explore new experiences that are perhaps not available at home (Elfer et al., 2003). This requires skill in getting to know the family's background and child's specific needs and to use this knowledge to complement the care given in the setting with the care given at home.

Parent and practitioner partnerships

Involving parents in early years education and care has grown over the past 50 years, with the establishment of organisations such as the Pre-school Learning Alliance, and the development of the early years education and care sector by both Labour and Conservative governments. Families, particularly those living in poverty, have recently become the central focus of wider social policy. *Supporting Families in the Foundation Stage* (DfE, 2011) brought together health and education services to support parents, by targeting services such as relationship counselling and parenting skills towards the most vulnerable families. Families continue to be at the centre of the current political agenda which focusses heavily on economic growth and full employment, with the result that poverty will be eradicated (The Prime Minister's Office and The Rt Hon David Cameron MP, 2016). In today's society, parents not only have busy and challenging lives but are being increasingly encouraged to balance work and family life to adequately meet the needs of their families. Social policies therefore have real implications for parental involvement.

What constitutes parental involvement, and the nature of parent/practitioner relationships, is the subject of much debate. By using the word 'partnership', the government paints a picture of harmonious relationships between parents and professionals, hiding many tensions that often exist in reality (Bastiani, 1989). Parental involvement is surrounded by terminology that has a variety of meanings and is open to different interpretations. Whilst in the setting, students may hear terms such as 'partnership', 'involvement', 'engagement', 'collaboration' and 'working alongside' which are used synonymously. Hornby and Lafaele (2011) observe that the relationship between parents and teachers is fundamentally defined by the difference in expertise, reinforced by the use of the word 'professionals'.

Parental involvement is considered by some as a process rather than a relationship (Hornby and Lafaele, 2011). McMillan (2005) cites Rennie's Stages of Parental Involvement as an example of the process that parents go through when engaging with a setting (see Table 12.1).

Thinking activity

Consider the parents that attend your placement setting.

Can you identify the different stages that parents are at on Rennie's Stages of Parental Involvement?

Can you identify parents who are not engaged at all? Why do you think this is the case?

Table 12.1 Rennie's (1996) Stages of Parental Involvement

Progression
Confidence building
Awareness raising
Real involvement
Partnership
Parents as co-educators

Source: McMillan, D. J. (2005). 'Close Encounters: Issues in Pre-school Parental Involvement in Northern Ireland' *Child Care in Practice* 11 (2): pp. 119–134

Judgements and stereotypes

As students on placement, you might observe different types of family groups involved in the setting. Families today come in many different shapes and sizes. The Office for National Statistics (ONS) published a report on national family trends in the UK, defining the family as falling into the following categories:

- married or civil partner couple families
- cohabiting couple families and
- lone parent families.

(ONS, 2015)

The term 'family' however, can mean different things to different people, and our understanding is shaped by past experiences. Wilson (2015) suggests that family structures have changed, in particular the role of women; equally Abela and Walker (2013) discuss changes in contemporary society, and describe families moving away from perceived traditional models where fathers were often identified as the bread winners and mothers as the carers. Gender roles are being transformed, especially for women, through increased opportunities in education and careers. However, there is also pressure on women to contribute to the family income and an increasing need for women to be involved in the workplace, creating a tension between work and parenting (Abela and Walker, 2013). For the student practitioner this means that defining the contemporary family is difficult. Significantly, the 2015 ONS statistics confirm that fewer and fewer children are being parented in families that follow the traditional nuclear family pattern of two parents, mother and father (ONS, 2015).

The early years practitioner is in a unique position when working with children, as they will encounter and become involved with different family structures and carers. In your student placement you will become aware of many different adults, you will hear the term *parents and carers* widely used, and you will be aware of adults with parental responsibility, grandparents and wider family members. Their experiences as parents and carers will be influenced and shaped by personal history and their previous understanding and knowledge of parenting practices. Whilst acknowledging that parents and carers do not fit into set categories, contemporary families consist of a diverse and rich mix of cultures, religions and traditions and all have the potential to nurture, educate and influence young children.

Positive interaction between children and their parents can provide an environment where children can feel able to explore but know they are safe. In her early work, Diana Baumrind studied behaviours believed to impact on parenting and identified three distinct parenting styles – authoritarian, permissive and authoritative (Baumrind, 1971). Further research by Macoby and Martin (1983) supported these definitions and identified a fourth, neglectful, style. Although somewhat dated, Baumrind and Macoby and Martin's research is still found to be relevant and features in contemporary reports (Wilson, 2015).

The Economic and Social Research Council (ESRC) highlights a connection between parenting style and children's development, suggesting that positive parenting offers children structure, opportunities for learning and a supportive home environment. Using data from the *Millennium Cohort Study*, the report concludes that the benefits of a positive and supportive relationship between a parent and child are regarded as the most desirable and supportive in today's society, and are associated with positive

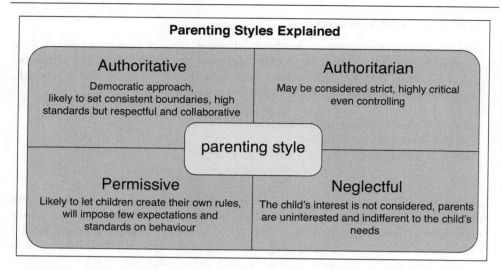

Figure 12.1 Parenting styles explained, adapted from Baumrind (1971) and Macoby and Martin (1983)

early achievement and outcomes (ESRC, 2012). This preferred style can be equated with Baumrind (1971) and Macoby and Martin's (1983) 'Authoritative' parenting style as one that is respectful, fair and able to set consistent boundaries.

Strong, positive early relationships between parents, carers and practitioners are important for healthy development and have the ability to influence a child's future outcomes (Asmussen et al., 2016). The unique child experiences the world holistically; therefore, it is important that his/her environment, including home and setting, support him/her to become a resilient individual. This view of the child as capable and strong can sometimes be in conflict with the beliefs and values of both practitioners and parents (Elfer and Page, 2015). Evidence highlighted in a number of key reports published in the past ten years charts the influential role of parents and carers on early years development, but the impact can be both positive and negative (Field, 2010; Allen, 2011; Tickell, 2011).

Thinking activity

Consider the four identified parenting styles. Do you recognise any similarities with your own childhood or maybe combinations of one or more styles?

Think about your observations of parental engagement on placement. Can you recognise different approaches to parenting? How can this help you to develop your practice?

Conflict can potentially arise when adults have differing views about childhood and what children need to grow and develop. There are two key concepts for practitioners to consider when thinking about the child as an individual; both are reasonable and will hold truth depending on the family's experiences and viewpoints

(Desforges and Abouchaar, 2003). The first concept is that that children are regarded as vulnerable and in need of protection; the second is that they are competent and capable individuals with the ability to act on and influence their own agency. It can be argued that both perspectives have credibility. Whilst as adults we have the responsibility to safeguard and protect children (HM Government, 2015a), it is equally important that adults respect the rights of children and value them as individuals. This concept needs thoughtful consideration by the adults who care for and educate them.

Developing partnerships is not without challenges, and success will take many different forms. There needs to be a strong emphasis on relationships, cooperation and collaboration between practitioners, parents and the wider family. Key to this is a reciprocal partnership between all parties and a commitment to engage in respectful dialogue, which develops a shared understanding when attending to the needs of the child. This requires a holistic, integrated view of raising children and partnerships that are built on honesty and trust (Jackson and Needham, 2014). The student, therefore, needs to be aware of their own values and beliefs when working with children and families. Whalley (2007) simplifies this concept, explaining that valuing parents as partners requires the practitioner to understand how their own philosophies can influence their work with others. Students need to be reflective and reflexive in their practice, and to understand that both parents and children have rights.

Practitioners often talk about not making judgements about the families they meet. This involves being open-minded, considerate and respecting that people have different approaches and beliefs when parenting their children. The Equality Duty (2011), an addition to the Equality Act 2010, places a duty on public bodies to consider the needs of others in their 'day to day work' (Government Equalities Office, 2011). In early years practice, this means respecting that parents make choices based on their own individual situations, and in the majority of cases believe that they do this in the best interests of the child. As a student you therefore need to be aware of how you perceive others and how others perceive you; your body language, what you say and how you say it, are all important considerations. When working together with children, adults can influence each other in both positive and negative ways through language, behaviour and actions. Wilson (2015) suggests it can be helpful to recognise each other's strengths, requiring practitioners and parents to work collaboratively, ideally resulting in stronger partnerships.

Thinking activity

Look back on your placement and try to think about occasions when you came into contact with parents.

Can you think of a time when you observed a situation between a parent and child that made you question your own beliefs and values?

What did you do?

Can you think of a way that you could work in partnership in a respectful way?

Barriers to Parental Involvement (PI)

Involving parents in their children's learning is sometimes a challenge. Parents do generally want to be involved in their children's learning, but may be faced with barriers that make involvement difficult. Hornby and Lafaele (2011) created a model to explain the factors that present barriers to parents becoming involved in their child's education, which have a negative impact on the setting's ability to work with parents. This model groups the factors into four areas (See Table 12.2).

Parent and family factors

Parental beliefs, their current life contexts, class, ethnicity and gender all influence parental involvement (Hornby and Lafaele, 2011). According to Harris and Goodall (2008), involvement is more likely if parents believe that it is part of their parenting role. Some parents experience barriers to involvement, but McMillan (2005) found that about 16 per cent of parents make a conscious decision not to be involved. A lack of confidence in skills and abilities, or a previous negative experience of schooling, contribute to feelings of powerlessness and exclusion (Hornby and Lafaele, 2011). LaRocque et al. (2011) state that ideally parents should be advocates for their children, but research by Whalley (2007) revealed that this was not always possible for parents who experience the re-emergence of deep rooted feelings that reinforce blindness to the benefits of education.

Family life context, particularly socio-economic status and material deprivation, presents physical and emotional barriers to parental involvement (Harris and Goodall, 2008; LaRocque et al., 2011). Education, employment, health, family care responsibilities and support networks are influential factors, and in a challenging modern world, meeting basic needs is the preoccupation of many parents. LaRocque et al. (2011) warn that presence in the setting should not be taken as a measure of interest or involvement. Practitioners need to be proactive. Parents need to be recognised as a valuable resource, but not treated the same, acknowledging their individual needs (LaRocque et al., 2011; Pugh, 1989). Whalley (2007) stresses the importance of getting to know parents, so that a variety of options for parental involvement can be offered. Practitioners need to give real consideration to the social and economic complexities of families and local communities (Bastiani, 1989), but it can be unlikely that practitioners gain sufficient insight in the short time that some families are involved with the setting.

Table 12.2 Hornby and Lafaele's Explanatory Model of the Potential Barriers to Parental Involvement (PI)

Individual parent and family factors	*Child factors*
• parents' beliefs about PI	• age
• perceptions of invitations for PI	• learning difficulties
• current life contexts	• gifts and talents
• class, ethnicity and gender	• behavioural problems
Parent-teacher factors	*Societal factors*
• differing goals and agendas	• historical and demographic
• differing attitudes	• political
• differing language used	• economic

Source: Hornby, G. and Lafaele, R. (2011). 'Barriers to parental involvement in education: an explanatory model' *Educational Review 63* (1): pp. 37–52

> **Thinking activity**
>
> Having spent time in your placement setting, observe how the setting engages parents in their children's learning.
>
> How are parents encouraged to engage?
>
> Consider how this affects different parents and how changes might be made to encourage more involvement.

Parent and teacher factors

Parents can often find the attitudes of professionals difficult to negotiate. Many parents, especially those from ethnic minority groups, are frightened of "overstepping some unwritten mark" and perceive settings as "closed systems" that are hard to reach (Harris and Goodall, 2008, pp. 280, 285). Many parents are uncertain about their role, are wary of being judged and do not consider their knowledge to be of value (McMillan, 2005; Pugh, 1989). Some suggest that professionals assume that parents are generally not interested (Hornby and Lafaele, 2011), and become preoccupied with parents who are difficult to deal with (Harris and Goodall, 2008), whereas others assume, often incorrectly, what parents want (LaRocque et al., 2011).

Understanding these factors when developing partnership working is important. Recognising that parents have different needs will help students to develop their practice around communicating effectively with parents. Most parents simply want to know about their child's day, the progress they are making and what can be done at home to support them. It is important, therefore, to value all efforts that parents make to support their children's learning, and to provide the support they need in doing so.

> **Thinking activity**
>
> Think about the parents at your placement setting and reflect on how you might break down some of the barriers to involvement that are created from the way education is perceived.
>
> How might you as an educator make parents feel that their knowledge and information is valued?

There is a broad consensus that parental involvement is an ethos central to practice, but there is a lack of training in this area (Bastiani, 1989; Harris and Goodall, 2008; McMillan, 2005). The most important resource for effective parental involvement is time. Whalley (2007) expresses the need to adopt a clear pedagogy, a good understanding of child development and a shared language to bring parents and practitioners together.

Child factors

As a student, you may observe the way in which parents become involved according to their child's abilities and needs. Parental involvement has a positive effect on behaviour (Harris and Goodall, 2008), but Hornby and Lafaele (2011) observe that fear and embarrassment inhibit involvement from parents of children with behaviour problems. Parents of gifted and talented children take particular pleasure in their involvement, but disagreements over the commitment to a particular skill or talent may arise (Hornby and Lafaele, 2011).

Societal factors

The influence of class, ethnicity and gender prompt reflection on where the power lies in the parent/teacher relationship. Hornby and Lafaele (2011) believe that working class families are acutely aware of the gap between them and middle class professionals. Both Harris and Goodall (2008) and Hornby and Lafaele (2011) relate the existence of class inequalities amongst parents to social capital, described by Bourdieu as the ability to connect socially (Haralambos et al., 2013).

Research has found that middle class professional parents are more able to speak the language of early years practitioners, are comfortable in a relationship with them and are more likely to be treated as equals (Harris and Goodall, 2008; Hornby and Lafaele, 2011). Parents who have feelings of being connected are those who have access to childcare, transport and support from friends and family (Harris and Goodall, 2008; Hornby and Lafaele, 2011). Conversely, working class parents experience multiple barriers to parental involvement, resulting in reduced social capital and feelings of disconnectedness (Hornby and Lafaele, 2011).

More mothers than fathers are involved in supporting the transition between home and pre-school. However, fathers and other relatives are becoming increasingly involved. Hornby and Lafaele (2011) attribute this to changing family structures and the employment status of women. Whalley (2007) found that fathers responded better to invitations to formal meetings that focussed on maths, science and technology, rather than the informal gatherings preferred by mothers. This might affect the type of opportunities for involvement that settings offer parents.

Thinking activity

Find out how your placement setting has provided opportunities for parents to be involved in their child's learning, for example, a workshop, a library facility or a parents evening.

How successful was the setting at engaging fathers?

Were there particular barriers that prevented particular groups from engaging?

What other factors might have prevented involvement?

Research carried out at the Pen Green Centre in Corby, Northamptonshire (Whalley, 2007), demonstrates how a carefully structured approach successfully engages parents facing multiple barriers to parental involvement. The study shows how establishing an agreed set of principles concerning decision making, pedagogy, information sharing and mutual respect has a greater impact on parental involvement than parental involvement strategies themselves. The emphasis on acknowledging the personal feelings of all parties concerned and reflecting on attitudes to other people is particularly striking. Whilst some of the principles are transferable, the amount of time, money and external support needed to replicate the Pen Green approach is likely to be beyond the reach of most early years settings.

Case study: Hamza

Hamza is 2 and lives with his mum Rabia and his dad Yousuf. Yousuf was born in England and Rabia came to England from Pakistan after they were married. Rabia comes from a small village and speaks little English. She has not been living in the UK very long, has no transport and sometimes has difficulty in understanding what is expected of her. She is also quite shy. Hamza's dad works shifts, usually at night, at a local factory whilst his mum stays at home and looks after him and the house. Rabia brings Hamza to pre-school on the bus every afternoon. Hamza has had some health issues from birth and as a result he misses some pre-school sessions. Rabia doesn't call the pre-school on these occasions. Hamza is very excited because his mum is 7 months pregnant and he will soon become a big brother. His limited language skills mean that he finds it difficult to tell the staff how he feels. Hamza's key person, Julia, has made a particular effort to communicate regularly with Rabia, asking her how her pregnancy is progressing and keeping informed about Hamza's medical condition and appointments. She gets help from a Punjabi-speaking staff member to communicate important information but generally speaks with Rabia directly in English. As a result Rabia's ability to communicate is improving, and she asks specifically to speak to Julia if she has a problem. Julia arranged for Hamza to borrow a doll, some doll's clothes and feeding equipment to take home so that he could practice looking after the baby when it comes.

Now go back to the thinking activities with Hamza and his family in mind. How has this affected the way you think about working with parents?

Current thinking and practice

Parents and carers are often described as having the "biggest influence on children's future outcomes", and their role as their children's most influential educators from pre-birth is well documented (Gutman and Feinstein, cited in Tickell, 2011, p. 5). But what does this mean for students and practitioners? There are a number of significant reports highlighting the importance of parental involvement in children's early years, particularly emphasising the significance of the home as a learning environment. Bonci (2008), Field (2010), Allen (2011) and Tickell (2011) conclude that a focus on parenting and a stimulating home learning environment have the potential to make a difference to children's future outcomes and development.

Families and early years practitioners together can play an influential role in the first five years of a child's life (Hallet, 2016), as early experiences are shaped by the people they come into contact with. Social policy, especially in the last 20 years, has placed a greater emphasis on local services to work together with parents and carers in order to improve educational outcomes for children and young people. Indeed, this increased focus places the key role that parents play in their children's learning and development at the heart of integrated family services (Field, 2010). Labour government initiatives in the late 1990s challenged the existing culture of children's services to provide an environment where agencies worked in an integrated way. Of particular significance, the Labour's government flagship Sure Start programme invested heavily in local services from 1998–2005, focussing on improving the lives of the most disadvantaged families (National Audit Office, 2006). During this period, Sure Start local programmes initiated a rapid expansion of early learning and childcare services, alongside support for families affected by poverty, high unemployment and social problems (Anning and Ball, 2008).

The development of services continued with Children's Centres succeeding Sure Start programmes alongside the Ten Year Childcare Strategy (DfES, 2004), aspiring to increase parental choice by expanding childcare services and improving quality through a professionally led workforce (Envy and Walters, 2013). Changes to the landscape continued with the Coalition government, elected in 2010, making a number of changes to Labour's previous initiatives, including a revision of the Early Years Foundation Stage and the introduction of funded nursery places for 2-year-olds (Lloyd, 2015). Critics of the Coalition's position, however, describe contradictory trends and competing demands (Lloyd, 2015), as a disconnection emerged between education and care, with families struggling to balance their finances as a result of tax and benefit reforms. Policy developments in ECEC continue to be an agenda item for the current Conservative government, albeit less prominently, due to competing priorities following Brexit in June 2016.

The role of parents and the home learning environment do not impact upon children's outcomes in isolation. All 3- and 4-year-olds and 40 per cent of disadvantaged 2-year-olds are currently entitled to 15 hours per week of statutory early education and care (DfE, 2014). Plans for a further 15 hours per week of free childcare for working parents were announced in July 2015, and later incorporated into the Childcare Act 2016. This development is particularly crucial as, once implemented from September 2017, it will double the universal offer, albeit only for working parents, enabling their children to attend early education for 30 hours per week, 38 weeks of the year (DfE, 2014). It is too early to know the impact that this policy change will have on children and their families; however, it heralds the start of children accessing early years provision for increasing amounts of time, with a potential impact on partnerships with parents and the home learning environment.

Thinking activity

Take some time to read the latest news about the hours children spend in nursery settings on the foundation years website, www.foundationyears.org.uk.

Can you think of creative ways to foster parental involvement in your placement setting when both parents are working full time?

Alongside practitioners, students are tasked with meeting the standards set out in the EYFS framework (DfE, 2017), developing a relationship with parents and supporting them in maintaining enabling environments. The EPPE Project (Sylva et al., 2004) explored the importance of the home learning environment, emphasising that what parents do with their children and their involvement and engagement in learning activities has far greater impact on their future achievements than their socio-economic status. This notion builds on the findings of Feinstein and Symons (1999) and recognises the importance of parental interest above other socio-economic factors. It also challenges assumptions that social class, family size and parental education have the most impact when predicting future academic performance. If the home environment is influential in early learning, and the role of parents is the key to its success, practitioners play a part in supporting all parents to provide rich experiences for children to learn and develop.

Conclusion

As a student, you must be aware of the responsibility to work in partnership and engage parents in their children's learning alongside the competing demands of family life. Working together to build respectful relationships that support children's learning, both in the setting and at home, are skills needed in practice. A good practitioner will be aware of the different needs of the children and families who access their provision, and will take this into account when forming working relationships with them. Whilst on placement in a setting, you have an opportunity as a student to observe the different ways in which this is achieved and to reflect on your practice when working with parents.

Further reading and research

The Foundation Years website provides excellent information for people working with parents in the early years. You can find information about working with parents on their Knowledge Hub at www.foundationyears.org.uk/working-with-parents

The National Children's Bureau offer training in working with parents. You can read more about their approach at www.peal.org.uk

You can read more about the Pen Green Centre on their website at www.pengreen.org

National College for Teaching and Leadership – Teacher's Standards (Early Years). This chapter provides underpinning knowledge for Standards 2.7, 6.2, 6.3 and 8.3.

References

Abela, A. and Walker, J. (2013) *Contemporary Issues in Family Studies: Global Perspectives on Partnerships, Parenting and Support in a Changing World*, 1st edn., Chichester: Wiley-Blackwell.

Allen, G. (2011) *Early Intervention: The Next Steps*, London: Crown Copyright.

Anning, A. and Ball, M. (2008) Improving Services for Young Children: From Sure Start to Children's Centres, London: Sage.

Asmussen, K., Feinstein, L., Martin, J. and Chowdry, H. (2016) *Foundations for Life: What Works to Support Parent and Child Interaction in the Early Years*, Early Intervention Foundation (EIF), Retrieved from www.eif.org.uk/wp-content/uploads/foundationsforlife/EIF_Foundations-for-Life.pdf

Bastiani, J. (1989) *Working with Parents: A Whole-School Approach*, Windsor: NFER Nelson.

Baumrind, D. (1971) Current patterns of parental authority, *Developmental Psychology Monograph*, 4: pp 1–103.

Bonci, A. (2008) *A Research Review: The Importance of Families and the Home Learning Environment*, London: National Literacy Trust Childcare Act 2016.

Department for Education (DfE) (2011) *Supporting Families in the Foundation Years*, London: Crown Copyright.

Department for Education (DfE) (2017) *Statutory Framework for the Early Years Foundation Stage: Setting the Standards for Learning, Development and Care for Children from Birth to Five*, London: DfE.

Department for Education (DfE) (2014) *Early Education and Childcare: Statutory Guidance for Local Authorities*, London: DfE.

Department for Education and Skills (DfES) (2003) *Every Child Matters* (Cm.5860), Norwich: HMSO.

Department for Education and Skills (DfES) (2004) *Choice for Parents, the Best Start for Children: A Ten Year Strategy for Childcare*, London: HMSO.

Desforges, C. and Abouchaar, A. (2003) *The Impact of Parental Involvement, Parental Support and Family Education on Pupil Achievement and Adjustment: A Literature Review: Research Report No. 433*, Nottingham: Department for Education & Skills (DfES).

Economic and Social Research Council (ESRC) (2012) *Parenting Style Influences Child Development and Social Mobility: Evidence Briefing*, Swindon: ESRC.

Elfer, P., Goldschmied, E. and Selleck, D. (2003) *Key Persons in the Nursery: Building Relationships for Quality Provision*, London: David Fulton.

Elfer, P. and Page, J. (2015) Pedagogy with babies: Perspectives of eight nursery managers, *Early Child Development and Care*, 185(11–12): pp 1762–1782.

Envy, R. and Walters, R. (2013) *Becoming a Practitioner in the Early Years*, London: Learning Matters.

Feinstein, L. and Symons, J. (1999) Attainment in Secondary School: Oxford Economic Papers, 51, in A. Bonci (ed.) (2008) *A Research Review: The Importance of Families and the Home Learning Environment*, London: National Literacy Trust, pp 300–321.

Field, F. (2010) *The Foundation Years: Preventing Poor Children Becoming Poor Adults*, London: Crown Copyright.

Goldschmied, E. and Jackson, S. (2004) *People under Three: Young Children in Day Care*, 2nd edn., Abingdon: Routledge.

Government Equalities Office (2011) *The Equality Act 2010: Public Sector Equality Duty. What do I Need to Know: A Quick Start Guide for Public Sector Organisations*, Crown Copyright, Retrieved from www.pfc.org.uk/pdf/equality-duty.pdf

Hallet, E. (2016) *Early Years Practice: For Educators and Teachers*, London: Sage.

Haralambos, M., Holborn, M., Chapman, S. and Moore, S. (2013) *Sociology: Themes and Perspectives*, 8th edn., London: Collins.

Harris, A. and Goodall, J. (2008) Do parents know they matter? Engaging all parents in learning, *Educational Research*, 50(3): pp 277–289.

HM Government (2015a) *Working Together to Safeguard Children: A Guide to Inter-Agency Working to Safeguard and Promote the Welfare of Children*, London: Crown Copyright, Retrieved from www.gov.uk/government/uploads/system/uploads/attachment_data/file/419595/Working_Together_to_Safeguard_Children.pdf

Hornby, G. and Lafaele, R. (2011) Barriers to parental involvement in education: An explanatory model, *Educational Review*, 63(1): pp 37–52.

Jackson, D. and Needham, M. (2014) *Engaging with Parents in Early Years Settings*, London: Sage.

LaRocque, M., Kleiman, I. and Darling, S. M. (2011) Parental involvement: The missing link in school achievement, *Preventing School Failure: Alternative Education for Children and Youth*, 55(3): pp 115–122.

Lloyd, E. (2015) Early childhood education and care policy in England under the Coalition government, *London Review on Education*, 13(2): pp 145–156.

Macoby, E. E. and Martin, J. A. (1983) Socialization in the Context of the Family: Parent-Child Interaction, in P. H. Mussen (ed.) and E. M. Hetherington (vol. ed.) *Handbook of Child Psychology, Vol. 4: Socialization, Personality, and Social Development*, 4th edn., New York: Wiley, pp 1–101.

McMillan, D. J. (2005) Close encounters: Issues in pre-school parental involvement in Northern Ireland, *Child Care in Practice*, 11(2): pp 119–134.

National Audit Office (2006) *Sure Start Children's Centres*, Report by the Comptroller and Auditor General/HC 104 session 2006–2007/19 December 2006, Retrieved from www.nao.org.uk/wp-content/uploads/2006/12/0607104.pdf

Office for National Statistics (ONS) (2015) *Families and Households: Statistical Release*, Retrieved from www.ons.gov.uk/peoplepopulationandcommunity/birthsdeathsandmarriages/families/bulletins/familiesandhouseholds/2015-11-05

The Prime Minister's Office and The Rt Hon David Cameron MP (2016) *Prime Minister's Speech on Life Chances*, Retrieved from www.gov.uk/government/speeches/prime-ministers-speech-on-life-chances

Pugh, G. (1989) Parents and Professionals in Pre-School Services: Is Partnership Possible? in S. Wolfendale (ed.) *Parental Involvement: Developing Networks between School, Home and Community*, London: Cassell Educational, pp 1–19.

Rennie, J. (1996) Working with Parents. In G. Pugh (Ed.), *Contemporary Issues in the Early Years: Working Collaboratively for Children* (2nd ed). London: Paul Chapman Publishing.

Sylva, K., Melhuish, E., Sammons, P., Siraj-Blatchford, I. and Taggart, B. (2004) *The Effective Provision of Pre-School Education (EPPE) Project: Final Report*, London: Institute of Education.

Tickell, C. (2011) *The Early Years: Foundations for Life, Health and Learning – An Independent Report on the Early Years Foundation Stage to Her Majesty's Government*, London: Crown Copyright.

Whalley, M. (2007) *Involving Parents in Their Children's Learning*, 2nd edn., London: Paul Chapman Publishing.

Wilson, T. (2015) *Working with Parents, Carers and Families in the Early Years: The Essential Guide*, London: Routledge.

Chapter 13

Working in partnership with placement

Amanda Crow and Samantha McMahon

Chapter aims

By the end of this chapter you will:

- be clear about what the university and placement can do to support your work-based learning
- understand the role of the work-based mentor
- be clear about how to have a successful placement.

Introduction

This chapter complements and builds on Chapter 2 to help you work in partnership with your placement to develop your professional skills. This chapter provides an overview of what you might expect from university and from your placement to help you to feel confident and gain from your experience. The intention of this chapter is to help you maximise your experiential learning and to understand that placement is a site for application of knowledge and skills. Jones and Dallal (2016) suggest that until recently work-based learning has been viewed as a poor relation to academic learning, but in the last two decades it has been understood that academic learning alone has not met the needs of employers and employees. Therefore, this chapter provides insight into how the university and placement can support your learning through, and at, work. Your placement experience is central to your studies, and should be valued and given equal status to your academic work.

If learning on placement has equal status to your academic work, then it needs to be carefully planned and organised; clear communication between the university, student and setting is vital in order to ensure that placement preparation is a success. The following table is a collection of expectations that will help you to be clear about your own responsibilities and give you some ideas about what you can reasonably expect from both the university and placement staff.

Chapter 2 explored your responsibilities on placement and this chapter will now explain how the university and the setting might support you on placement.

Table 13.1 Placement expectations

Students	Settings	University
Will attend the setting as agreed, attending consistently and being punctual. Agreed absence reporting procedures will be followed when necessary.	Will provide experiences in line with course guidelines and complete and sign evidence of achievements as necessary.	Will enter into contractual agreement in order to ensure safe practice, including health and safety and DBS clearance.
Will maintain confidentiality and respect for colleagues, children and their families.	Will provide an experienced member of staff to supervise and support the student.	Will raise students' awareness of professionalism.
Will seek to learn through applying theory to practice, and will work as a member of the team following the routines in the setting.	Will support student through induction and regular support meetings, identifying and reviewing progress.	Will provide support through appropriate course structures; this is likely to involve at least one placement visit.
Will comply with course and setting requirements.	Will communicate any concerns to the appropriate tutor and be prepared to work collaboratively to resolve difficulties.	Will respond to concerns and liaise with student and staff members as appropriate.
Will treat the needs of children as paramount.	Will report on students' progress on completion of placement and contribute to assessment.	Will support setting staff with regards to paperwork and assessments.

Support from the university

Preparation and support for success on placement often begins before the student has enrolled on the course. The university will organise a check with the Disclosure and Barring Service (DBS), which prevents unsuitable people from working with young children. The student will also normally complete a medical declaration and may have to attend a health check with the Occupational Health Service at the university. This is to ensure that the university and placement can make reasonable adjustments for disabled students. Working with children can be physically and mentally demanding; however, the university and setting must work together to extend inclusive practice to students, and to prevent discrimination. On occasion, students suffer from anxiety or depression and this can make attendance at placement very challenging. If the student, university and setting work together, it is often possible to alter placement requirements to enable the student to be successful.

The university will have structures in place to support you whilst on placement. Often you will be provided with a placement handbook, which clearly sets out the professional requirements of the course. It is likely that you will need to document your time on placement and complete a final report. You will also attend lectures and workshops, which will support your developing professional and theoretical knowledge. You will have opportunities in class to engage in reflective conversations with your colleagues and tutors. These can help you find answers to challenges, sustain motivation and help you maintain your professional records.

In addition, it is likely that you will be visited by a tutor whilst on placement. This reinforces the link between the student, university and placement and is a great opportunity to review progress, solve problems and establish a partnership which underpins your work-based learning. You should ensure that you notify placement in advance of the visit and have all relevant paperwork on hand. Make a note of any questions or issues you want to raise with your tutor. The tutor is there to help you draw out the connections between theory, policy and practice, to help you transition successfully from level 3 to levels 4 and 5, and to help you understand the assessment requirements.

The university may have an established partnership with the placement built upon many years of collaboration. Sometimes practitioners in the setting may have themselves studied at the university and will have a good understanding of the course requirements. However, the university will still provide a handbook for the placement, which presents an overview of the course, and outlines their responsibilities to the student. The university may offer mentor training and will ensure that the placement has contact details should they need to get in touch with the university.

Thinking activity

Take some time to reflect on what you have read so far in this chapter. Then identify what you have to do to ensure the university can meet its responsibilities in ensuring you have a successful placement experience.

Support from the setting

Consider the following case study, which presents the view of one manager and how she supports a student in her setting.

Case study

Ellie is the owner and manager of a small, private day nursery. She is an EYP and believes that it is important to help develop a professional, graduate-led workforce. Ellie describes her role: "Well I set the tone, you know, friendly but not a friend, professional. The student has to see me behaving in the way I expect them to behave; I'm a role model, and a mentor. But if I see something I don't like, I'm going to tell them. I have to always put the children and their families first." Ellie goes on to talk about one of the students she recently supported. "When she first came she was so quiet and the children tended to ignore her. I asked her to shadow one of the experienced practitioners and to keep a diary of what she had seen. Every Friday we would sit together and go through her diary and talk through what she had to do the following week. She came to the training on sustained shared thinking and put together a display about it for the parents. It was great. Now she sits with the children, they hang onto her every word. . . . It's very rewarding. She's completely turned it around."

How does Ellie "set the tone" in the setting for the student?

What actions did Ellie take to support the student?

What actions did the student take to "turn around" her placement into a positive learning experience?

Role model

We know from social learning theory that children look to their peers as models and learn from more experienced colleagues. It is the same for students on placement. Ellie described herself as a role model, and also asked the student to shadow a more experienced practitioner. By observing and recording what the practitioner did, the student then had the opportunity to analyse her practice. She did this in partnership with Ellie, who was able to identify good practice; in this way Ellie scaffolds the student's learning. You can gain confidence in your practice by imitating experienced practitioners in the setting.

Activity

In placement, identify a practitioner that you would like to shadow. With their permission observe and record their practice. With them or your work-based mentor, analyse their practice and identify the strategies they use to support children's learning and development. Make links to appropriate theory.

These observations can help you to progress your knowledge and understanding of the practitioner role (Hayes, 2014). Spending time in a setting is an ideal time to reflect on situations together with the staff team, as opening up your thoughts and sharing in reflective dialogues will help you to practise problem-solving techniques and prepare you for future practice.

Action learning, attributed to Revans, is a theory that is helpful when thinking about solving problems and finding solutions, as it is associated with professionals solving real-life problems and issues that can arise daily in practice (Coughlan and Coughlan, 2010). The most important aspect of placement experience is having the time and space to link your understanding of theory to practice. McGill and Beaty (2001) suggest that imagining action learning as a bridge between the world of action and the world of learning can be a helpful way to understand how action learning might apply to your own practice. Whilst this is only one theoretical approach to consider, being an active learner will help you to make sense of the various policies and procedures, become familiar with routines and understand the implications that professional decisions have on the lives of children and families.

Thinking activity

Use your university library to research Revans's theory of action learning. There will be books and journals that you can access. You will find that there are many sources as action learning is used in many disciplines; you are particularly looking for 'action learning in education and early years'.

Revans's philosophy is that: "there can be no learning without action and no action without learning" (1998).

Can you relate to this as a student practitioner?

Reflective practice, when combined with active learning, recognises the importance of collaboration, an active process of thinking, discussing and testing out ideas with others. During your placement this collaboration will involve you working collectively with your mentor, families and tutors. Building on the theory by Revans and reflecting on your daily experiences together with your mentor has the potential to encourage deeper learning and knowledge of child development. Coughlan and Coughlan (2010) suggest this approach can be motivating and encouraging and will offer you opportunities to critically engage in reflective practice.

The role of the placement mentor

The EYFS requires all staff including students to have an induction to the setting; this involves a member of staff, usually the manager or senior practitioner on duty, to take you through a training programme that includes your expected roles and responsibilities (DfE, 2017). There will be a number of important policies for you to read and understand, of particular importance will be health and safety, safeguarding and the setting's equality policy. You will usually be asked to sign to say you have understood them. During the induction, you will usually be introduced to your allocated supervisor or mentor who will support you in developing your practice.

Case study

Placement mentor in Private Day Care:

We are asked in advance if we are willing to take a student on placement, this is usually in the summer before the new term starts and this helps us to plan. As a nursery staff team, we feel it is really important to have a settled team, and this can affect whether we can offer placements. We want to make sure students have the best opportunities to learn here and if we have had staff changes, it can hinder the support we can offer.

When we are contacted by the student or university to place a student, we ask them to come and meet us first. This is similar to having an interview but a lot less daunting. It is a chance to talk about the setting and the way we work with the children and a chance for the student to ask questions. This meeting will be short but will involve being shown around the nursery; I will ask to see the handbook/course requirements so that we can offer the right kind of help. This meeting serves two purposes: it is important the student feels happy with the placement but also that we can be sure the placement is right for the student. I think it is best to be open and honest. If the student really wants to work in a different kind of setting, a school for example, then a day nursery might not be suitable for them.

Once we have agreed together then we will arrange a start date. The nursery has a student policy. This includes all the information the student will need and they are asked as part of their induction to read and sign it. I meet with the student regularly to discuss their work, usually this is weekly. If there are times when this can be difficult due to staffing or time of day, we can e-mail then meet the following week.

As the setting mentor I have the responsibility to coordinate students. Sometimes we have more than one and I need to make sure that the children come first. I think it is important to help students to integrate and to settle into the staff team. We also make sure parents are aware we are training future early years staff.

Brockbank and McGill (2012) define mentoring as a process which leads to a change in thinking, and a mentor as someone who supports a mentee in the process of thinking things through, and is respectful and empowering. Ultimately the professional development of the mentee is the focus for both parties. There are different approaches to mentoring but the key principles remain the same, i.e. the setting of goals, achievement criteria and timescales. There must be a commitment to action from both parties, and you should always ensure that you prepare in advance and keep detailed records of each meeting (McMahon et al., 2016). As a mentee, it is important that your professional development needs are the focus; however, at the start of your placement it can be difficult to know exactly what your needs are. Refer to your professional handbook from the university, build on your strengths and reflect honestly on aspects of your practice which need to be improved. There is no one approach to mentoring which suits every student; as you gain in confidence you can shape your mentee/mentor relationship to meet your needs.

Remember mentors are often busy and it is a voluntary role. You are expected to take the initiative and make the most of your mentor's time. Establish the reasons for your meeting, summarise what you have discussed, agree on actions and importantly set the date for the next meeting.

Lauren enthusiastically described her first two meetings with her mentor:

She's already helped me identify about seven things I should be doing. She knows what I need to do for university, what's expected of me and she's really happy to look at my observations and stuff. . . . That's great you know, to know that you are on the right track.

What if it goes wrong?

It is necessary to note that placement experiences are on the whole positive, but there can be times when relationships breakdown and difficulties occur. With support from your tutor and mentor, issues can easily be resolved; however, it is important that you communicate any issues as soon as they arise, as the earlier they are managed, the more successful the outcome. There will be procedures in place to help you, but it is necessary that you take a professional approach. Depending on the circumstances, you may feel confident to discuss and reflect with your mentor directly. If, for any reason, you cannot address the situation in the setting, make sure you bring it to the attention of your tutor as soon as possible. If the situation is irretrievable, the decision might be taken to support you to move placement; this is usually a last resort and will be managed in a respectful way for both the setting and you.

The Care Council in Wales (2011) have identified the following common barriers to effective mentoring:

- a lack of standards or guidance for the process
- a lack of time and space
- interruptions
- poor recording of meetings and a lack of training for the mentor
- unplanned and infrequent meetings.

Thinking activity

Reflect on the barriers to effective mentoring as presented above and identify the conditions which will support effective mentoring.

How to have a successful placement

The following activity was carried out with first year undergraduate students before starting to attend placement; using the metaphor of baking a cake, the following recipe is a collection of their ingredients for a successful placement. You might find it helpful to think about the recipe when planning placement and for avoiding placement breakdown, or perhaps the method will offer you some ideas for a checklist.

Method

1   Plan ahead to make sure you arrive on time, before the children and ready to start the day.
2   Ask questions and use your initative. Do not be scared of not knowing, as this is the only way to develop your learning.
3   Do not wait to be told what to do; once you know the routines try to be proactive and a team player.

4 Keep a weekly log or diary as this will help to manage your time.
5 Be enthusiastic, ask to see the setting's planning documents, offer ideas for activities or maybe read a story.
6 Communicate with your mentor and university tutors; if things start to go wrong, try to talk.

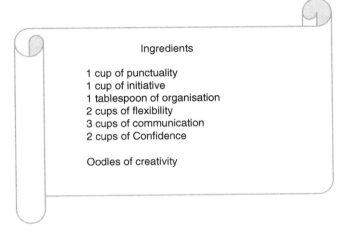

Ingredients

1 cup of punctuality
1 cup of initiative
1 tablespoon of organisation
2 cups of flexibility
3 cups of communication
2 cups of Confidence

Oodles of creativity

Figure 13.1 The ingredients of a successful placement

Making the most of placement: a view from a manager

We look forward to helping students by offering placements; it takes us back to the time when we were new to early years. All we ask is that you are committed to the children and to learn while you are here. This includes being consistent, attending on agreed days, being on time but also being flexible; most of all your enthusiasm will be welcome. As a manager I will always try to support the student and help them to benefit from placement.

Conclusion

This chapter has provided an overview of how the university and the setting can support you to have a successful placement. Success requires an effective partnership between you, the university and the setting. The chapter explains how you can work with your tutor and placement mentor to make links between practice, policy and theory. Remember, early years practice is an enjoyable and influential profession; you are in a privileged position as you are helping to shape the lives of future citizens. Making the most of your placement opportunities will help you to develop as a conscientious and knowledgeable practitioner. As a student you have a responsibility to the children and families, and that involves behaving in a professional and courteous manner, and working in an honest and ethical way (NCTL, 2013). By following these principles you will be making a positive contribution to children's education and care and be a valuable asset to the setting.

Some useful websites

Michael Reed and Rosie Walker have produced together with Sage a companion website to their book *A Critical Companion to Early Childhood*; it has useful activities to support your reading and the references to Michael Gasper; information can be found at: https://study.sagepub.com/reedandwalker.

The Foundation Years website offers a range of advice through their knowledge hub; further information can be found here: www.foundationyears.org.uk/pedagogy-early-learning.

Universities have website links to their own individual placement information, search through your chosen institution for more information.

National College for Teaching and Leadership – Teacher's Standards (Early Years). This chapter provides underpinning knowledge for Standards 1.1, 1.3, 8.1, 8.2.

References

Brockbank, A. and McGill, I. (2012) Supporting early childhood practitioners through relationship-based reflective supervision, *NHSA Dialogue: A Research-to-Practice Journal for the Early Childhood Field*, 15(3): pp 286–301.

Care Council Wales (2011) *Supervising and appraising well: A guide to effective supervision and appraisal*, Care Council Wales [online] Retrieved from http://ctb.ku.edu/en/table-of-contents/leadership/effective-manager/staff-supervision/main (Accessed 29 October 2016).

Coughlan, D. and Coughlan, P. (2010) Notes toward a philosophy of action learning research, *Action Learning: Research and Practice*, 7(2): pp 193–203, doi:10.1080/14767333.2010.488330.

Department for Education (2017) *Statutory Framework for the Early Years Foundation Stage: Setting the Standards for Learning, Development and Care for Children from Birth to Five*, London: DfE, Retrieved from www.gov.uk/government/uploads/system/uploads/attachment_data/file/335504/EYFS_framework_from_1_September_2014__with_clarification_note.pdf2014

Gasper, M. (2015) Professional Practice and Early Childhood Today, in M. Reed and R. Walker (eds) (2014) *A Critical Companion to Early Childhood*, London: Sage.

Hallet, E. (2016) *Early Years Practice: For Educators and Teachers*, UK: Sage.

Hayes, C. (2014) The Nature of Reflective Practice, in C. Hayes, J. Daly and M. Duncan (eds) (2014) *Developing as a Reflective Early Years Professional: A Thematic Approach*, London: Critical Publishing.

Jones, C. and Dallal, J. (2016) Work-Based Learning, in L. Trodd (ed.) *The Early Years Handbook for Students and Practitioners: An Essential Guide for the Foundation Degree and Levels 4 and 5*, Abingdon: Routledge, pp 28–43.

McGill, I. and Beaty, L. (2001) *Action Learning: A Guide for Professional, Management & Educational Development*, rev. 2nd edn., London: Routledge Falmer.

McMahon, S., Dyer, M. and Barker, H. (2016) Mentoring, Coaching and Supervision, in L. Trodd (ed.) *The Early Years Handbook for Students and Practitioners: An Essential Guide for the Foundation Degree and Levels 4 and 5*, Abingdon: Routledge, pp 433–447.

Musgrave, J. and Stobbs, N. (2015) *Early Years Placements: A Critical Guide to Outstanding Work-Based Learning*, London, UK: Critical Publishing.

National College for Teaching and Leadership (NCTL) (2013) *Teachers Standards (Early Years) from 2013*, Crown Copyright, Retrieved from www.gov.uk/government/uploads/system/uploads/attachment_data/file/211646/Early_Years_Teachers__Standards.pdf

Nicholson, N. (2016) The Issue of Professionalism, in I. Palaiologou (ed.) (2016) *The Early Years Foundation Stage: Theory and Practice*, London: Sage.

Revans, R. W. (1998) *ABC of Action Learning*, London: Lemos and Crane.

Index